Democratic Deficit?

Democratic Deficit?

Institutions and Regulation in the European Union, Switzerland and the United States

Thomas D. Zweifel

LEXINGTON BOOKS
Lanham • Boulder • New York • Oxford

LEXINGTON BOOKS

Published in the United States of America
by Lexington Books
A Member of the Rowman & Littlefield Publishing Group
4501 Forbes Boulevard, Suite 200, Lanham, Maryland 20706

PO Box 317
Oxford
OX2 9RU, UK

Copyright © 2002 by Lexington Books

All rights reserved. No part of this publication may be reproduced, stored in a retrieval system, or transmitted in any form or by any means, electronic, mechanical, photocopying, recording, or otherwise, without the prior permission of the publisher.

British Library Cataloguing in Publication Information Available

Library of Congress Cataloging-in-Publication Data

Zweifel, Thomas D., 1962–
  Democratic deficit?: Institutions and regulation in the European Union, Switzerland, and the United States / Thomas D. Zweifel.
    p. cm.
  Includes bibliographical references and index.
  ISBN 0-7391-0451-9 (alk. paper)
  1. European Union. 2. Democracy—European Union countries. 3. Democracy.
  I. Title.

JN40 .Z94 2002
341.242/2 21   2002010328

Printed in the United States of America

∞™ The paper used in this publication meets the minimum requirements of American National Standard for Information Sciences—Permanence of Paper for Printed Library Materials, ANSI/NISO Z39.48–1992.

For my parents
Dr. Eva and Dr. Heinz Wicki-Schönberg
who believed in me and made me curious about the world

WE DON'T WANT A BUNCH OF FACELESS BUREAUCRATS IN WASHINGTON TO TELL US WHAT TO DO.
AND WE DON'T WANT A BUNCH OF INCOMPETENT ELECTED OFFICIALS TELLING FACELESS BUREAUCRATS TO TELL US WHAT TO DO.
TOLES
UNIVERSAL PRESS SYND
©2000 THE BUFFALO NEWS
WHAT WE WANT IS A BUNCH OF NAMELESS SPECIAL INTERESTS TELLING INCOMPETENT ELECTED OFFICIALS TELLING FACELESS BUREAUCRATS TO TELL US WHAT TO DO.
THEN YOU'RE IN LUCK —

6·12·00

Contents

Tables	ix
Preface	xi
Acknowledgments	xv
1 Democratic Deficit?	1
2 Democratic Deficit Arguments	11
3 Institutions Compared	45
4 Bureaucratic Democracy	65
5 Case 1—Regulating Mergers	83
6 Case 2—Regulating Biotech	105
7 Democratic Surplus?	135
Bibliography	147
Subject Index	163
Author Index	171
About the Author	175

Tables

Table 2.1	Taxonomy of Democratic Deficit Arguments	41
Table 3.1	Democracy Scale: Alvarez, Cheibub, Limongi, Przeworski 1996	46
Table 3.2	Democracy Scale: Bollen 1993	48
Table 3.3	Democracy Scale: Coppedge and Reinicke 1990	52
Table 3.4	Democracy Scale: Freedom House 1995-1996	53
Table 3.5	Democracy Scale: Gasiorowski 1990	56
Table 3.6	Democracy Scale: Gastil 1990	58
Table 3.7	Democracy Scale: Gurr, Jaggers, and Moore 1990	59
Table 3.8	Overview of Democracy Scales	61
Table 5.1	Key Actors in Merger Regulation by Polity	84
Table 5.2	The European Merger Procedure	85
Table 5.3	The United States Merger Procedure	92
Table 5.4	The Swiss Merger Procedure under 1995 Cartel Law	96
Table 5.5	Bureaucratic Democracy Ratings in Merger Regulation	100
Table 6.1	Key Actors in Biotech (GMO) Regulation by Polity	106
Table 6.2	The European GMO Foods Labeling Procedure	109
Table 6.3	The United States GMO Foods Labeling Procedure	116
Table 6.4	The Swiss GMO Foods Labeling Procedure	123
Table 6.5	Bureaucratic Democracy Ratings in GMO Foods Labeling Regulation	128
Table 7.1	Bureaucratic Democracy Ratings, Merger and GMO Regulation Combined	136
Table 7.2	Assumptions: Traditional Democracy vs. Bureaucratic Democracy	141
Table 7.3	Anticipated Criticisms	143

Preface

If men were angels, no government would be necessary.
If angels were to govern men,
neither external nor internal controls on government would be necessary.
In framing a government which is to be administered by men over men,
the great difficulty lies in this:
you must first enable the government to control the governed;
and in the next place oblige it to control itself.

James Madison, The Federalist Papers 51, 1787-88

No form of government, therefore,
can be a perfect guard against the abuse of power.

James Madison, Letter to Thomas Ritchie, 1825

As he opened the European Convent in March 2002 to democratize the European Union, Valéry Giscard d'Estaing said the Convent would "listen constantly and attentively." The former French president was serious: a generation earlier, he had set a personal example for European integration in the 1970s by playing chess with then German chancellor Helmut Schmidt (Putnam and Bayne 1984). Now, the "professional Convent" of politicians from the European Parliament, Council of Ministers, European Commission, and current and future member state governments from twenty-eight countries would be complemented with a "forum of civil society," so that unions and employers, universities and think tanks, associations and nongovernmental organizations, as well as individuals, would have a voice in shaping a more democratic Europe. In line with the twenty-first century, an

Internet portal was established at http://european-convention.eu.int, and any interested parties were invited to submit contributions to sg-forum-convention@cec.eu.int.

But this time, the elder statesman has taken on an ambitious promise. Can the Convent make the European Union (EU) really representative of citizens' preferences and their everyday concerns? Does the EU really stand in the shoes of the "end user"? This book is about these questions.

The importance of the European Union as a pioneer of international organization cannot be overstated. Erected after World War II—after three centuries of bloody warfare ever since the foundation of the modern state system at the 1648 Peace of Westphalia—as the European Coal and Steel Community to assist European reconstruction and serve as a bulwark against the Soviet Union, the EU has evolved into a decision-making body that often acts as a unified entity in international affairs. In many ways, Winston Churchill's vision of the "United States of Europe" has become a reality: the EU is a regulatory state with centralized government institutions.

This brings up the question: *quis custodiat custodes*? Who, or what institutional features, ensures that the leadership of the EU is held accountable by citizens of EU member states? Nationalists, realists, and other proponents of state sovereignty voiced fears of excessive supranational powers exercised by international institutions ever since the proliferation of these institutions after World War II. Since the Treaty of the European Union in 1992, monetary union and an independent European Central Bank, such fears have arisen newly under the banner of a "democratic deficit" in the EU.

Writing in the British daily *Financial Times*, Martin Taylor, the chairman of W. H. Smith, charged that "large numbers of sensible citizens have deep misgivings over the authoritarian, undemocratic direction of the European Union." Taylor compared the EU to the "late medieval papacy": "Now as 500 years ago, powerful and unaccountable institutions develop an arrogance which, unchecked, fuels resentment and eventually rebellion."[1] And in Switzerland, a coalition of eleven groups, including two right-wing parties, forced a May 2000 referendum with 70,000 signatures against bilateral Swiss-EU treaties. The referendum was defeated at the polls, but Swiss EU opponents said that by spurning Austria because of its inclusion of the far right wing Jörg Haider in its government, the EU showed that it is too big and bureaucratic and not democratic enough.[2]

The issue became only more salient during the December 2000 Nice European Council meeting of the member states, who had to decide whether to transfer even more national powers to Brussels as the Union prepares for further enlargement by as many as twelve, mostly Eastern European, states by 2005. Since Europe has an aging and shrinking population, its leaders see enlargement as a key strategy to preserve its economic vitality in both world politics and world markets. But enlargement carries the danger of diluting democratic values: potential members like Rumania or Cyprus do not exactly bring a long-standing tradition of free elections.

So far, research in the area of EU institutions has been largely descriptive and shows a notable dearth of systematic analysis. Many studies are based on assertions, backed by their authors with those case studies that favor their assertion—if any. Based on the premise that the EU is *sui generis* and cannot be compared, most such assertions are made in a vacuum.

This book aims to help fill this gap through a systematic comparative analysis that straddles the fields of international relations and comparative politics. In order not to merely speculate, the book compares the real, currently existing EU to the United States and Switzerland. Based on a comparison of the institutions of the three polities, and on a comparison of their regulatory processes in both merger policy and biotechnology regulation, I reach a surprising conclusion. The EU does *not* suffer from a democratic deficit greater than that of most liberal democracies. At least in terms of democracy, neither current smaller EU member states (such as Denmark or Sweden) nor potential members (such as Hungary, Latvia, or Switzerland) have grounds for fear of a tyrannical EU. In certain policy areas, liberal democracies may even benefit from adopting EU procedures that strike a prudent balance between accountability and independence in the regulatory state.

The book might be important for another reason. International organization has been on the rise in the latter part of the twentieth century and will become a defining feature of international affairs in the twenty-first century. International institutions will receive more and more expansive competences in order to tackle a proliferation of transnational issues—terrorism, AIDS, environmental pressures, or migration, to name but a few—that transcend national boundaries and cannot be tackled by the individual nation-state alone. The present integration of the EU, and the surrender of national sovereignty by its members, is unprecedented. The question whether this experiment in transnational integration is democratic—whether it represents the interests of affected citizens—matters far beyond the EU for the future of all international organization. May this study serve as a small contribution to building an EU, and perhaps ultimately other international institutions, that truly represent their member states' citizens.

NOTES

1. *Financial Times*, Personal View, 19 October 2000, 17.
2. *New York Times*, 10 February 2000.

Acknowledgments

To do justice to all my intellectual debts, I would have to write my autobiography. Hence, here just a few words of gratitude to some selected guides in writing this book. Adam Przeworski introduced me to the topic of democracy and instilled in me a healthy hunger for questioning assumptions. Mike Gilligan helped me structure the book and guided me along the path. Walter Mattli gave me crucial insight into European institutions. Bernard Manin helped me evaluate democratic deficit arguments, and Lawrence Broz reminded me of relevant distinctions of international political economy.

Chris Matthews of the European Commission made time for countless interviews, phone calls, and correspondence on EU institutions and case studies. Grace Lui sifted through an ocean of cases. Robert Weissman guided me through the labyrinths of U.S. regulation. Felix Heusler and Valentin Zellweger helped me understand Swiss law. Peter Zweifel and Damien Neven furnished key sources on Swiss competition policy, and Elisabeth Stern on Swiss biotech regulation. A special thanks goes to Yoram Wurmser for his assistance in crossing the finish line. But as always, all mistakes are mine alone.

1

✢

Democratic Deficit?

One of the developments that set the twentieth apart from previous centuries was the proliferation of international regimes, particularly over the past fifty years, in virtually all fields of policy-making. Transnational issues such as the environment and AIDS, debt and trade, nuclear weapons and arms sales, population and migration pressures, hunger and poverty, and international terrorism and drug trafficking present challenges that individual nation-states can no longer confront alone. With globalization and regional integration, national governments are increasingly forced to delegate rule-making and adjudicative powers to transnational or supranational institutions.

Organizations are seen as "international" when they consist of at least three nations as contracting parties (Slomanson 1995:99–100). International regimes have been defined as sets of values, norms, rules, and decision-making procedures around which actor expectations converge in a given issue-area (Krasner 1983:1). International organization is a framework of trilateral or multilateral governance, in which parties subject themselves and their negotiation to an institutional authority acting as arbitrator (Williamson 1985:70–78). But the European Union has moved far beyond an international organization. In less than fifty years, it has evolved from an intergovernmental treaty to an increasingly unified entity with many features of a state: its own territory and flag, its own currency and central bank, its executive, legislature and court, and soon its own army [1]. Much like the United States, the EU has been called a "regulatory state" (Seidman and Gilmour 1986; Sunstein 1990; Rose-Ackerman 1992; Majone 1996:55, 1998) in which budget constraints lead the government to rule by regulation rather than by taxation and spending, and where extensive policy-making powers are delegated to nonmajoritarian institutions that fulfill public functions but are not directly accountable to voters or to their elected representatives (Majone 1996:55, 1998).

The renaissance of the EU in the last decade, and its likely expansion in the next, has renewed questions whether European institutions are sufficiently democratic to represent the interests of member states' citizens. As Robert Dahl wrote, the boundaries of any nation-state are "now much smaller than the boundaries of the decisions that significantly affect the interests of its citizens," thus eroding the autonomy of those states and hence democratic control of their decisions (Dahl 1989:2, 318–20; Pinder 1999:2–3). Policymakers and scholars alike have asserted that the EU suffers from such erosion of democratic control—in other words, from a "democratic deficit." The term implies a gap in the EU between democratic practice in theory and in reality (Lodge 1993:22).

The issue came onto the European agenda in the wake of the Maastricht Treaty and subsequent European Monetary Unification (EMU). It followed the rejection of the treaty in a Danish referendum, its narrow approval in a French referendum and the British Parliament, and the German constitutional court ruling that the EU cannot be integrated further unless its institutions are made more democratic (Weiler, Haltern, and Mayer 1995; Scharpf 1997a).

Does the EU suffer from a democratic deficit? The question can be split into two: First, *are* EU institutions and rules democratic? Second, does the EU *work* as a democracy in its policy-making processes? The first question is static, the second dynamic. To answer both, I first compare the EU "regulatory state" with two federal democracies that continually receive the highest grades in classifications of democratic regimes—Switzerland and the United States. Second, by tracing two specific and analogous cases of legislation in the EU, the United States, and Switzerland, I compare the three polities in action.

IS THE EU COMPARABLE?

Much of the existing literature on the EU's democratic deficit is overly descriptive, lacks a systematic methodology, and sees the EU as an idiosyncratic, unique entity that cannot be compared to international organizations or to national polities. This dearth of comparison makes for assertions that are rarely verified or falsified. By comparing the EU with Switzerland and the United States, I plan to test democratic deficit arguments systematically for their validity.

But can the EU, obviously not a nation-state, be matched with national polities? The question itself is controversial and hotly debated, and the three entities vary widely in their cultures and political institutions. Some assert that the EU is still an international organization subject to national supremacy. In this view, the EU is scarcely more than the sum of its parts, a collection of sovereign nation-states, but far from a federal "state." Already in 1967, in a direct and self-conscious challenge to European Community law, the German Bundesverfassungsgericht ruled that certain fundamental rights protected by the German constitution could not be effectively protected by the Community order (Mancini 1989:609). As recently as 1993, the German constitutional court ruled again, this time on the Maastricht Treaty, that the Community fell short of statehood and was a mere "union of states." The high court argued that like all European treaties, the Treaty on European Union is merely an international agreement among sovereign states who remain the "lords of the Treaties" and never surrendered their power to secede the Union (Majone 1998:7).

Others argue that the EU is *sui generis*, a unique organizational hybrid that cannot be compared to anything but itself. Wallace wrote in the early 1980s that the Community was "less than a federation, [but] more than a regime" (Wallace 1983). Burley and Mattli argued ten years later that if the Community remains something well short of a federal state, it also has become something more than an international organization of independent sovereigns (Burley and Mattli 1993:41). First, compared to nation-states, the EU has more decision-making centers and access points, less authoritative control over its territorial area, and fewer powers of implementation (Peterson 1995). The EU can be seen as an additional layer to the democratic nation-state, added on to fully fledged national governments. The resulting peculiar interconnectedness between national and European layers leaves policy implementation mostly in the hands of the member states. Second, the Community lacks the use of violence and coercion, a defining characteristic of the state in classic political theory (Wincott 1995). Finally, the EU's taxation powers are minimal relative to those of nation-states. Second, the EU is not a Keynesian welfare state, since it has little powers of taxation or redistribution. Its limited budget allows for only modest economic and social policies (Scharpf 1997b, Majone 1998).

Nevertheless, core similarities between the EU, the United States, and Switzerland beg for comparison. First, to protect smaller member states, all three polities combine the twin rules of proportional representation and member state representation (Linder 1999:386). Second, compared to parliamentary systems, all three polities have weak parties (Hix 1998:40).[2] Third, like the United States and Switzerland, and by virtue of its independent executive, legislative, and judicial branches, the EU is characterized by checks and balances and by territorial fragmentation (see Pollack 1997). And fourth, in all three polities, the major glue of union has been a federalizing court (Goldstein 1977).

Legal practice in the EU, like in Switzerland and the United States, has been federal since the precedent of the 1963 *van Gend* ruling, which interpreted Community law as a new kind of international law. "Independently of the legislation of Member States, Community law therefore not only imposes obligations on individuals but is also intended to confer upon them rights which become part of their legal heritage" (Case 26/62 van Gend en Loos [1963] ECR:12). This doctrine of direct effect required the principle of supremacy of European law over national law. The case illustrates the political activism of the court, which fundamentally altered the legal character of the Community from one negotiated by the member states. In the following year, the court cemented its supremacy in the *Costa* case by differentiating European law from "ordinary" international law. The court wrote: "By contrast with ordinary international treaties, the EEC Treaty has created its own legal system which, on the entry into force of the Treaty, became an integral part of the legal systems of the Member States and which their courts are bound to apply" (Case 6/64 Costa v. ENEL [1964] ECR:593).

Another expression of the legal unity of the EU is the Rome Treaty's Article 177, whose objective was the uniform application of Community law in the member states (Weiler 1991:2420–21). The article in effect allows individuals to raise matters of Community law before their national courts and have the interpretation of that law referred to the European Court. The court applied Article 177 again in January 2000 when it ruled that a twenty-three-year-old German woman was allowed to bear arms in the German army, despite a German constitutional ban on women bearing arms. The electrical engineer had brought her case in 1996 to a Hanover court, which referred it to the European Court. Invoking Article 177, the EU in effect told a member state how to interpret its own constitution—in this case in the vital matter of Germany's own national security.

Since its adoption, Article 177 has "been transformed into a quasi-federal instrument for reviewing the compatibility of national laws with Community law." This resulted in "the Court of Justice acquiring a power of review which is analogous to—though of course narrower than—that routinely exercised by the Supreme Court of the United States and the constitutional courts of some Member States" (Mancini and Keeling 1994:184–85).

In short, conceptualized as a system of government, the EU shows a "new federalism" (Pinder 1998:266) and resembles federal states such as Germany, Switzerland, Canada, and the United States in important respects (Peterson 1995; Hix 1998:24). Already in 1994, Hix argued that "politics in the EC is not inherently different to the practice of government in any democratic system." He called the EU a "quasi-federal state" and wrote that describing the EU in terms of "cooperative federalism[3]... allows further comparisons to be drawn from politics in other federally organized and territorially pillarised systems" (Hix 1994:1, 20).

By the way, Scharpf showed that the EU can be both unique *and* comparable to national federal entities. He argued that the EU is one of a class of political systems in which decision-making authority is not allocated in zero-sum fashion between different levels of government, but instead shared. Just as the German federal government shares authority with the *Länder* through the need to secure a majority in the Bundesrat, so the EU shares authority with national governments through the pivotal decision-making role of the Council of Ministers (Scharpf 1988:42).

The bottom line: comparative research (Sbragia 1992; Greenwood, Grote, and Ronit 1992; Andersen and Eliassen 1993; Majone 1996; Goldstein 1997) demonstrates the value of comparing the EU to other systems of government. Tools of comparative politics, rather than of international relations, can be gainfully deployed in explaining change in the EU. Sbragia gave the *sui generis* view the *coup de grâce* when she wrote: "thinking about the Community comparatively will prove to be more fruitful analytically than simply describing the Community as 'unique' and consequently analyzing it exclusively on its own terms. Theories, concepts, and knowledge drawn from the study of other polities can in fact be illuminating when applied to the study of the Community" (Sbragia 1992:12–13).

CASE SELECTION

Why choose the United States and Switzerland as bases for comparing the EU? First, as we just saw, all three polities are federalist. Second, the United States and Switzerland are both "model" liberal democracies. Indeed, the EU and the United States have been usefully compared before (Majone 1996; Goldstein 1997), but what is the added value of comparing the EU to Switzerland? There are at least four reasons for including Switzerland in the equation. First, both polities are governed by a collegial executive (Hix 1998:24). Second, the distribution of powers between European states and Brussels is remarkably similar to Switzerland's structure, where canton governments enjoy vast policy-making powers and the overwhelming majority of tax revenue from their citizens. Switzerland's cantons have remained largely autonomous units vis-à-vis Berne. According to the Swiss constitution, "The Cantons are sovereign as long as their sovereignty is not constrained by the federal constitution; they exercise all the rights that are not delegated to the federation" (Bundesverfassung, Title 1, Art. 3). Unlike the governments of more centralized countries, the proportion of Swiss personnel at the federal level is only some 30 percent, but some 70 percent at the cantonal and community level (Germann 1984). This concentration of power at the member level is akin to the EU, whose budget equals less than 3 percent of the public spending of EU member states (Majone, 1997a:14).

Third, like the EU's, Switzerland's juridical system is based principally on the tradition of statutory law; in contrast, the U.S. system is based on common law. Since the EU is a hybrid between the two, this difference might help in explaining variation in legislation and/or jurisdiction.

Finally, much like in Europe, four national languages are spoken in Switzerland (German, French, Italian, and Romantsch), not to mention dozens of other languages spoken by immigrants. With 20 percent of its population being foreign nationals, Switzerland boasts "the highest rate of foreign influx of refugees from all over the world" and faces continuous challenges of linguistic integration.[4]

Fine, but why the cases in chapters 5 and 6, merger policy and biotech regulation? Why not compare other policy fields, for example Common Foreign and Security Policy (CFSP) or Justice and Home Affairs (JHA)? Doubtlessly, these policy fields would be fascinating case studies too; but given our concern with the European democratic deficit, we need to select policy fields where the EU, and especially the nonelective European Commission, enjoy broad discretion and wield power in policies that directly affect European citizens from Barcelona to Belfast. This is true in both merger and biotech regulation.

DEMOCRACY, REPRESENTATION, DELEGATION

What is democracy? Many definitions have been offered (see Inkeles 1990:3–6). A few original conceptions should suffice here. Over half a century ago, Schumpeter wrote that "the democratic method is that institutional arrangement for arriving at political decisions in which individuals acquire the power to decide by means of a competitive struggle for the people's vote" (Schumpeter [1942] 1976:269). Similarly, Downs stated that a democracy must have periodic elections decided by majority rule with a one-person one-vote standard (Downs 1957:23). Lipset defined democracy as "a political system which provides regular constitutional opportunities for changing government officials . . . [and] permits the largest possible part of the population to influence decisions through their ability to choose among alternative contenders for political office" (Lipset 1960:71).

Four decades later, Huntington followed these theorists by defining "a twentieth-century political system as democratic to the extent that its most powerful collective decision makers are selected through fair, honest, and periodic elections in which candidates freely compete for votes and in which virtually all the adult population is eligible to vote" (Huntington 1991:7). That same year, Przeworski built his definition on Dahl's and Linz's: "Democracy is a system in which parties lose elections. . . . [O]ne elementary feature—contestation open to participation (Dahl 1971:20)—is sufficient to identify a political system as democratic." He boiled the definition down to three words: "Democracy is, as Linz (1984) put it, government pro tempore" (Przeworski 1991:10).

All these definitions of democracy require the criterion of voting in elections. Can governments be democratic without elections? Governments are representative if they do what is best for the people, if they act in the best interests of at least a majority of citizens. There are four possible reasons why governments would represent interests of the people (Manin, Przeworski, and Stokes 1999:1):

(1) Because only those persons who are public-spirited offer themselves for public service and they remain uncorrupted while in office.
(2) Because, while individuals who offer themselves for public service differ in their interests, motivation, and competence, citizens use their vote effectively to select either those candidates whose interests are identical to those of voters or those who are and remain devoted to the public service while holding office.
(3) Because, while anyone who holds office may want to pursue some interests or values different from and costly to the people, citizens use their vote effectively to threaten those who would stray from the path of virtue with being thrown out of office.
(4) Because separate powers of government check and balance each other in such a way that, together, they end up acting in people's best interest.

Unfortunately, possibility (1) can only be hoped for but not assumed because institutions cannot guarantee moral virtue. Possibility (2) or (3) is not necessarily a given in the modern administrative state, which is quite different from the state envisioned by the framers of representative government. Lawmaking has become much more complex and voluminous. Thousands of laws are enacted every year. A great deal of lawmaking is no longer done by elected lawmakers but delegated to agencies charged by the legislature with developing regulations to fill out the framework and details of statutory policy. This is the way delegation is usually defined in the legal literature (Eskridge and Ferejohn 1992:534). Commonly accepted reasons for delegation are the complexity of decisions, the quality of decisions, and expertise needed for decisions (Fiorina 1985).[5]

These agencies, for example the European Commission bureaucracy, the U.S. federal agencies, or the Swiss bureaus; the Federal Reserve, the Nationalbank, or most recently the European Central Bank (ECB), are not directly selected by or accountable to voters. To be sure, delegation need not be incompatible with representation. Elected officials usually predetermine agency goals; thus the bureaucracy is subject, indirectly, to the discipline of elections. John Dunn, for example, gives a thin definition for democracy that avoids the criterion of elections: "Democracy is a system in which the demos can expect to play at least some causal role, sooner or later, in the activity by which changes in their leaders are engineered" (Dunn 1999). Indeed, leadership changes can come about without elections: public opinion can force them, for example.

But delegation presents us with the issue of information asymmetries. "And if the people do not know what [government officials] would have done because the government, by virtue of being the government, knows what people do not, who is to judge its actions?" (Manin, Przeworski, and Stokes 1999:9–10).[6]

OVERVIEW

In order to determine whether EU institutions are representative, we need to first determine whether Manin et al.'s possible reasons (2) and (3) above can be assumed in the EU. Can citizens use their votes effectively to select lawmakers and/or threaten them with dismissal? Do legislative institutions in the EU empower citizens to influence lawmaking through votes? Second, we need to see whether possible reason (4) above, the separation of powers that check and balance each other, is a guarantor of representative government. Are EU institutions designed in a way that they end up being and acting in EU citizens' best interests?

To tackle the two tasks, this book is constructed much like a funnel. Each chapter is designed to narrow the scrutiny of the democratic deficit arguments. Chapter 2 classifies and critically evaluates the democratic deficit literature and its arguments that the EU is not democratic enough. The chapter shows that plausible arguments for the existence of a democratic deficit can be grouped into five sets. It examines these arguments for their validity, and eliminates weak, inconsistent, or erroneous arguments.

Once we have refuted the invalid claims, we will be left with the arguments that need further testing. Chapter 3 will begin this process by systematically comparing EU institutions with those of the United States and of Switzerland along widely accepted scales of democracy. By the end of chapter 3, we will see that most EU institutions do not suffer from a democratic deficit significantly greater than that of their counterparts in the United States and Switzerland. However, the jury will still be out on other institutions; particularly the Commission and its bureaucracy will require further scrutiny.

To examine agency actions, we will need a theoretical framework. Chapter 4 will examine the Commission in the framework of agency theory, and aim to derive a theory, including seven dimensions, of bureaucratic democracy. Chapters 5 and 6 apply the indicators of bureaucratic democracy from chapter 4 to specific cases. The chapters compare two stories of regulation in the three polities. Chapter 5 compares European merger regulation, and Chapter 6 European regulation of labeling genetically modified foods, to analogous regulation in Switzerland and the United States. Chapter 7 offers conclusions and some normative recommendations.

We want to know whether legislative institutions and processes in the EU are less democratic than analogous institutions and processes in the United States or Switzerland. The answer has potentially far-reaching implications for the integration of Europe. If we find that the EU is less democratic, or works less democratically, than Switzerland or the United States, then further European integration and enlargement should stop, because it could jeopardize democracy and the rights of European citizens. If, on the other hand, we find that the EU is as democratic as Switzerland or the United States, then further EU integration and expansion is safe for European citizens, at least on grounds of democracy.

In sum, this book seeks to add to the existing body of knowledge in four ways. First, building on earlier classifications of democratic deficit arguments in the EU (Majone 1998; Sanchez de Cuenca 1997), it classifies and evaluates key arguments and assumptions. Second, it goes beyond assertions about the EU made in a vacuum and instead compares the EU, Switzerland, and the United States systematically along quantifiable scales of democracy. Third, it suggests clear dimensions and criteria of bureaucratic democracy. Fourth, it offers a comparison of specific legislative processes across polities, and might reveal some best practices to policymakers attempting to fashion more democratic institutions in Europe or elsewhere.

John Dunn suggests that being ruled is unpleasant. Government is of course necessary to protect citizens from the horizontal hazard of each other; but it is also discomfiting because ruling exposes citizens to the vertical hazard of rulers (Dunn 1999). There is no easy solution to this dilemma. With this study, I hope to make a contribution to the understanding of how institutions can be designed to minimize the hazards of being ruled.

NOTES

1. On 3 June 1999, in the aftermath of the Kosovo crisis, the leaders of fifteen European countries decided to make the European Union a military power, with command headquarters, staffs and forces of its own for peacekeeping and peacemaking missions in future crises. "European Union Vows to Become Military Power," *New York Times*, 4 June 1999, page A1/A22.

2. "One could hence conclude that this [European Parliament parties] is in fact more similar to the dynamics of party organization in the Swiss parliament or in the US Congress than in parliamentary systems" (Hix 1998:40).

3. In "cooperative federalism . . . most policy areas are the joint responsibility of both levels, and the central level is usually responsible for setting policy frameworks whereas the local level is responsible for policy details and implementation. Moreover, the holders of executive office at the lower level are directly involved in the making of legislation at the central level—usually in the second chamber of the legislature. This is often referred to as 'executive federalism'" (Hix 1998:23).

4. *Swiss Review*, June 2000, xiv.

5. As we will see in chapter four, Fiorina argues that legislators delegate for another reason, too: to avoid or disguise their responsibility for failure. Benefits and costs of government programs are not perfectly perceived. Legislators spend considerable efforts improving perception of program benefits or lessening their perceived responsibility for failed programs.

6. Information asymmetries may or may not be innocuous, as we will see in chapter four. Schumpeter (1942) defended them as part of the division of labor between voters and politicians. Voters "must understand that, once they elected an individual, political action is his business not theirs. This means that they must refrain from instructing him what he is to do. . . ."

2

✣

Democratic Deficit Arguments

> All gin bottles will soon have to be round rather than square under new Single Market rules.
>
> *The Times* (London)[1]

The European Union has moved far beyond a mere international institution. According to Weiler, "it has, *inter alia*, the capacity

- to enact norms which create rights and obligations both for its member states and their nationals, norms which are often directly effective and which are constitutionally supreme;
- to take decisions with major impact on the social and economic orientation of public life within the member states and within Europe as a whole;
- to engage the Community and consequently the member states by international agreements with third countries and international organizations;
- to spend significant amounts of public funds. (Weiler 1997:502)

This unprecedented delegation of powers to the EU has spurred concerns about a "democratic deficit" of its institutions and decision-making processes. The EU, critics argue, must tolerate more than other communities of states being measured against standards of democracy, because it—by lawmaking and imposing law—executes immediate sovereign might. One has asked: "With what good, verifiable reasons can we justify that the European Union exercises legislative power over more than 360 million citizens?" (Kielmannsegg 1996:47–51; my translation)

But the label "democratic deficit" includes so many claims that at first glance it is little more than a justification for all kinds of grievances and dissatisfactions with the EU (Sanchez de Cuenca 1997). Partly because the EU is a moving target that has evolved over the years, we encounter a bewildering jungle of arguments and opinions whose underlying assumptions are seldom explicit. This chapter is an attempt at some "clearing and cleaning": to look underneath the arguments, unearth the assumptions that drive them, and distinguish viable plants from weeds. This weeding-out process should enable a systematic analysis of EU institutions along transparent criteria of democracy in the next chapter. Democratic deficit arguments can be bundled into five sets (the literature references are for illustration only and far from exhaustive):

1. *Lack of legitimacy:* Eurobarometer data and low voting turnout indicate insufficient trust in EU institutions. Most public discourse over European politics is still driven by national interests, and member states have an incentive to shift blame to the EU while claiming credit nationally. Institutional channels for legitimacy transfer from the national electorates to the EU level are too narrow to make European citizenship a meaningful concept (Weiler 1991a; Scharpf 1997b). In short, democracy presupposes one European *demos*, but Europe consists of many *demoi*.
2. *Lack of transparency:* EU institutions, especially the Council of Ministers, suffer from too much secrecy (Sbragia 1992; Hayes-Renshaw and Wallace 1995; Franklin, van der Eijk, and Marsh 1996).
3. *Lack of consensus:* the EU is increasingly majoritarian, as epitomized by the rise of qualified majority voting in the council. It is ruled by a tyranny of the majority that crushes the will of minorities (Weiler 1991a).
4. *Lack of accountability:* EU agencies (such as the European Commission, the European Central Bank, and standardization bodies) and the European Court of Justice are unaccountable to the electorate, as their principal, since they are staffed with nonelected officials who expand their competencies away from public scrutiny. The Parliament, the only supranational institution that is directly elected, is too weak to make up for the democratic deficiencies of the other EU institutions (Seidman and Gilmour 1986; Eichener 1995; Shapiro 1997; see Burley and Mattli 1993).
5. *Lack of protection:* negative integration has led to a "race to the bottom," where the most competitive member states are the ones with the lowest level of social policy. The EU's social policy cannot replace this drop of welfare at the national level (Scharpf 1997b, 1999; Streeck 1997; see Held 1987).

Let us look more closely at each argument; then we can evaluate each for its validity.

LACK OF LEGITIMACY

Far from being a unified society, Europe is a multitude of societies and cultures. In addition to now eleven official EU languages, dozens of "lesser used" languages are spoken by significant minorities: Mirandese in Portugal, Gaelic and Welsh in Britain, Occitan and Basque in France and Spain, or Francoprovençal and Friulian in Italy.[2]

Based on this multiplicity of languages and cultures, Weiler argues that the use of a classical vocabulary of citizenship in the discourse on European integration is problematic, since the Treaty of Rome set out to "lay the foundations of an ever closer union among the peoples of Europe"—a union not of one people (as in "the people of the United States") but of many peoples (Weiler 1997:498). Europe consists of "Demoi, then, rather than demos" (Weiler, Haltern, and Mayer 1995:1); and "if there is no demos, there can be no democracy" (Weiler 1997:502). On this view, the EU is not democracy-capable because such a capability would require a community of communication, of experience, and of memory:

> To what degree is a construction such as the European Union "democracy-capable"? . . . It is communities of communication, of experience, and of memory in which collective identity builds itself, stabilizes, and is traded. Europe, also the narrower Western Europe, is hardly a memory community and only in a limited sense an experience community. Europe is not a communication community, because Europe is a multilingual continent—the most banal fact is simultaneously the most elemental. (Kielmannsegg 1996:54–55; author's translation)

Without such a collective European identity, there is no shared language in which a political discourse could take place:

> The conditions for the possibility of a civil-society constitution will also in future be bound to the communication communities that we call nations. . . . The public political discourse carried by mass media, which alone makes politics a cause of the general public and which alone makes democracy democracy, is naturally bound to language spaces. A European discourse, carried by European media, led before and with a European audience–that may be a vision, reality it is not. (Kielmannsegg 1996:57–58; author's translation)

This diversity of languages reflects diverse cultures of democracy. There is not one understanding of democracy, but many competing national understandings (Weiler et al. 1995:1).

In a related vein, Scharpf and Sbragia argue that even if EU institutions were democratized, the structural preconditions on which authentic democratic processes depend are still lacking. There are no European parties, no European political leaders and no European-wide media of political communication; hence no Europe-wide controversies and debates on political issues and policy choices, and no Europe-wide competition for government offices that could assure democratic accountability (Scharpf 1997b). For Sbragia, the dominant role of the Council of Ministers in the EU means that European politics results from the compromise between particular interests of the member states. A judicious European politics that releases itself from these interests cannot exist in her view. It can only demonstrate itself as *European* politics if it is conceived from a European perspective (Sbragia 1993:32); but parliamentary elections in member states from which governments emerge are national—they are not European elections focusing on Europe, in which competing programs of European politics are decided. European topics play at most an occasional and marginal role.

This poses a dilemma: the EU derives its legitimacy from the member states, but the possibilities of legitimacy transfer are increasingly narrow. If democracy means that governments derive their legitimate power from the consent of the governed, then this means not consent that is granted once and for all, but consent that must be given again and again newly, and can be withheld (Kielmannsegg 1996:53). But there is no institutionalized vote in which European voters can withhold their consent. Without these basic guarantees, EU citizenship is a phony concept. Weiler accuses EU "managers" of offering European citizenship as an empty package, an exercise in brand development to placate dissatisfied shareholders—"Saatchi and Saatchi European citizenship" (Weiler 1997:502).

What is more, the EU lacks a constitution built on diffuse consent, which "is surely not a sufficient condition for a sustainable foundation built upon diffuse support, but in any case a necessary one" (Kielmannsegg 1996:50–51). And the current EU "constitution" is merely a system of contractual arrangements between states, not a true constitution (Sbragia 1992:271).

Enlargement of the EU can make things only worse, argues Scharpf. Without minimally necessary constitutional reforms, the accession of new EU member states will compound its existing problems of heterogeneity. Once Central and Eastern European states enter the Union, the economic, institutional, cultural, and linguistic differences between member states will further preclude a European collective identity and European-wide political discourses that could legitimize majority decisions on contested issues. This may exacerbate the perception of an "irremediable European democratic deficit" (Scharpf 1999:188).

The December 2000 Nice Summit about enlarging the Union to the east brought these fears of current, Western European, member states to a head. Most of the twelve candidates for accession by 2005 (Bulgaria, Cyprus, Czech Republic, Estonia, Hungary, Latvia, Lithuania, Malta, Poland, Rumania, Slovakia, and Slovenia) are former Eastern bloc nations and lack long-standing traditions of democratic regimes. Would their membership weaken the overall adherence to democracy in the EU?

LACK OF TRANSPARENCY

The second line of democratic deficit arguments denounces the lack of transparency of EU policy processes to citizens. The EU constitutes yet another layer of government, removing decision-making even further from concerned citizens than the national state does already (Weiler, Haltern, and Mayer 1995:2). EU committees, working groups, and agencies have grown to over a thousand, according to some estimates. The overlap of their activities and the divergence of the rules governing them create a real lack of transparency (Dehousse et al. 1992:30).

A significant difference between a democratic legislature and the Council of Ministers, the European institution analogous to the U.S. Senate or the Swiss Ständerat, is that a democratic legislature is obligated to publicize the minutes of its deliberations. Parliaments vote publicly, and the act of voting and being seen to vote is a crucial identifier of the parliamentarian's role and performance. But in the council, voting is more implicit than explicit, and decisions are reached mainly by persuading potential opponents to demur. Much like in a national cabinet, votes are not willingly made public. Compounding this opacity is the proliferation of procedures, especially those involving the Parliament. There are some twenty-three different combinations of procedures for decisions shared between the council and the Parliament on legislation. Proceedings are concealed from scrutiny, which raises problems of trust (Hayes-Renshaw and Wallace 1995). The Parliament is much more public, but its role in the European legislative process is not transparent to voters either. This lack of transparency allows for collusion by particular interests. For example, some critics assert that major parties collude in European Parliament elections by avoiding discussion of divisive European issues (Franklin, van der Eijk, and Marsh 1996).

The root of this lack of transparency could be that the EU lacks a clear separation of powers. Manin reminds us of the important distinction between separation of powers on the one hand, and checks and balances on the other. In a system of separation of powers, Parliament is the "unchecked checker" that expresses the popular will. By contrast, in a system of checks and balances each function of government is performed by more than one branch. For example in the United States, the framers devised checks and balances to rein in the supremacy of the legislature. The legislature does not have the last word; its laws can be vetoed by the executive or ruled unconstitutional by the Supreme Court. The executive's actions can be checked by the legislature, by independent agencies, or by courts. The courts are controlled through appointment by the executive and legislature, and through the legislature's censure procedures The Central Bank is checked by appointment, censure procedures, and the threat of legislation (Manin 1994). The EU is organized along similar checks and balances among the Parliament, council, commission, and court. While such a system of checks and balances is designed for greater accountability of institutions, it can obscure responsibilities, which makes it difficult for citizens to hold rulers accountable.

LACK OF CONSENSUS

As we have seen above, enlargement creates fears of more heterogeneity, more *demoi* that weaken the democratic fiber of Europe. But member states may have a far more concrete fear of new member states: that their accession will reduce the voting weight of each existing member state and its citizenry. The analogy is a corporation: when a company issues new voting shares, the value of each share shrinks (Weiler et al. 1995:2).

This fear has become salient with the decline of the unanimity principle. The 1966 Luxembourg Compromise, an informal practice that gave every single member state the power to veto policies by invoking its vital national interest, was "the single most legitimating element" of the Community's constitution (Weiler 1991:189).

The threat of a tyrannical majority did not exist as long as all decisions required unanimity, but majoritarian voting rules might offer insufficient protection for the minority. The December 2000 Nice Summit renewed fears among member governments of being outvoted. EU heads of state agreed to expand qualified majority voting (QMV) in the Council of Ministers into thirty-five new policy areas. Powerful member states, such as Germany, France, the United Kingdom, Italy, and Spain, by virtue of their greater voting weights, can impose decisions on weaker member states. The Nice Treaty reinforced this trend by changing the voting weights in the Council. After Nice, ninety-one of the 345 council votes will be a blocking minority; alternatively, countries constituting at least 38 percent of the EU population can block a policy. The 38 percent rule gives Germany plus two other large member countries de facto power to block policies under QMV.

The council's legitimacy derives from its members being elected office holders in their own countries. But this no longer seems an adequate base for legislation under the first pillar (European Communities) or much beyond coordination under the second (Common Foreign and Security Policy, CFSP) and third (Cooperation in Justice and Home Affairs, JHA) pillars. Ensuring ratification of council decisions by national legislatures has become harder, since QMV creates a compliance problem when member governments are outvoted in the council. The problem might actually become more acute if voting records become more public (Hayes-Renshaw and Wallace 1995).

This majoritarian trend is bound to continue. "If decisions are made unanimously, all governments bear responsibility collectively for the decision, and each can be held responsible by its parliament and its electorate—this may in some cases be difficult or improbable, but it is not impossible," writes one EU critic. But "with the continuation of the integration process, majority rule will gain increasing significance for the Council of Ministers. Majority decisions in the Council of Ministers—this means nothing other than that a group of member states imposes its will on other member states" (Kielmannsegg 1996:48; author's translation).

LACK OF ACCOUNTABILITY

Weak Parliament

The European Parliament is the only EU institution directly elected by European voters. Critics assert that despite its growing powers, the Parliament is too weak to compensate for the democratic deficit of other EU institutions, that its influence on European legislation is still quite limited, and that its powers are feeble relative to those of most national parliaments. Most importantly, the Parliament has no right of initiative in legal terms, although its committees can and do submit reports to the Commission for future legislation.

Parliament elections suffer from low voter participation, as few voters think their vote matters:

> Concerning the elections to the European Parliament, one will certainly not be able to interpret the low participation level (56.6% in 1994—tendency since 1979 declining) as a vote against Europe—it is above all expression of the widespread conviction that the elections to the European Parliament are insignificant because they are inconsequential. (Kielmannsegg 1996:50; author's translation).

Finally, compounding the weakness of the Parliament is the absence of a European party system that would allow steering European politics through elections (Kielmannsegg 1996:53; Scharpf 1997b).

Unaccountable Agencies

The weak Parliament is unable to check another key actor: European agencies. EU bureaus are independent of national-level control. They are guilty of inappropriate intrusion into areas of national sovereignty. As a regulatory state, the EU poses problems of oversight and accountability not posed by the traditional tax-and-spend state, not least the problem of multiple functions. "That this nonelective bureaucracy executes, legislates, and adjudicates raises questions of excessive power and accountability" (Wood and Waterman 1994).

The European Commission embodies the claim that unaccountable bureaus hold excessive competencies. Some critics argue that the Commission usurps power and springs decisions on member states. With its initiative monopoly, the Commission plays unquestionably a significant part in the European "ruling power," but is far removed from any electoral vote (Kielmannsegg 1996:53). Though the Parliament vets and approves the Commission's president and the College of Commissioners, the Commission is not directly elected.

Besides, not nearly all EU legislation passes through the Council of Ministers or the Parliament. The Commission can act alone in certain instances, for example in regulating common markets in fruit and vegetables under the Common Agricultural Policy (CAP) or in imposing an EU-wide ban on British beef. And the 1992 Treaty on European Union permits the Commission unprecedented leverage over the finances of member states. Article 104c of the Maastricht Treaty enjoins member states to avoid excessive government deficits, and requires the Commission to "monitor the development of the budgetary situation and of the stock of government debt in the Member States with a view to identifying gross errors" (Majone 1997:5).

We need to keep in mind that the Commission is more political than other bureaus. The major fields of Commission activity—proposing legislation and supervising the implementation of decisions—are highly politicized tasks. The Commission has been called a "politicized bureaucracy" (Christiansen 1997). One legal observer noted that "the Commission combines, not only within the competition division, but within individual officials, the role of prosecutor and judge. . . [this] has left the Commission the master of its own procedural destiny" (Brent 1995:278). The Commission has adopted the role of guardian of rules and procedures as much as that of big spender—a dangerous combination.

Suspicions about these multiple and expansive competencies are reflected in the commission's low popular credibility. The Eurobarometer of November 2001 reported that only every second European citizen trusts the Commission, while 30 percent mistrust it.[3]

The Commission is only one EU agency accused of excessive powers. Another is the European Central Bank. The Maastricht Treaty authorizes the ECB, not a Community institution within the meaning of Article 4 of the Treaty of Rome, to make regulations that become European and member states' law without the involvement of national parliaments, the European Parliament or other Community institutions. With minor exceptions, the bank's status can be modified only through treaty amendments, which require unanimous consent of all member states. Elected officials can override bank decisions only through a very arduous procedure. The one formal accountability requirement for the bank is to present an annual report on the activities of the European System of Central Banks and on the monetary policy of the previous and current years to the European Council, the Parliament, the Council of Ministers, and the Commission. The bank's income and expenditures do not fall under the Community budget, which gives it yet another dimension of independence (Majone 1998:15). It has the power to determine the livelihoods of EU citizens from Sicily to Ulster unconstrained by a sufficient structure of accountability.

Majone explains the lack of oversight in the EU-bureaucracy with the emergence of the regulatory state, which is taking the place of the tax-and-spend state. The EU, with its extremely low budget, has no choice but to be a regulatory apparatus:

> Despite significant growth in recent years, the EU budget represents only 2.4 per cent of all the public sector spending of the member states, and less than 1.3 per cent of the gross domestic product of the Union... [T]he only way for the European Commission to increase its influence is to expand the scope of its regulatory activities: rule making puts a good deal of power in the hands of the Brussels authorities, in spite of the tight budgetary constraints imposed by the member states. In other words, since the EC lacks an independent power to tax and spend, it could increase its competences only by developing as an almost pure type of regulatory state. (Majone 1997:14–16)

Such regulatory activity lends itself less to oversight than budgetary activity does. Therefore the EU is characterized by a lack of regulatory accountability:

> The absence of a binding budget constraint for regulatory policy making has several important consequences. First, neither parliament nor the government systematically determine the overall level of regulatory activity in a

given period. Second, no office is responsible for establishing regulatory priorities across the government. Finally, while spending programmes are regularly audited, no such control is exercised over regulatory programmes. (Majone 1997:14)

One such problem of oversight lies in the area of standardization. Critics maintain that, while European standards promulgated by CEN (Comité Européen de Normalisation) or CENELEC (Comité Européen de Normalisation Electrique) are binding on all participating countries, these institutions and their decisions are not accountable to public or legislative scrutiny.

Excessive Court Authority[4]

The caseload of the European Court of Justice (ECJ) is growing at more than 10 percent per year, with over 1,000 cases pending.[5] The limits of EU jurisdiction are unclear, and the court's constantly expanding authority raises the danger of excessive power that threatens to curtail the powers of member states and their courts.

Over time, the court has quietly transformed the Treaty of Rome into a de facto European Community constitution and steadily increased the impact and scope of EC law. Already in the 1960s, in a series of landmark decisions, the court succeeded in moving the review of member-state acts from the sphere of international law to that of constitutional law. Until 1963 the enforcement of the Rome Treaty depended entirely on national legislatures of member states. By 1965, a member-state citizen could ask a national court to invalidate any provision of domestic law found to conflict with directly applicable provisions of the treaty. By 1975, this right of EU citizens was extended to secondary legislation or "directives" passed by the Council of Ministers. And by 1990, EC citizens could ask their national courts to interpret national legislation consistently with EC legislation in case of undue delay in application by national legislatures (Burley and Mattli 1993). The court is even authorized to impose penalties on member states that violate their treaty commitments (Article 171 TEC) and to rule at the request of ordinary member-state courts on the authoritative interpretation of Community law (Article 177 TEC). In sum, the court transformed the Treaty of Rome into supranational law with direct effect on member states (Weiler 1991; Volcansek 1992). This decision liberated European law from the control of national governments, parliaments, and courts over the domestic implementation of international agreements (Scharpf 1999:53); and it was a decision not taken by the people or their elected representatives (Sanchez de Cuenca 1997).

The doctrines of direct effect and supremacy have had significant impact on policy making. For example, when the council could not agree on a common transport regime, the court backed the Commission, effectively bypassing the Council, to liberalize the transport sector (Héritier 1997a). Hence, both institutions assumed lawmaking powers in politically contested areas (Scharpf 1999:64). As we will see in chapter 5, the doctrines have also profoundly affected European competition law. Direct effect turned neoliberal ideology into constitutional competition law to a degree unprecedented in the member states; and supremacy placed neoliberalism even beyond the control of parliamentary supermajorities in EU member states. "By judicial fiat, in other words, the freedom to sell and to consume had achieved constitutional protection against the political judgement of democratically legitimized legislatures" (Scharpf 1999:54–58).

Remarkably, member-state courts and governments have been willing, by and large, to go along with the direct effect and supremacy doctrines of European over national law (Weiler 1992; Burley and Mattli 1993) and have effectively condoned a monopoly of the European Court in the substantive interpretation of European law (Scharpf 1999:55).

LACK OF PROTECTION

Scharpf has argued that globalization and regulatory competition are forcing a reduction of social services in EU member states, but that this loss of national competencies is not balanced by a corresponding build-up of EU competencies. As economic integration deepens globally and even more so in the EU, national capacities to regulate and to tax mobile capital and firms are reduced, whereas governance at European or international levels is constrained by conflicts of interest among the governments involved (Scharpf 1997c). The result can be a "race to the bottom" (Vogel 1995) or a "Delaware effect" named after the American state that attracted companies by offering the least demanding standards for incorporation (Cary 1974). The nation-state can no longer, and the EU cannot yet, protect the interests of European citizens (Scharpf 1997c). In this view, the EU lacks legitimacy because it is a "welfare laggard" failing to provide social justice and economic redistribution.

Other critics have warned that this type of "regime erosion" in countries with high standards, unless kept in check within those countries themselves, will lead to further regime erosion in countries with lower standards (Streeck 1997:658–659) or that the gap between rich and poor creates an inequality in the structure of the Union (Held 1987:289).

Scharpf suggests that the purposes originally served by national regulations would be better protected if what is lost in national problem-solving capacity is regained through reregulation at the European or international level (Scharpf 1997c). National governments are losing democratic legitimacy not in the input dimension but in the output or effectiveness dimension. If effective self-determination is to be maintained, the responsibility for redistribution must be shifted from the national to the European level (Leibfried 1992; Leibfried and Pierson 1995). But this would move political responsibility to a level where legitimacy is not yet available and where decisions could not be taken by majority vote in the Parliament or by a democratically legitimated EU government. The freedom of choice at the national level is massively constrained, while at the European level, where action might be effective, democratic legitimacy is weaker or nonexistent (Scharpf 1997b).

Scharpf revisits Tinbergen's distinction between "negative" and "positive integration" (Tinbergen 1965). Negative integration means the removal of tariffs, quantitative restrictions, and other barriers to trade or obstacles to undistorted competition, and is usually consistent with a neoliberal or anti-interventionist approach. Negative integration was already enshrined in the "primary law" of the Treaties of Rome, and could be pushed by the commission and the court without much political attention. Positive integration, by contrast, means the reconstruction of economic regulation at the level of the larger economic unit and can be either interventionist—Keynesian—or anti-interventionist (Scharpf 1999:45).

From the neoliberal, anti-interventionist viewpoint, most legitimate aspirations of economic integration are realized through negative integration—the achievement of a common market. From an interventionist perspective, however, the common market is a constraint that reduces the capacity of national polities to pursue democratically legitimized policy goals.

Scharpf does not doubt the output-legitimacy of European policies that take these high hurdles of negotiated agreement. Positive integration depends on agreement in the intergovernmental council and in the pluralist Parliament, in which diffuse interests of consumers and environmentalists have gained a strong foothold (Pollack 1997). Since majority voting is not generally available for positive integration and market-correcting policies, opposing arguments must be heard, and solutions adopted are more likely to reach the Pareto frontier (Scharpf 1999:190). But he warns that ideological, economic, and institutional differences among member states will make agreement on common European regulations—positive integration—extremely difficult and often impossible. Since positive integration depends on high levels of agreement among member governments, positive integration policies are unlikely to be dealt with effectively at the European level.

The institutional structure of the EU makes negative integration (i.e., taking down barriers between nations) the dominant alternative. This restricts the capacity of national governments to pursue redistribution at home, thus reducing the accountability of rulers. Interventionist policies and the people they could serve are systematically disadvantaged in European integration. If simultaneously negative integration and pressures of globalization undercut national idiosyncratic solutions, the overall result will be a general loss of problem-solving capacity in the European polity and a "loss of output-oriented democratic legitimacy" (Scharpf 1999:49, 83).

This argument asserts that this race to the bottom happens not only in the economic but also in the political sphere. With integration, national parliaments suffer a loss of competence that is not offset by gains in the European Parliament (Bogdanor and Woodcock 1991; Neunreither 1994; Williams 1991).

Now that we have classified the various democratic deficit arguments, we can turn to analyzing and evaluating each.

LACK OF LEGITIMACY?

Recall that the lack-of-legitimacy argument comes in several guises: the EU cannot be democratic because it lacks a community of communication, of experience, and of memory; it lacks European parties, European political leaders, and European media; and it lacks a constitution able to engender consent and command legitimacy.

Let us begin with the last of these subarguments. In contrast to liberal democracies (but like the United Kingdom and Israel, for example), the EU lacks a written constitution based on the consent of the European citizenry. A 2000 Eurobarometer survey asked Europeans for the first time whether they support a European constitution. The survey defined a constitution as a "fundamental document combining the various treaties currently in place." Seven of ten respondents were in favor, with the lowest level of support in the United Kingdom (47 percent) and the highest in the Netherlands (88 percent).[6] Although EU citizens already enjoy rights granted by their respective member states, a European constitution would certainly help forge European citizenship.

Another valid concern that European leaders recognized is the possibility that enlargement might weaken European democratic values. The 1993 Copenhagen Summit established clear political criteria for membership, including democratic institutions. Candidate countries must have achieved stable institutions that can guarantee democracy, the rule of law, human rights and respect for and protection of minorities.[7] It remains to be seen whether and how the EU will ensure ongoing compliance with these steep criteria with the anticipated growth to twelve new members by 2005.

But arguments that deny the existence of a European *demos* go deeper. They can come dangerously close to asserting that ethnic and linguistic homogeneity is necessary for democratic legitimacy (Scharpf 1997b). A common language or culture has little to do with national community: quite the contrary. It is in the very nature of democracy that it allows for a multitude of peoples and cultures to cohabit a political entity and strive for a common understanding. Democratic, multicultural nations such as Canada, Switzerland, or the United States show that cultural homogeneity is not a prerequisite for democracy.[8] And a *demos* is not a given, but historically constructed. There is no reason why Europe could not construct a European culture; and even if it will not, a single government can still rule a fragmented polity. Both Switzerland and the United States have integrated their multiple *demoi* over time (note the plural "United *States*").

Switzerland, for example, has been a multilingual, multicultural *and* homogenous democracy ever since 1848, when the then 25 cantons chose the path toward federation, notwithstanding their linguistic and religious diversity. Instead of installing one prime minister as in most other European countries, the framers of the Swiss constitution formed an executive body, the Bundesrat (Federal Council) consisting of seven ministers. This collective structure granted proportional representation in the executive to linguistic minorities from the start to provide for collective and balanced decision making in all matters of government. Today, Switzerland is a well-known example of peaceful multiculturalism that conducts all government business in three official languages.

Theories of state formation allow us to generalize from the Swiss example. Benedict Anderson, for example, defines the nation as "an imagined political community . . ."

> My point of departure is that nationality, or, as one might prefer to put it in view of that word's multiple significations, nation-ness, as well as nationalism, are cultural artifacts of a particular kind. To understand them properly we need to consider carefully how they have come into historical being, in what ways their meanings have changed over time, and why, today, they command such profound emotional legitimacy." (Anderson 1983:4–6)

A government apparatus constructs communities of communication, of experience or of memory through schooling, the army, and other institutions. Take France: as late as 1863, half of the French recruits in the French army did not speak French (Weber 1976). If national identity is not a natural given but a historical construction, then it is conceivable that a supranational European identity can be formed over time just as well as national identities can. The first steps were taken in the Maastricht and Amsterdam Treaties. The citizenship clause in Maastricht stated: "Citizenship of the Union is hereby established. Every person holding the nationality of a Member State shall be a citizen of the Union." The Amsterdam clause added: "Citizenship of the Union shall complement and not replace national citizenship." And while some of their parents are still often troubled by the idea of belonging to "Europe," many young people consider it natural to feel European as well as, say, German or Italian. Already in 1993, polls by the European Community found that three out of four young Europeans between the ages of fifteen and twenty-four supported its efforts to achieve regional union.[9]

In another refutation of the *demoi* argument, Héritier suggests that Europe's very diversity, far from being an impediment, might actually be an important source of democratic accountability. Because European decision making involves a consensus among different actors who monitor each other suspiciously, every step in policy development involves a high degree of horizontal control (Czada 1996) among knowledgeable actors. This horizontal control is often more substantial than vertical control by citizens and their elected representatives. The same distrust that hinders swift decision making also functions as a powerful mechanism of accountability (Héritier 1997b, 1999:26).

This idea is not exactly new. Madison wrote in the *Federalist* that the diversification of society is an important factor of fair democratic government, because the variety of parties and interests in the large republic makes it less likely that factions "[w]ill have a common motive to invade the rights of the other citizens; . . . where there is consciousness of unjust or dishonorable purposes, communication is always checked by distrust in proportion to the number of whose concurrence is necessary" (Madison [1787] 1981:22).

European integration has ebbed and flowed ever since the inception of the European Coal and Steel Community (ECSC) in 1953. Periods of supranationalism preceded and followed periods of intergovernmentalism. But it would be wrong to conclude that the European super state is not capable of federal unity because its member states still command considerable autonomy. Taking Switzerland once again as a somewhat analogous example, we have seen that the Swiss cantons retain significant independence in collecting taxes and shaping policy. Such autonomy, or lack of federal unity, does not make Switzerland undemocratic—quite the contrary.

Now to the next subargument within the lack-of-legitimacy claim: the "disconnect" between the content of national elections and the European level at which national governments participate. This gulf is serious, but is a common obstacle to aggregating particular interests in any polity. The analogous claim in the United States would be that the governor of California or a congresswoman from New York is unable to make policy at the aggregated, national level. Even if this were true, it would not negate the democratic nature of congressional or governmental institutions.

Similarly, we cannot conclude that national-level elections and EU-level business are incompatible, let alone that EU institutions are undemocratic that a European civil society is impossible, or not backed by the consent of the governed. Low election turnouts in European Parliament elections do not correlate with a democratic deficit, as Switzerland shows, where voter participation has often been lower than in European elections (see Bollen 1980). The debate on European institutions is potent and public, and polls have shown repeatedly that members-state citizens are in favor of further European integration.[10]

In 1993, the *Bundesverfassungsgericht* (the German constitutional court) derived the constitutionality and legitimacy of the Treaty on European Union from the democratic legitimacy of the countries signing it. The EU is founded upon contracts that member states have ratified under rules given by their constitutions. Except perhaps during the founding years, popular votes have played a significant role in the extension and deepening of the EU (Kielmannsegg 1996:51).

In sum, the absence of a viable party system at the European level is a serious deficiency, since stronger European parties might act as better watchdogs for voters and against corruption.[11] But if the EU suffers indeed from an insufficient civil society, it shares this affliction with many nation-states. And according to Eurobarometer surveys, the legitimacy of the EU seems not to be declining but growing apace: in November 2001, 50 percent of European citizens said they trust the European Commission, up from 45 percent in July 2001, 40 percent in spring 1999 and 35 percent in 1998.[12]

LACK OF TRANSPARENCY?

The lack of transparency in EU policy making, however, is a serious problem, above all in the Council of Ministers. Hayes-Renshaw and Wallace suggest several remedies for the council's lack of accountability and transparency: simple one-page summaries of key features of decisions; the publication of who voted which way in votes; public council sessions; or indirect accountability through national parliaments (Hayes-Renshaw and Wallace 1995).

An argument against greater transparency of EU decision making, especially in the council, is that it has downsides for efficiency or freedom of action, since much council business is transacted confidentially and since the intergovernmental brokering of agreements would be much harder in the fishbowl of publicity, where positions harden easily. Also, the members of the council are subject to electoral pressures in their respective member states (Goldstein 1997:182); these pressures act as a democratic check on the council's discretion. But lack of transparency makes it hard for outsiders to believe that the council is efficient, since it cannot marshal evidence to the contrary; and the council's comitology system has long been seen as a gap in democracy.

A *modus vivendi*, approved at an Inter-Institutional Conference in December 1994, permits Parliament to deliver an opinion and compels the council to take "due account of the European Parliament's point of view without delay." While this provision is open to interpretation, it increases the information available to Parliament, thus improving the transparency of the council.

But lack of transparency goes beyond the council; and opacity creates opportunities for collusion, which tend to occur in any political system, whether democratic, authoritarian or totalitarian. The question is whether there are checks against collusion, and whether it is publicized if and when it takes place. To deter against collusion, monitoring and decentralization efforts are being undertaken. For example,

> the declarations attached to the Treaty on transparency and access to information, and on the cost-benefit evaluation of Commission proposals, should be seen as part of the same effort to monitor more closely the regulatory process.... Many new provisions give the impression that their main objective is not so much to legitimise the regulatory power of the EC in a number of new fields, but rather to make sure that this power is not used beyond certain limits—an impression which is only strengthened by the inclusion of the subsidiarity principle in the Treaty. (Majone 1997:16)

Subsidiarity means that policies should be decided at national, and perhaps even regional or local, levels whenever possible (Nugent 1994:69). The subsidiarity principle, Article 3b in the Treaty on European Union (TEU), reads:

> The Community shall act within the limits of the powers conferred upon it by this Treaty and of the objectives assigned to it therein.
> In areas which do not fall within its exclusive competence, the Community shall take action, in accordance with the principle of subsidiarity, only if and in so far as the objectives of the proposed action cannot be sufficiently achieved by the Member States and can therefore, by reason of the

scale or effects of the proposed action, be better achieved by the Community.

Any action by the Community shall not go beyond what is necessary to achieve the objectives of this Treaty.[13]

But despite such efforts to increase transparency and minimize collusion, it remains to be seen whether Council of Ministers deliberations will become more transparent to the public. And unless they do, this democratic deficit argument is justified. Opacity, however useful for efficiency and however compatible with representation it may be, is not conducive to democratic accountability. The EU's lack of transparency is a significant liability on the balance sheet of democracy.

TYRANNY OF THE MAJORITY?

The argument that enlargement lowers the voting weights of existing members is easily refuted. As the population of any democratic system grows, each individual has less voting power. A recent example is the unification of the Federal Republic of Germany and the German Democratic Republic, which increased the population of Germany to some 85 million people, each of whom now has a smaller voting weight than before that "merger" of the two countries. But this fact has no bearing on the democracy of the German polity. Conversely, the claim that some member states' greater voting weight is undemocratic is simply false, since those voting weights are based upon the number of European citizens who can vote there.

The move away from unrestricted unanimity in the Council of Ministers on the other hand, undertaken in the interest of greater efficiency and to break deadlocks, is indeed a threat to those member states whose vote is in the minority. Under the informal Luxembourg Compromise, the only occasion where member states can invoke their veto power is when their vital national interest is at stake. "The unanimity rule guarantees, under some conditions, that the result of collective choice is efficient in the Pareto sense, since anybody adversely affected by the collective decision can veto it" (Majone 1997a:27–28). In this sense, a shift away from unanimity, while likely permitting more innovation because conservative member states can no longer stop legislation that they do not like, might lead to Pareto-inferior outcomes: it can make some member states worse off. But this argument for unanimity is less an argument for democracy than one for Pareto-efficiency.[14]

The criticism of majoritarian voting rules as oppressing the minority does not stand scrutiny for several reasons. First, as long as redistribution remains an issue, majority voting is bound to remain. Where redistributive concerns prevail, legitimacy can be assured only by majoritarian means (Majone 1996:296). Second, two-party systems in majoritarian democracies, for example in the United Kingdom or the United States, engender majorities (for example the Republican-led U.S. Congress), but nobody would claim that these systems suffer from a democratic deficit. Finally, the European rules adopted by qualified majority voting (QMV) have often been more innovative and more representative of voter preferences than those of all or most countries of the EU (Majone 1996:74–78); for example, in health or immigration policy.[14]

To grasp the significance of this last point, we need to make a distinction between the intergovernmental and supranational fields in the EU (Majone 1998:8). The intergovernmental field—the second pillar (a common foreign and security policy), the third pillar (cooperation in justice and home affairs), the European Council of Heads of State and Government, and the Council of Ministers—is international. The supranational field is everything else: the first pillar (the European Communities), the Parliament and courts, and the Commission. This distinction matters because the democracy of the member states can lend democratic legitimacy only to the former, not the latter. Why? Because the supranational field is designed to safeguard the rights and interests of EU citizens, if need be against the majoritarian decisions of their own government or even against the majority of EU member states. The supranational institutions do not gain legitimacy from the democratic regimes of the member states; they must legitimize themselves, either through elections (as for the Parliament) or through procedural or substantive legitimacy (Majone 1998:8). This brings us to the next democratic deficit argument: that a weak European Parliament cannot effectively constrain the other supranational EU institutions.

LACK OF ACCOUNTABILITY?

Weak Parliament?

Recall that the European Parliament is the only supranational EU body directly elected by the European citizenry. Direct elections began in 1979 and have taken place every five years since then. As we saw, national parties essentially organize Parliament election campaigns at the national level. The voter turnout for these elections has been low and declining (62 percent in 1979, 61 percent in 1984, 58 percent in 1989, 56.5 percent in 1994, and 52.8 percent in 1999), probably because EP elections do not offer prospects of changing a government, switching a policy, or breaking political reputations. However, we should not conclude based on low participation levels in European Parliament elections that European citizens see the Parliament as inconsequential. Participation levels of less than 60 percent are typical for, and often higher than, the voting level of national elections in most member states.

The Parliament has been gaining influence steadily since the adoption of the Single European Act (SEA) in 1986; we will see in the next chapter exactly how. Suffice it to say for now that parliamentary committees may exert more control, especially over bureaucratic agencies, than is visible at first glance, "especially through the appointment process and by conducting oversight hearings" (Majone 1997a:20). Under codecision, the Parliament is a more equal partner alongside the council in several important policy areas, despite the weighting of the procedure toward the council. For example, under codecision, the presidents of the council and Parliament sign acts jointly. The net result is an increasingly bipartite bargaining process.[15] In some cases (e.g., the Fourth Research and Technological Development [RTD] Framework Programme), interinstitutional "trialogues" (Peterson 1995:86), where the Commission and council informally court Parliament, underscore the increasing formal powers of the EP under co-decision. Parliament is beginning to "exercise its new veto power under the procedure" (Docksey and Williams 1994:141). However, codecision is not applicable to all areas in which the council legislates; for example, in European economic or Central Bank policy, where the Parliament is merely consulted or informed.

Finally, a weak Parliament may not matter as much as democratic deficit critics suspect. Majone argues that the "Westminster" or pure majoritarian model of democracy, which sees the directly elected Parliament as the only, or at least the main, repository of democratic legitimacy does not directly fit federal or quasi-federal systems, whose component units are autonomous because of institutional arrangements—vertical or horizontal separation of powers, checks and balances, over-representation of small jurisdictions, judicial review—designed to prevent the crushing of minorities by majorities. Such nonmajoritarian institutions are just as important as the legislature, not only in federal-type systems but in all "plural" societies, that is, in "societies that are sharply divided along religious, ideological, linguistic, cultural, ethnic or racial lines into virtually separate subsocieties with their own political parties, interest groups, and media of communication" (Lijphart 1984:22). The EU is a prime example of such a plural society in need of cleavage management and the protection of minorities through nonmajoritarian mechanisms (Majone 1998:19).

Nonetheless, despite all the above reasons, the Parliament needs more power, especially agenda-setting power to initiate policies, as we will see in chapter 3.

Unaccountable Agencies?

What about other supranational actors? The European Central Bank (ECB) and the European bureaucracy are not subject to popular elections, thus not subject to popular control and increasingly independent of national-level control.

One EU agency with much power is the ECB. We will review agency independence, and specifically theories of central bank independence, in chapter 4. For now, the bank's independence should not be seen as a democratic deficit. Rather, an independent central bank, much like an independent court, is a meaningful check on the executive. As the Federal Reserve does in the United States, the ECB acts as a check on economic policy, as long as it explains its targets and actions to the public. And who says that the United States suffers from a democratic deficit because of the Federal Reserve's independence?

Other new bodies, such as the European Environmental Agency and the European Centre for Drugs and Drug Addiction, are information agencies—structures which lack coercive power of their own, and whose primary purpose is to provide policymakers with the information they need to carry out their policies (Majone 1997b). In 1958, the court ruled (case 9/56, *Meroni v. High Authority*) that Community law prohibits delegation of discretionary powers to bodies not created by the treaty—namely to information agencies. But their lack of discretionary power should not be perceived as a sign of irrelevance. The court admitted the legality of the delegation of executive powers so long as these are clearly circumscribed and the delegating body retains control over agency decisions. Hence these agencies operate under Commission control: for example, with the European Agency for the Evaluation of Medicinal Products (AMEA), the Commission takes formal decisions; with the Trademark and the Plant Variety Offices, the Commission controls the legality of agency decisions.

One new competence delegated to nonelective bureaus is standardization. In 1985 most European standardization was delegated to the Comité International des Normes (CEN). Standardization processes are also accountable to the commission, which issues directives, then delegates their implementation to CEN. Although they are private processes, standard-setting processes appear to be more accountable and legitimate than American standard-setting processes, which Europeans incidentally criticize for insufficient democracy. For example, CEN's eighteen members have weighted voting rights, similar to the national voting weights in the Council of Ministers. In the beginning, there was no provision for consumer participation in CEN, but in 1995, ANEC (European association for the representation of consumers in standardization) was founded to enable involvement of consumer interests. At the behest of high-standard countries, especially Germany and France, the Commission funded consumer representatives to be sent to CEN meetings. While today consumers and industry are generally satisfied with CEN's process, unions and small and medium enterprises complain of still having no voice in standard setting.

Later, chapter four will theorize agency discretion; here just a preliminary word on European agencies, which act as network coordinator, rather than as central regulators, as in the United States. They have been given limited powers, and national representatives play a crucial part in European agencies. The fact that EU agencies enjoy limited autonomy is precisely why member states did not oppose their creation, and why the legitimacy problem posed by American independent agencies was bypassed.

European agencies are less problematic than their American counterparts for several other reasons. First, as we saw, the EC treaty has not realized a neat separation of powers, but a system of checks and balances between the interests of the Community and those of the member states. The discretion of European agencies is checked by this system. Second, agencies are more transparent than the obscure comitology system. "Would we be better off if the powers of the Drug Monitoring Centre were exercised by the Pompidou Group, or if the authorization of new medicines was left entirely to some unknown committee? Seen in this light, the establishment of European agencies can indeed appear as a net gain in terms of legitimacy" (Dehousse 1995). Agencies are subject to greater controls than comitology committees.

Third, Gatsios and Seabright show that EU agencies can help national governments make credible policy commitments to their electorates, which can produce Pareto-superior outcomes. "The delegation of regulatory powers to some agency distinct from the government itself is . . . best understood as a means whereby the governments can commit themselves to regulatory strategies that would not be credible in the absence of such delegation" (Gatsios and Seabright 1989:46). We have already seen that Pareto-efficiency is not tantamount to democracy; but by making no one worse off and at least one person better off, it is in the best interests of the governed. We can say that Pareto-optimality enhances representation.

Fourth, we have seen above that the subsidiarity article leaves policy implementation in the hands of the member states, and effectively rules out the notion of a community continuously moving the boundary posts of its own competence (Dashwood 1996).

Finally, and most importantly, agencies are subject to the noncompulsory part of the EC budget, where Parliament has the last word. A substantial part of funds earmarked for agencies are frozen until Parliament is satisfied that its concerns have been addressed. Like in the United States, this power of the purse is likely to be one of the main instruments of parliamentary control of agencies.

Notwithstanding these optimistic views of agencies, the claim of excessive authority for supranational EU institutions must be taken seriously. If nonelected bureaucrats make policy decisions that cannot be voted on by the European electorate, democracy is potentially jeopardized. In subsequent chapters, we will need to keep a watchful eye particularly on the nonelective European bureaucracy.

Unaccountable Commission?

The European Commission consists of a political level—the president, two vice-presidents and currently twenty commissioners—and a bureaucratic body of some 15,000 officials. These are practically two different institutions. A variety of contradictory institutional logics—bureaucratic, political, diplomatic, democratic—are at work within the Commission (Christiansen 1997). But any executive in any state may perform multiple functions.

More importantly, Nugent argues that the Commission's leadership capacity has increased over time. The Commission has seized on Article 155 of the EC Treaty, which permits it to launch new initiatives and shape the ongoing debate about EU policies and structures. It has exploited this provision to shape political and policy agendas, bring forward specific policy and legislative proposals, mobilize support for initiatives, and navigate proposals through the maze of EU procedures from draft to final decision making (Nugent 1995). Also, decision making early in the EU policy process is a critical determinant of eventual policy outputs. Hull estimates that once the Commission has agreed on a proposal and sent it to the Parliament and council, scope for changing the proposal exists only at the margin, involving about twenty percent of the total proposal (Hull 1993:83).

The Commission is more capable of acting as a cohesive institution than are the European Council of Heads of Government, the Council of Ministers, or the Parliament, for four reasons. First, commissioners are occupied fulltime with their focus on Europe, while members of the European Council or the Council of Ministers are often consumed by managing affairs in their own countries. Second, commissioners hold office much longer than do heads of state or national ministers; this longer tenure enables them to build loyalty to their post and expertise, as well as a long-term perspective. Third, in contrast to national or European parliamentarians, commissioners are not supposed to be politically or nationally partisan. The Treaty of Rome stated that "the members of the Commission shall, in the general interest of the Community, be completely independent in the performance of their duties. . . . They shall neither seek nor take instructions from any government or from any other body" (TEC, Article 157). Finally, the Commission president has greater potential of forging cohesion than do the six-monthly rotating council president or the weakly empowered Parliament president. Although the TEU barely differentiates the Commission president from the College of Commissioners—formally he [there has yet to be a female president] is little more than a *primus inter pares*[16]—in practice his stature and visibility have increased (Nugent 1995).

Three additional changes in recent years are worth mentioning here. First, the European Council of Heads of State has become the forum where major political decisions—on enlargement, institutional reform, budgetary development, or policy guidelines—are taken. This trend has enhanced the agenda-setting and drafting power of the Commission. Second, the greater use of qualified majority voting (QMV) in the Council of Ministers since the mid-1980s, and the expansion of policy areas in which QMV is constitutional, have emboldened the Commission. Under QMV, it need no longer water down its proposals if there is resistance in one or two states. Third, the TEU Social Protocol has had an effect similar to the one of QMV even in areas where unanimity is still required, since often two-track agreements[17] have been reached where once a dissenting view might have derailed a proposal for good (Nugent 1995).

In most single-market policy areas the Commission has focused on harmonizing national policies. Compared to other regulatory techniques, harmonization preserves national prerogatives. The Commission has been conceived on the model of the French *administration de mission*, whose principle is, in Jean Monnet's own words, *non pas de faire, mais de faire faire* (Dehousse 1997).

The Commission can only propose, not ratify legislation; and compared to other systems of government, the agenda-setting process is relatively open (Peters 1994). The Commission's initiative monopoly does not mean "ruling power," since the Council of Ministers (i.e., the member states) is free to refuse policy initiatives unacceptable to the majority of member-states delegates. The tripartite process of codecision (which we will discuss in chapter 3) places the Commission in a considerably more ambiguous and weaker position than in the cooperation or consultation procedures (Earnshaw and Judge 1995).

Majone argues that the treaties grant the Commission powers of initiative—not to give a supranational bureaucracy excessive powers, but to link council and Parliament more closely to European law and supranational objectives. According to him, the excessive-power argument is not even an issue anymore:

> At least since the Maastricht Treaty on European Union (TEU), the continuous accretion of powers to the Community is no longer on the political

agenda. In fact, the new precise delimitation of Community powers was a major result of the TEU. Article 3b of the Treaty, which enacts the principles of the constitutional order of the EC, marks a shift in the Community's deep structure." (Majone 1998:18)

Héritier shows in the case of environmental policy how the Commission uses institutional and informal strategies for policy innovation and expansion. First, the Commission can play the "treaty base game" (Ross 1995), where decision making is shifted from unanimity to QMV under Article 130. Second, it can present a policy issue as product regulation, which lies technically outside the political decision-making process. Third, it can use a "Russian doll strategy" (Ross 1995), where the initial passage of mere framework legislation ("mother-directives") meets with less initial resistance but later necessitates more specific legislation ("daughter-directives") and triggers gradual self-commitment and a self-promoting dynamic of consent (Eichener 1995:38). Fourth, in "coalition-building," subnational actors (local governments, interest groups, or expert communities) operate against their respective governments to get a foot in the door of a policy field. Finally, as a "process manager" (Eichener 1995), the Commission has a view of the overall situation of European policy making and can seize windows of opportunity or integrate policies into package deals (Héritier 1997b). All of these strategies strengthen the Commission's influence and likely not just in environmental policy.

Institutional models confirm the Commission's powers, showing that under majority voting, the agenda setter (in this case the Commission) has an influential role, since it can select its preferred solution among several options that might be supported by majorities of different members (Shepsle and Weingast 1987). Even under unanimity rule, assuming imperfect information in multilateral negotiations, a central agent like the Commission can lower transaction costs by searching for a solution in a series of bilateral negotiations. It will be rational for all governments to vote for the Commission proposal, as long as each prefers the proposal to no agreement at all (Scharpf 1997a).[18]

As we will see in chapters 5 and 6, in merger policy and biotech regulation, the Commission has been endowed with direct monitoring and enforcement powers. It remains to be seen whether these powers are democratically legitimate.

Court as Unchecked Checker?

The European Community lacks the use of violence and coercion, a capacity considered a defining characteristic of the state in political theory. Consequently the European Court of Justice (ECJ) had to rely on its ability to persuade other actors to obey its rulings. Not only in Europe, "the growth of the regulatory state has converted the one unelected branch of government, the Judiciary, from a relatively neutral referee to an active player in the administrative game" (Seidman and Gilmour 1986:132).

The court has been depicted as a "purposeful opportunist" (Wincott 1995) that, like the Commission, uses subterfuge to push its integrationist agenda. In a "linking up" strategy, the court has encouraged national and subnational actors to refer cases to it. It introduces new doctrines step-by-step: it states a new general principle while clarifying that the principle is subject to various qualifications. It then reaffirms the principle in later cases, when the qualifications can be whittled away and the full extent of the new doctrine revealed (Hartley 1994:87–88).

But instead of looking at the court in isolation, we need to compare it to another federal court, for example the U.S. Supreme Court. Goldstein shows that the early U.S. Supreme Court encountered much more resistance from member states than did the ECJ. The numbers speak for themselves. The federal Supreme Court in the antebellum United States, 1790–1859, was defied by nineteen states in 132 incidents, while only three European member states in 23 incidents disobeyed the ECJ. A nominally sovereign US government was regularly and officially disobeyed by the states, while nominally sovereign European nation-states regularly, and virtually from the start, obeyed the federal authority of the EU as set forth by the ECJ (Goldstein 1997).[19]

The Supremacy Clause (Article VI, Clause 2) in the United States made clear that federal law was to be "the supreme law of the land; and judges in the several states shall be bound thereby, anything in the constitution of laws of any state to the contrary notwithstanding." But beginning with Georgia's refusal to carry out the first Supreme Court decision in 1793, *Chisholm v. Georgia,* for five years before a constitutional amendment overturned that decision, individual states, on intensely controversial issues, resisted this national authority for seventy years. By contrast, ECJ judges took a treaty and its rules and turned them into enforceable, supreme law that takes precedence within each member state, even over subsequent national legislation (*Costa v. ENEL,* ECJ Case 6/64 [1964] E.C.R. 585). European law overrode even constitutional provisions contrary to it (see *Internationale Handelsgesellschaft v. EVGF,* ECJ Case 11/70 [1970] E.C.R. 1125, and *Simmenthal II,* ECJ Case 106/77 [1978] E.C.R. 629).

While European states willingly and even eagerly accepted the court's augmentation of authority, state governments in the early United States did not. Of course, most states, most of the time, and on most issues, accepted federal authority as legitimate. But *Tassel v. Georgia* serves as an illustration of how some states challenged federal authority and jurisdiction. In 1829, the Georgia legislature passed laws, as an act of its purported sovereign power, nullifying the federal treaties with Cherokee Indian tribes. This move allowed whites to seize Indian property by using violence. Georgia proceeded to arrest, try, convict, and sentence to hanging an Indian, Corn Tassel, for a murder committed in defense of his property. *Tassel v. Georgia* was appealed to a federal court on grounds that under the treaties Indian courts, not state courts, had jurisdiction over Tassel. The federal Supreme Court subpoenaed Georgia's governor. When the governor informed the Georgia legislature that he would forcibly resist any attempt to enforce this subpoena, the legislature ordered him and every other state official to disregard any federal process that might be served on them. Tassel was executed. Two years later, in a separate Cherokee Indian case, the Georgia legislature again defied the federal government and went as far as to call for a national convention to reconsider the jurisdiction of the Supreme Court.

To be sure, EU member states have far from passively accepted the court's activism. The Maastricht Treaty reflects a determination of member states to limit the court, which is entirely excluded from two of the three treaty "pillars," namely foreign and security policy, and cooperation in justice and home affairs (Burley and Mattli 1993). But why did the European Court, on the whole, encounter much less resistance than did the U.S. Supreme Court? One possible answer is that the court's activism has not deprived member-state governments of their power. Vaubel asserts that supremacy of European law over national law has paradoxically strengthened the hand of the member-state governments. Meeting in the council, they can control their own parliaments rather than being controlled by them (Vaubel 1995).

Goldstein suggests another answer: the ECJ's rules appear to be, and often are, more democratic. She shows that the European Court allowed for a federation of rules that had long been advocated by John C. Calhoun in the United States (Calhoun [1848] 1963). For example, because of the unanimity principle of the 1966 Luxembourg Compromise, which gave each member state de facto veto power, the member states were willing to hand over significant portions of their sovereign authority to federal European governing organs. A similar veto-power suggestion had been made unsuccessfully in the U.S. Senate in 1823 and in the House in 1867: to require a unanimous Supreme Court vote in order to declare unconstitutional state or federal legislation. While the ECJ does not require unanimous voting, its practice is to issue unsigned opinions without dissents, which creates an appearance of unanimity and legitimacy of court rulings.

Another proposal in the United States, also in 1821 and 1867, was to empower either the U.S. Senate (with two senators by state) or a new institution (with one representative from each state) to draw the line between state and federal power (Warren 1991). The ECJ wisely incorporated this idea by having one judge from each member state. No state can legitimately claim that it lacks input into ECJ decision making (Goldstein 1997).

A third proposal of U.S. constitutional amendments in 1831–32 was to change federal judges' terms of office from life to a fixed number of years (Warren 1991:165). The ECJ has that provision: judges serve fixed six-year renewable terms that have enhanced their accountability. They have also fostered member-state acceptance of European jurisprudence, not least by the fact that judges return to their home countries where they serve as eminent jurists and spread the pro-European law message (Burley and Mattli 1993:65).

A fourth European arrangement was sought in vain in the United States: the EU leaves it to nation-state judges to adjust their national law to European supreme law requirements. This face-saving measure—an "all-important fiction"—allows member-state judges to appear autonomous while the specificity of an ECJ ruling dictates, for practical purposes, the state-level outcome (Burley and Mattli 1993:64–65). In the early nineteenth century, the Virginia Supreme Court (*Martin v. Hunter's Lessee*, 1815) demanded precisely such a face-saving arrangement that would have allowed each state its own judiciary to interpret its laws and would have given a surface appearance of coequal sovereignties (Goldstein 1997:177).

The EU has prudently omitted a fifth and final U.S. provision. The Eleventh Amendment states that no lawsuit against a state can be "commenced" in federal court "by citizens of another state" or by foreigners. But in *Cohens v. Virginia* (1824), the Supreme Court made a massive jurisdictional exception to this amendment, namely appeals on federal grounds that challenged resolutions of cases originally commenced by state authorities. Hence American state officials were routinely brought into federal court by private citizens who appealed state decisions on grounds of conflict with federal law. In Europe, private citizens do not have this power. While citizens may challenge their member-state law in a member-state court, only the Commission (Article 169), other government officials (Article 170), or in-state judges seeking guidance (Article 177) can bring a national government before the court. Goldstein recapitulates:

> When sovereign states join together into a federal union they can minimize member-state resistance to central authority by adopting institutions that create the appearance or reality of limiting federal action to measures that reflect the sentiment of a substantial majority—consensus, if not unanimity—of the member states and that foster the appearance that member-state governments are not directly taking orders from the center. Such features of the Eu-

ropean Community include (a) super-majority decision-making (Council of Ministers), or the appearance of it (ECJ) at the center, such that federal rules appear to be the product of consensus; (b) equal representation of member states on federal decision-making bodies (ECJ); (c) limited terms of office for federal-level legislative (Council) and judicial (ECJ) officials, who thus remain at least indirectly accountable to member-state voters; and (d) an appearance of honoring member-state sovereignty in decision-making structures of the judiciary (i.e., federal judges cannot give direct orders to state judges as though they were all part of the same system) (Goldstein 1997).

LACK OF PROTECTION?

Now we come to the fifth and last democratic deficit argument: the lack of protection or redistribution. Scharpf argues that the future viability of national welfare states is directly challenged by European economic integration, which drastically reduces the effectiveness of democratic national self-determination. This is the core problem confronting democratic governance not in the EU but *in Europe* (Scharpf 1997b; emphasis in original). Scharpf assumes that regulatory competition and regime-shopping produce a race to the bottom or "Delaware effect," as states (like Delaware in the United States) seek to attract firms or capital by offering them the lowest taxes—meaning less redistribution and less services for citizens. In fact, to kick off a race to the bottom, capital need not actually move to another country; it need only threaten credibly to move and will engender preventive deregulation by member states (Streeck 1996:85–86; Streeck 1997). But as Vogel and others have demonstrated, such a Delaware effect is not inevitable; on the contrary, regulatory competition may at times push the level of regulation upwards, for example when a small coalition of member states can benefit from cooperative momentum. Regulatory competition then produces a "California effect" named after the state that was allowed under the 1970 Clean Air Act to exclude from its home market cars that did not meet its stricter emission standards. Since California was a big market, this forced the car industry to lobby for uniform national standards that were stricter than the ones it favored initially (Vogel 1995; Genschel and Plümper 1997).

In fact, Scharpf himself concedes that price competition, cost-cutting, beggar-thy-neighbor strategies, and a race to the bottom are not the only, and not necessarily even the preferred, policy choices for high-cost countries (Scharpf 1999:194). Exploiting the advantages of specialization, and distinguishing their "unique selling proposition" to attract highly mobile, highly skilled and knowledgeable companies and workers with quality of work-life policies, may well produce a race to the top instead. Not all companies or workers want to be in low-tax Delaware—many more are quite happy to locate in high-price New York City.

Scharpf's contribution is his inclusion of economic redistribution as an aspect of democratic legitimacy. At the European level, welfare policies are impeded not only by the democratic deficit, but also by deep-rooted conflicts of economic interest among member states, and by the widely divergent structural characteristics of national welfare states (Scharpf 1997b). But Scharpf's critique conflates the basic distinction between (a) a change in regulation and (b) a change in jurisdiction from states to the EU level. The former, deregulation, is a fact of life not only in the EU, but in all states under globalization. All national governments are now forced to compete against each other to attract or retain mobile capital and firms. In that sense their situation is now comparable to that of subnational (state, provincial, or cantonal) governments in federal states like the United States, Canada, Germany, or Switzerland, as Scharpf himself recognizes (Scharpf 1997b). Besides, the "race to the bottom" argument is largely discredited by Rodrick's analysis, which shows that the more open an economy, the bigger, *not smaller*, its government. Rodrick finds that there is a strong positive statistical relationship between size of government and degree of trade openness in a sample of over one hundred countries. He suggests that the explanation for this can be found in the role that government spending plays in reducing the role of external risk to which economies are exposed. Since more open economies have higher degrees of such risk, they compensate by having larger public sectors, with the result that "globalization may well require, big, not small, government" (Rodrick 1996:26). At least, we would expect the argument to hold for social security and welfare spending in industrialized countries.

Majone argues that the very modest role of social policy in the EU is a result of the reluctance of member states to surrender control of politically sensitive policies of redistribution to the Community. Article 118 in the Rome Treaty clearly limits the Community competence in social policy (with a few exceptions, such as the social security regime for migrant workers). The Single European Act, Maastricht, or Amsterdam did nothing to provide true legislative competencies in this area. Besides, Eurobarometer data show that European integration of health and social security is opposed by a majority of citizens. And the delicate value judgments of balancing efficiency and equity for redistributive and social policies cannot be made legitimately in a heterogeneous polity like the EU. In fact, trying to legitimate the Community by integrating social policy or push redistribution would actually aggravate the democratic deficit problem by creating a highly centralized bureaucracy, which would be against the clearly expressed preferences of the governments and citizens of the member states (Majone 1998:20; 1996:299). If a central government in Brussels were to set general levels of income redistribution and taxation in a community of member states that differ greatly in their levels of economic development, political systems, and legal traditions, the consequences for democracy could be disastrous. All redistributive policy areas affecting capital, labor and welfare state policies depend on democratic legitimization and should be left to each member state.

CONCLUSION

Table 2.1 sums up my classification and evaluation of key democratic deficit arguments.

Table 2.1. Taxonomy of Democratic Deficit Arguments

	Arguments	Proponents	Their Cases	My Findings
1	Not one demos but many demoi, no European debate / parties / competition. Enlargement will only increase heterogeneity.	Weiler 1991, Kielmannsegg 1996, Scharpf 1997, 1999	Up to 12 new member states by 2005.	Not valid. A demos is constructed: Switzerland and the U.S. have integrated their demoi into one *demos*. Democracy is a key accession criterion.
2	Lack of transparency and comitology breed collusion.	Sbragia 1992, Hayes-Renshaw and Wallace 1995, Franklin et al. 1996, Majone 1997	Council of Ministers.	Valid. Secret Council deliberations are a significant agency problem.
3	Qualified majority voting (QMV) means tyranny of the majority.	Weiler 1991, Kielmannsegg 1996	Council votes.	Not valid. The EU is less, not more majoritarian than the U.S.
4a	Weak Parliament.	Scharpf 1997	European Parliament.	Valid. Parliament without power of initiative, but stronger post-Amsterdam.
4b	Nonelected agencies have excessive powers. Standardization by private organizations is not accountable.	Sandholtz & Zysman 1989, Cameron 1992, Hull 1993, Wood & Waterman 1994, Eichener 1995, Ross 1995, Christiansen 1997, Shapiro 1997,	Commission competition and electricity policy. European Central Bank. CEN, CENELEC.	Valid. Commission has power of initiative. Significant agency problem and possible capture by special interests. But EU standardization

Table 2.1. (*continued*)

	Arguments	Proponents	Their Cases	My Findings
		Christiansen 1997, Héritier 1997b, 1999, Krislov 1997		is more accountable than in U.S.
4c	ECJ acts unilaterally, with excessive powers.	Seidman and Gilmour 1986, Burley and Mattli 1993	Fundamental HR rulings by ECJ.	Not valid. Supreme Courts are not elected in U.S. and Switzerland either. Independent courts can enhance democracy. ECJ is in some respects more accountable than the U.S. Supreme Court.
5	Regulatory competition and negative integration weaken redistribution at national level, but do not replace them at EU level.	Leibfried & Pierson 1992, Scharpf 1997, Streeck 1997	Social policy, industrial relations, business & capital taxes.	Not valid. A problem of political economy, not of democracy. EU is not a welfare state but a regulatory state. Open economies have bigger, not smaller governments.

After weeding out the arguments that cannot withstand the test of logic or evidence, three important arguments for the existence of a democratic deficit remain:

1. The deliberations of the Council of Ministers are not transparent, making the council insufficiently accountable to voters, and posing dangers of collusion at the European level. While opacity and collusion are of course not unique to the workings of the EU—they doubtless occur in many national governments, too—that is no excuse for secret council decision making.
2. The European Parliament is still too weak as the only supranational EU institution directly acting as a voice for the European electorate. Despite gains in its powers over time, the Parliament can still not initiate legislation.
3. EU agencies, above all the Commission, may enjoy unaccountable authority for at least three reasons. First, most bureaucrats are not

subject to elections or individual vetting by the legislature. Second, most agencies are appointed by and report to the nonelective Commission. Third, negative integration may tie the hands of national rulers and reduce their accountability to their electorates. Fourth, not all legislation passes through the Council of Ministers or the European Parliament as checks on the executive or the bureaucracy.

But this chapter has only scratched the surface, and these points require more systematic examination in subsequent chapters. By comparing EU rules and decision-making rules to those of the United States and Switzerland along verifiable indicators of democracy, chapter 3 takes the democratic deficit arguments out of the vacuum in which they have been made and puts them into a comparative framework. As we saw in chapter 1, the tools of comparison can be, and have been, used effectively by EU scholars.

NOTES

1. This piece of Euromythology was in reality an April Fools' joke carried by *The Times* (London). It was widely believed, with letters and telephone calls of protest arriving at the European Commission.

2. The EU spends about $3.8 million annually on fostering minority languages—a fraction of the amount it spends on translating documents and meetings to and from the official EU languages (*Christian Science Monitor* 23 May 2000).

3. Compared to the same survey six months earlier, confidence in the Commission increased in ten member states while it decreased in four: Austria, Italy, Portugal, and Sweden (Eurobarometer No. 53, 24 July 2000).

4. In chapter 5, we will not only examine the European Court of Justice (ECJ), but also the Court of First Instance (CFI). Here I speak generically of "the court."

5. *New York Times*, 14 January 2000.

6. Eurobarometer No. 53, July 2000.

7. Copenhagen Summit, European Council 1993; interview with Commission 2000.

8. This is beside the fact that on logical grounds, concluding from the assumption that Europe has "no demos," that the EU is undemocratic has a strong whiff of tautology.

9. *New York Times*, 9 August 1993.

10. According to Eurobarometer 56 (December 2001), 54 percent (up 6 percentage points from the previous poll in July 2001) responded that membership in the Union is a good thing; 52 percent (up 7 percentage points) said that their country had benefited from EU membership; 61 percent (up 2 percentage points) supported the euro common currency; 66 percent supported in principle a common foreign policy, and 73 percent in principle a common security and defense policy.

11. But note that at least one study of national parties has shown that stronger parties do not necessarily produce more accountability to citizens. It seems that parties have neither the incentive nor the ability to allow citizens to sanction representatives themselves (Gandhi 1997).

12. Incidentally, those who assert that the EU lacks legitimacy would need to explain why virtually nobody saw the Swiss government as illegitimate before 1971, when women, over half its population, were finally granted suffrage.

13. *Treaty on European Union, Official Journal of the European Communities,* C224, 31 August 1992.

14. Democracy and Pareto-efficiency are not entirely unrelated, since the latter is compatible with representation. But to conclude from Pareto-inferiority that majoritarian voting is undemocratic would be tantamount to condemning all majoritarian systems, including the United States, as undemocratic.

15. For a detailed description of codecision, see chapter 3.

16. Although the Nice Treaty empowers the Commission president with the special authority to dismiss other commissioners, its collective composition makes the Commission similar to the Swiss Federal Council.

17. Two-track agreements allow the states in favor of a new but controversial policy to adopt that policy while a minority of one or more states holds off on adopting it.

18. Scharpf writes that his own earlier conception of a "joint decision trap" (Scharpf 1988) failed to sufficiently consider the role of the Commission as agenda setter in reducing transaction costs and facilitating agreement. "To that extent, my present conclusions would be more optimistic with regard to the European capacity for consensual policy-making" (Scharpf 1999:76).

19. This section relies heavily on Goldstein (1997).

3

✥

Institutions Compared

What is a good measure of democracy? This chapter compares the EU to Switzerland and the United States along seven established scales of democracy. I use these scales because their criteria and findings are generally accepted, prominent, and diverse, yet robust. Not that alternative scales lack merit, but more scales would not produce meaningfully different findings. While democracy is measured differently by different analysts, their indicators come from a limited pool of common measures, and a high degree of agreement exists about classifying nations as democratic or not. For example, Coppedge and Reinicke (1990) use an independent model, but their scale of polyarchy correlates .94 with Gastil's (1990) civil liberties measure for some 170 countries in 1985. Gurr, Jaggers, and Moore's (1990) measure performs similarly to Bollen's: Gurr's ratings of 118 countries circa 1965 correlate .83 with Bollen's measure and .89 with a score combining Gastil's separate measures of political and civil liberties for 113 countries in 1985. Alvarez et al. (1996) also find high correlations between their own and other scales: Coppedge and Reinicke's scale for 1978 predicts .92 of Alvarez et al.'s dichotomous regimes. Gurr's scales of autocracy and democracy for 1950–1986 jointly predict .91, Gastil's scale of political liberties for 1972–1990 predicts .93, the same scale of civil liberties predicts .92, and the two scales jointly predict .94 of Alvarez et al.'s regimes. "Different views of democracy, including those that entail highly subjective judgments, yield a robust classification" (Alvarez et al. 1996:21).

ALVAREZ, CHEIBUB, LIMONGI, AND PRZEWORSKI

Alvarez et al. build on Przeworski's minimal definition of democracy. "What is essential to consider a regime as democratic is that two kinds of offices are filled, directly or indirectly, by elections—the chief executive office and the seats in the effective legislative body—and that the office holders are responsible only to the electors, not to any non-elected powers." (Alvarez et al. 1996: 5–6). Unlike others, Alvarez et al. use a nominal classification rather than a ratio scale to measure democracy. They argue that, like pregnancies, political regimes cannot be half-democratic: they are either democratic or not.

Table 3.1 shows that all three polities are classified identically, but the Exselec variable brings up two questions. First, which institution is the EU's executive branch? Second, is the executive elected?

We can answer the first question by exclusion. The European Council of heads of EU member states is not an executive branch, since the treaties have not endowed it with constitutional authority. The largely informal body emerged from summit diplomacy between heads of state in the 1970s (Putnam and Bayne 1984; Nugent 1994). Though the Council of Ministers does carry out some political tasks, it is not equipped for predominant executive responsibility either because it must balance a largely consensual process (Hayes-Renshaw and Wallace 1995). The council is often called a "co-legislature" analogous to the U.S. Senate or the Swiss *Ständerat* by both EU and national actors.

That leaves the European Commission. Although scholars have disagreed whether it is the EU executive branch, the legislative branch, or the bureaucracy (Hayes-Renshaw and Wallace 1995; Christiansen 1997:80; Dehousse 1997:249), the Commission is today widely regarded as the European executive for four reasons. First, it exercises wide executive responsibilities, including agenda-setting and rule-making powers; the supervision and implementation of EU policies; and external representation and negotiation on behalf of the EU. Second, as a process leader with

Table 3.1. Democracy Scale: Alvarez, Cheibub, Limongi, and Przeworski 1996

Indicators	Switzerland	USA	EU
• EXSELEC (chief executive elected)	yes	yes	yes
• LEGSELEC (legislative elected)	yes	yes	yes
• PARTY (2 or more parties)	yes	yes	yes
INCUMB	no	no	no
• Type II Error	0	0	0

Alvarez et al.'s variables are dichotomous. EXSELEC is coded as "yes" in all three polities, since the chief executive is elected directly in USA and indirectly in Switzerland and EU.

initiative monopoly, the Commission has an overall view of the European policy-making process and can seize windows of opportunity or integrate policies into package deals (Nugent 1994:103–121; Eichener 1995:273). Third, its bureaucratic apparatus can execute legislation and decisions. Fourth, its collective identity makes the Commission analogous to the seven-member federal council, the Swiss executive. It may be a weak executive, but an executive nonetheless.[1]

Now, is the Commission elected? Alvarez et al. clarify their criterion for Exselec: "For a regime to be qualified as democratic, the executive must be directly or indirectly elected in popular election. Indirect elections qualify as popular only if the electors are themselves elected. Elections by bodies which are themselves nominated are not qualified as popular elections" (Alvarez et al. 1996:7).

While the U.S. president is *de facto* directly elected,[2] the Swiss executive is elected indirectly. Article 175(2) of the Swiss Federal Constitution states: "The members of the Federal Council are elected by the Federal Assembly after every comprehensive election of the National Assembly" (Schweizerische Bundesversammlung 1999:42). In Alvarez et al.'s definition, the indirect election of the Swiss Federal Council qualifies as popular election.

Does the Commission's selection qualify as indirect election, too? Maastricht and Amsterdam have overhauled the selection procedure. First, after consulting the Parliament, the member-state governments nominate the commission president by common accord. Since Amsterdam, their nominee is subject to approval by the directly elected Parliament. Then the member states nominate the Commission members in consultation with the nominee for president. After individual hearings by the appropriate parliamentary committees, the entire Commission is then subject to approval by the Parliament, and is finally appointed by the member states in the council.[3] The election of the Commission would still qualify as indirect in Alvarez et al.'s definition, since the member-state governments nominating commissioners are themselves subject to popular election—even without Parliament approval.

"Party" is coded as 2 across the board since there are two or more parties in all three polities. There are no restrictions on the opposition in the three polities, so "Incumb" is irrelevant here. In sum, all three polities are democratic in Alvarez et al.'s scale.

BOLLEN

Bollen groups indicators of democracy into two sets: "I define liberal democracy as the extent to which a political system allows political liberties and democratic rule" (Bollen 1993:1208–9).

As table 3.2 shows, Bollen gives great weight to media freedom: two of his eight indicators are "freedom of broadcast media" and "freedom of print media." All three polities are equally democratic in seven of his eight criteria. The one doubtful indicator is "effectiveness/elective legislative body." First, what is the EU legislature? Second, is that legislature effective?

There is now widespread consensus that the European legislature consists of the Parliament and the council. On the RTD Fourth Framework Programme, council's reasons spoke of the council and Parliament as "two legislative bodies," two chambers of the EU legislature. Similarly, in the case of deposit guarantee schemes, Germany brought a case in the ECJ jointly against council and Parliament as "co-legislature" to annul the directive (see Earnshaw and Judge 1995:629, 638). The Commission now formally sends its proposals to both chambers simultaneously. This point is not trivial. In assessing the relative effectiveness of the European legislature, it is important that the council, usually seen as the European actor with teeth and made up of ministers appointed by elected member-state governments, is a factor in the equation.

Table 3.2. Democracy Scale: Bollen 1993

Indicators	Switzerland	USA	EU
• 4 political liberties indicators:			
(X1) freedom of broadcast media (Sussman 1980/81/82)	10	10	10
(X2) freedom of print media (Sussman 1980/81/82)	10	10	10
(X3) civil liberties (Gastil 1986/88)	10	10	10
(X4) freedom of group opposition (Banks 1971/79)	10	10	10
• 4 democratic rule indicators:			
(X5) political rights (Gastil 1986/88)	10	10	10
(X6) competitiveness of nomination process (Banks)	10	10	10
(X7) chief executive elected (Banks)	10	10	10
(X8) effectiveness/elective legislative body (Banks)	10(1)	10(1)	10(.5)
• Scales	100	100	94

Bollen linearly transformed each variable to range from 0 to 10, with 10 being the highest degree of liberal democracy. X8 is a combined variable indicating whether the legislature is elected or not, then multiplied with an effectiveness indicator. EU values are mine. Differences are emphasized.

Banks scores Legislative Effectiveness as (0) = *None* if no legislature exists. As (1) = *Ineffective* if the legislature is ineffective on three bases. First, legislative activity may be ssentially of a "rubber stamp" character. Second, domestic turmoil may make the implementation of legislation impossible. Third, the effective executive may prevent the legislature from meeting, or otherwise substantially impede the exercise of its functions. As (2) = *Partially Effective* if the effective executive's power substantially outweighs but does not completely dominate that of the legislature. As (3) = *Effective* if the legislature possesses significant governmental autonomy, including, typically, substantial authority with regard to taxation and disbursement and the power to override executive vetoes of legislation (Banks 1971:xvii).

The other question posed by Bollen's "effectiveness/elective legislative body" indicator is more complex: is the European legislature effective, compared to Switzerland or the United States? Consider each legislative chamber in turn. The council, much like the German Bundesrat, consists of officeholders elected in their member states. We saw in chapter two that the council stands accused of democratic deficiencies. First, the legitimacy derived from its elected membership seems inadequate for legislation under the first pillar (European Communities) or much beyond coordination under the second (Common Foreign and Security Policy) and third (Cooperation in Justice and Home Affairs). Second, we have seen that council proceedings lack transparency. Third, the rise of qualified majority voting (QMV) in the council, especially since the December 2000 Nice Treaty,[4] creates a compliance problem whenever member governments are outvoted in the council (Hayes-Renshaw and Wallace 1995). On the other hand, the Nice Treaty lifted the threshold for QMV from 71 percent to 74 percent, in effect toward unanimity; and since the council consists of cabinet members of democratically elected governments, it is widely seen as a democracy-enhancing institution. Those who refer to the weak EU legislature typically mean not the council but the Parliament.

But the Parliament has become a powerful actor since its humble beginnings in 1957 for several reasons: first, its procedural powers, for example its veto power; second, its powers of appointment and dismissal over the Commission; and third, its budgetary powers over European agencies. Its rise led one observer to write: "what the European Parliament most closely resembles is that most un-European of institutions, the United States Congress."[5]

Four procedures can be distinguished (Tsebelis and Garrett 1999). First, consultation between council and Commission since 1957 kept ultimate decision-making power with member governments. The Luxembourg compromise allowed any council member to block new legislation in any area it considered vital to its national interest. This oldest procedure gives Parliament no substantive role.

Parliament acquired that role in the second procedure, cooperation, in the 1987 Single European Act. Under Cooperation, Parliament may amend Commission proposals and becomes a "conditional agenda setter" (Tsebelis 1994). If the Commission accepts Parliament's amendments, they go to the council, which can either accept them under QMV or amend them unanimously. Parliament's rejections of proposals can be overridden only by an agreement between the Commission and a unanimous council.

Third is codecision, set up under the 1992 Maastricht Treaty. Now the council can no longer reject Parliament amendments accepted by the Commission, but has to request a Conciliation Committee of all council members and equal numerical representation from the Parliament. Where a joint text is agreed in conciliation, both council (by QMV) and Parliament (by simple majority) must adopt the measure in accordance with the joint text, or the proposed act is "deemed not to have been adopted" (Article 189b[5]). If agreement is prevented in conciliation, and council reconfirms its common position unchanged, Parliament must either accept the council's text or reject it by absolute majority (Earnshaw and Judge 1995).

The fourth procedure is modified codecision, since the 1997 Amsterdam Treaty, which gave Parliament full legislative powers for the first time. If the council and Parliament delegates to the Conciliation Committee do not agree on a joint text, the proposed legislation lapses (Amsterdam Treaty, Art. 189[6]): the last two stages of original codecision are now removed. When the Amsterdam provision came into force in May 1999, Parliament became a coequal legislator with the council; the EU legislative regime is now truly bicameral for the first time. The council can no longer overrule Parliament (not even unanimously, as under cooperation), nor can it present take-it-or-leave-it proposals to Parliament anymore. For the first time in EU history, the council and Parliament are equals.

Its appointment and dismissal powers give the Parliament additional authority. Since the Single European Act, Parliament has held hearings of prospective commissioners before their investiture (Jacobs 1995). And the Parliament showed its fangs when, in March 1999, it acted on its constitutional powers to force the Santer Commission out of office. The Commission has been very solicitous of the Parliament ever since.[6]

Lastly, Parliament has budgetary powers. Although legislatures potentially keep agencies more under control in presidential than in parliamentary systems (Shapiro 1997), the EC budget does put agencies under Parliament control. European bureaus fall under the noncompulsory part of the budget, where the last say rests with Parliament. Parliament is in a position to demand much from agencies in terms of reporting, hearings, or policy. Substantial funds earmarked for agencies are frozen and are released only once Parliament agrees that its concerns have been addressed (Brinkhorst 1996).[7] As with the congressional control of U.S. agencies, this power of the purse is one of the main instruments of parliamentary control of agencies in the EU.

However, the Parliament's effectiveness may be hampered by contextual factors. Even if its legal competencies were enlarged, the structural preconditions for its power are still absent. We have already seen that there are no potent European parties, no European political leaders and no European-wide media of political communication (Scharpf 1997c). The absence of a viable party system at the European level, for example, is a serious deficiency, as weak parties cannot act as watchdogs for voters and consumers against corruption. Given these reservations, given the lack of transparency of the council, and despite its increasing powers, the European legislature earns a substantially lower mark for its legislative effectiveness than do the U.S. House and Senate or the Swiss *Nationalrat* and *Ständerat*. Due to its lower effectiveness coefficient in indicator X8, the EU earns a score of 94 compared to 100 for Switzerland and the United States. This puts the EU on a par with Finland, Greece, Malta, and Portugal, and ahead of Germany (89) and Spain (83).[8]

COPPEDGE AND REINICKE

Coppedge and Reinicke, like Bollen, build their scale on Dahl's eight criteria for democracy. But in contrast to Bollen (and Gastil below), they see contestation as unidimensional, since political rights and political liberties are highly correlated: "Common sense dictates that a one-dimensional phenomenon be measured with a one-dimensional indicator. Once the unidimensionality of the phenomenon has been established, insisting on two-dimensional indicators is like trying to measure length in acres" (Coppedge and Reinicke 1990:56).

Coppedge and Reinicke combine Dahl's fourth requirement for democracy ("Eligibility for public office") with his seventh ("Free and fair elections") and eighth requirements ("Institutions for making government policies depend on votes and other expressions of preferences"). They fold these three criteria into one "FAIRELT" variable, "elections without significant or routine fraud/coercion."[9]

In table 3.3, Coppedge and Reinicke give four scores, one each for "FAIRELT" (from Dahl's criteria 4, 7, and 8), "FREORG" (Dahl's criterion 1), "FREXT" (Dahl's criterion 2), and "ALTINF" (Dahl's criterion 6). Each score ranges from 1 to 4, with 1 the most and 4 the least democratic. Coppedge and Reinicke's criteria for achieving the top score 1 are listed next to each indicator. Switzerland, the United States, and the EU all achieve top scores in all indicators. I am skeptical, however, whether the EU fully meets Dahl's eighth criterion, while Switzerland and the United States meet it without question. My skepticism is reflected by a "No?" and hence by a question mark in the "FAIRELT" indicator. Notwithstanding this question mark, the EU's democracy virtually equals that of Switzerland and the United States.

FREEDOM HOUSE

Freedom House, likely the most well-known of the scales, states a minimal definition: "At a minimum, a democracy is a political system in which the

Table 3.3. Democracy Scale: Coppedge and Reinicke 1990

Indicators	Switzerland	USA	EU
• Polyarchy Scale (Dahl 1971):			
(1) Freedom to form and join organizations	yes	yes	yes
(2) Freedom of expression	yes	yes	yes
(3) The right to vote	yes	yes	yes
(4) Eligibility for public office	yes	yes	yes
(5) The right of political leaders to compete for support	yes	yes	yes
(6) Alternative sources of information	yes	yes	yes
(7) Free and fair elections	yes	yes	yes
(8) Institutions for making government policies depend on votes and other expressions of preferences	yes	yes	no?
• FAIRELT (Dahl 4, 7, 8): 1 5 Elections without significant or routine fraud/coercion	1	1	1?
• FREORG (Dahl 1): 1 = Some trade unions or interest groups may be harassed or banned but no restrictions on purely political organizations	1	1	1
• FREXT (Dahl 2): 1 = Citizens express their views on all topics without fear of punishment	1	1	1
• ALTINF (Dahl 6): 1 = Alternative sources of information exist and are protected by law. If significant government ownership of media, they are effectively controlled by truly independent or multiparty bodies	1	1	1
• SUFF (Dahl 3): 1 = Universal adult suffrage	1	1	1
• **Unidimensional scales (for FAIRELT, FREORG, FREXT, and ALTINF)**	*1111*	*1111*	*1?111*

FAIRELT, FREORG, FREXT, ALTINF, and SUFF are each scored from 1 to 4 (1 = most democratic). EU scores are mine. Differences are emphasized.

people choose their authoritative leaders from among competing groups and individuals who were not chosen by the government.... In a free society this means the right of all adults to vote and compete for public office, and for elected representatives to have a decision vote on public policies. A system is genuinely free or democratic to the extent that the people have a choice in determining the nature of the system and its leaders" (Freedom House 1996:530).

In table 3.4, all three polities receive the top democratic grade 4 in all but one Political Rights indicator, number 4. Are European voters "able to endow their freely elected members of the European legislature with real power"? Since this is questionable, I rate the EU at 2. We have seen above that although the European legislature has gained power, it does not (yet)

Table 3.4. Democracy Scale: Freedom House 1995–1996

Freedom House 1995–1996	Switzerland	USA	EU
• Political Rights checklist	1	1	1
1. Is the head of state and/or head of government elected through free and fair elections?	4	4	4
2. Are the legislative representatives elected through free and fair elections?	4	4	4
3. Are there fair electoral laws, equal campaigning opportunities, fair polling and honest tabulation of ballots?	4	4	4
4. Are the voters able to endow their freely elected representatives with real power?	**4**	**4**	**2**
5. Do the people have the right to organize in different political parties or other competitive political groupings of their choice, and is the system open to the rise and fall of these competing parties or groupings?	4	4	4
6. Is there a significant opposition vote, de facto opposition power, and a realistic possibility for the opposition to increase its support or gain power through elections?	4	4	4
7. Are the people free from domination by the military, foreign powers, totalitarian parties, religious hierarchies, economic oligarchies, or any other powerful group?[10]	4	4	4
8. Do cultural, ethnic, religious and other minority groups have reasonable self-determination, self-government, autonomy or participation through informal consensus in the decision-making process?	4	4	4
• Civil Liberties checklist	1	1	1
1. Are there free and independent media, literature and other cultural expressions?	4	4	4
2. Is there open public discussion and free private discussion?	4	4	4
3. Is there freedom of assembly and demonstration?	4	4	4
4. Is there freedom of political or quasi-political organization?	4	4	4
5. Are citizens equal under the law, with access to an independent, nondiscriminatory judiciary, jare they respected by the security forces?	4	4	4
6. Is there protection from political terror, and from unjustified imprisonment, exile or torture, whether by groups that support or oppose the system, and freedom from war or insurgency situations?	4	4	4

(*continued*)

Table 3.4. (continued)

Freedom House 1995–1996	Switzerland	USA	EU
7. Are there free trade unions and peasant organizations or equivalents, and is there effective collective bargaining?	4	4	4
8. Are there free professional and other private organizations?	4	4	4
9. Are there free businesses or cooperatives?	4	4	4
10. Are there free religious institutions and free private and public religious expressions?	4	4	4
11. Are there personal social freedoms, which include such aspects as gender equality, property rights, freedom of movement, choice of residence, and choice of marriage and size of family?	4	4	4
12. Is there equality of opportunity, which includes freedom from exploitation by or dependency on landlords, employers, union leaders, bureaucrats or any other type of denigrating obstacle to a share of legitimate economic gains?	4	4	4
13. Is there freedom from extreme government indifference and corruption?	**4**	**4**	**2**

Polities are rated from 1 to 7 along the two dimensions of political rights and political liberties. (1 = closest to, 7 = farthest from, the ideals in checklist questions) based on countries getting 0 to 4 raw points for each checklist item. To get the top rating 1, a polity must have a total of 28–32 raw points in the 8 political rights indicators and a total of 45–52 in the 13 political liberties indicators. Switzerland and USA each get the maximum 32 and 52 raw points, while the EU gets 30 and 50 raw points. Raw point assessments and EU ratings are mine. Differences are emphasized.

command the authority vested in the U.S. Congress or the Swiss National Assembly. However, even if we subtracted all the raw points for this lack of real power, the EU would still meet the twenty-eight-point threshold that qualifies it, like Switzerland and the United States, for the top ranking of 1 across the board.[11]

In the Political Liberties checklist, all three polities achieve the top ranking 4 across the board in twelve of the thirteen indicators. The exception is the EU in indicator 13, "freedom from extreme government indifference and corruption." Given allegations of indifference in Brussels and corruption scandals during the Santer Commission in the late 1990s, the EU again gets a 2 here, but still exceeds the 48-point threshold that qualifies it for the top democracy ranking of 1.

GASIOROWSKI

Gasiorowski also borrows his definition from Dahl. A democratic regime is "a regime in which the state is highly responsive to the preferences of society because all adult citizens are free to formulate their preferences, to signify their preferences to other citizens and to the state, and to have their preferences weighed without discrimination in the conduct of state policymaking" (Dahl 1971:2–3).

Gasiorowski's operationalization is the most ambitious of the scales here. He is the only one who includes both dichotomous and continuous variables and, for example, indicators of the extent of state intervention in the economy or of the type of parties. He has provided only the categories, not the ratings. I rate all three polities in each category, using my subjective judgment.

The EU equals Switzerland and the United States in thirty of Gasiorowski's 35 indicators. In two indicators, the EU compares unfavorably: a high level of technocratic leadership (indicator 5f), and a moderate role of the state in economic planning (5i).[12] The EU differs from the United States in three indicators: it allows extremist parties on the left (indicator 2f); its system is "collegial-executive/independent," to use Hix's classification (Hix 1998), not presidential (3c); and representative not majoritarian (3d).

The bottom line: Gasiorowski's thirty-five criteria reveal few differences between the three polities, and no differences show the EU as being significantly less democratic than either of the other two polities.

GASTIL

Because "Democracy is a moving target," Gastil provides no definition, and freely admits to "the use of 'freedom' rather than democracy as the criterion for the rating system." He uses "a loose, intuitive rating system for levels of freedom or democracy, as defined by the traditional political rights and civil liberties of the Western democracies" (Gastil 1990:25–26).

Gastil's scale suffers from two problems. First, his annual survey has stuck with the same seven-point scale (1 = least, 7 = most undemocratic) for political rights and liberties over the years. He claims that changing the rating system would make comparison more difficult and confuse those who have followed the system over time. But too much consistency can become rigidity. Second, Gastil holds up the Western-style democracies as the standard that other countries should live up to, and his survey has been accused of right-wing bias. For example, does the U.S. system really provide freedom from gross socioeconomic inequality? Hardly. Did a recent shift in power through elections take place in Switzerland? Not quite.

Table 3.5. Democracy Scale: Gasiorowski 1990

Indicators	Switzerland	USA	EU
• 1) Exercise of Authority			
a) Representative Institutions and Law (yes,no;yes, no)	Y;Y	Y;Y	Y;Y
b) Existence of the Rule of Law (yes,no)	Y	Y	Y
c) Type of Official Ideology (totalists, guiding, none)	N	N	N
• 2) Political Participation			
a) Freedom of Speech and Press (yes, moderate, low)	Y	Y	Y
b) Freedom of Association (yes, moderate, low)	Y	Y	Y
c) Freedom of Organization (yes, moderate, low)	Y	Y	Y
d) Number & Character of Political Parties (0,1,2, >2)	>2	>2	>2
e) Party Fractionalization (index)	n/a	n/a	n/a
f) Extremist Parties (left, right, left+right)	*l+r*	*r*	*l+r*
g) Extremist Party Vote (%)	low	0	low
• 3) Leadership Selection			
a) Representative Selection Process (yes,no;yes,no)	Y;Y	Y;Y	Y;Y
b) Representative Government (yes,no)	Y	Y	Y
c) Executive-Legislative System (pres., parl., none)	*N/A**	*pres.*	*N/A**
d) Electoral System (majoritarian, representational, none)	*repr.*	*major.*	*repr.*
• 4) Fundamental Human Rights			
a) Existence of Political Prisoners (high, moderate, none)	none	none	none
b) Abuse of Political Prisoners (high, moderate, none)	none	none	none
c) General Climate of Repression (high, moderate, none)	none	none	none
• 5) Other Political Regime Characteristics			
a) Consociational Institutions (high, moderate, low)	low	low	low
b) Mobilizational Regime (high, moderate, low)	low	low	low
c) Populist Regime (high, moderate, low)	low	low	low
d) Traditionalistic Regime (high, moderate, low)	low	low	low
e) Military Leadership (high, moderate, low)	low	low	low
f) Technocratic Leadership (high, moderate, low)	low	low	high
g) Corporatist Institutions (high, moderate, low)	high	low	low
h) Personalistic Leadership (high, moderate, low)	low	low	low
i) State Role in Economic Planning (high, moderate, low)	low	low	mod
j) State Involvement in Political Socialization (high, moderate, low)	low	low	low
• 6) Miscellaneous Indicators			
a) Level of Popular Political Activity (high, moderate, low)	mod	mod	low

(*continued*)

Table 3.5. (*continued*)

Indicators	Switzerland	USA	EU
b) Degree of State Ownership of Means of Production (high, moderate, low)	low	low	low
c) Extent of State-Sponsored Social Welfare Program (high, moderate, low)	**high**	**low**	**mod**
d) International Alignment (east, west, non-aligned)	west	west	west
e) Changes of Government (0,1,2,>2)	0	0	0
f) Acts of Non-Violent Popular Unrest (0,1,2,>2)	0	0	0
g) Acts of Violent Unrest (0,1,2,>2)	0	0	0
h) Extremist Guerilla Groups (left, right, left+right)	none	none	none

Values are mine. Differences are emphasized.
*Based on Hix's (1998) classification of Switzerland as "Collegial Executive / Independent" and the EU as "Collegial Executive / Interlocking," I code indicator 3c as N/A.

Again, my intention is not to criticize Gastil's scale but to use it to compare. Two of Gastil's twenty-five indicators show a difference between the EU and the other two polities. In number 4, "Fair reflection of voter preference in distribution of power"; and number 25, "Freedom from gross government indifference or corruption," the EU misses the top grade. In the other twenty-three indicators, the EU is as democratic as the other two polities, and in one outperforms Switzerland (indicator 6, "Recent shifts in power through elections").

GURR, JAGGERS, AND MOORE

Instead of a definition, Gurr et al. combine the criteria of political rights, constraints on power, and civil liberties used in other scales:

> There are three essential, interdependent elements of democracy as it is conceived in the contemporary political culture of Western societies. One is the presence of institutions and procedures through which citizens can express effective preferences about alternative policies and leaders. Second is the existence of institutionalized constraints on the exercise of power by the executive. Third is the guarantee of civil liberties to all citizens in their daily lives and in acts of political participation. Other aspects of plural democracy, such as the rule of law, systems of checks and balances, freedom of the press, and so on are means to, or specific manifestations of, these general principles. (Gurr, Jaggers, and Moore 1990:83)

In five of Gurr et al.'s eight indicators to measure these three elements, all three polities get the top rating. All three have institutionalized participation, competitive participation, regulated recruitment of the chief

Table 3.6. Democracy Scale: Gastil 1990

Indicators	Switzerland	USA	EU
• 1) Exercise of Authority			
Checklist for Political Rights			
1. Chief executive recently elected by a meaningful process	1	1	1
2. Legislature recently elected by a meaningful process	1	1	1
3. Fair election laws, campaigning opportunity, polling and tabulation	1	1	1
4. Fair reflection of voter preference in distribution of power—parliament, e.g., has effective power	***1***	***1***	***2***
5. Multiple political parties	1	1	1
6. Recent shifts in power through elections	1	1	1
7. Significant opposition vote	1	1	1
8. Free of military or foreign control	1	1	1
9. Major group/groups denied reasonable self-determination	1	1	1
10. Decentralized political power	1	1	1
11. Informal consensus; de facto opposition power	1	1	1
• Checklist for Civil Liberties			
12. Media/literature free of political censorship	1	1	1
13. Open public discussion	1	1	1
14. Freedom of assembly and demonstration	1	1	1
15. Freedom of political or quasipolitical demonstration	1	1	1
16. Nondiscriminatory rule of law in politically relevant cases	1	1	1
17. Free from unjustified political terror/imprisonment	1	1	1
18. Free trade unions, peasant organizations, or equivalents	1	1	1
19. Free businesses or cooperatives	1	1	1
20. Free professional or other private organizations	1	1	1
21. Free religious institutions	1	1	1
22. Personal societal rights: including those to property, internal and external travel, choice of residence, marriage and family	1	1	1
23. Socioeconomic rights: including freedom from dependency on landlords, bosses, union leaders, or bureaucrats	1	1	1
24. Freedom from gross socioeconomic inequality	***1***	***2***	***2***
25. Freedom from gross government indifference or corruption	***1***	***1***	***2***
• Freedom Rating (= Political Rights + Civil Liberties)	2	2	2

EU ratings are mine. Differences are emphasized.

Table 3.7. Democracy Scale: Gurr, Jaggers, and Moore 1990

Indicators	Switzerland	USA	EU
• Regulation of participation	5	5	5
Competitiveness of participation	5	5	5
Constraints on chief executive	**7**	**7**	**6**
Regulation of recruitment of chief executive	3	3	3
Competitiveness of recruitment of chief executive	**2.5**	**3**	**2**
Openness of recruitment	4	4	4
Monocratism: characteristics of chief executive	**5**	**3**	**5**
Centralization of state authority	3	3	3
• **Democracy Scores**	**10**	**10**	**9**
Autocracy Scores	0	0	0

Regulation of participation ranges from 1 = unregulated to 5 = institutionalized. 5 = institutionalized means: "Relatively stable and enduring political groups regularly compete for political influence and position with little use of coercion. No significant groups, issues, or types of conventional political action are regularly excluded from political process."

Competitiveness of Participation ranges from 1 = suppressed to 5 = competitive. 5 = competitive means: "Relatively stable and enduring political groups regularly compete for political influence and position with little use of violence or disruption. No significant groups are regularly excluded."

Constraints on chief executive ranges from 1 = unlimited authority to 7 = executive parity or subordination. 7 = executive parity or subordination means: "Accountability groups have effective authority equal to or greater than the chief executive in most areas of activity." (6 = intermediate category.) 5 = substantial limitations means: "The executive has more effective authority than any accountability group but is subject to substantial constraints by them."

Regulation of recruitment of chief executive 1 = 5 unregulated to 3 = 5 regulated. 3 = Regulated means: "Chief executives are determined by hereditary succession or in competitive elections." "2 = designation/transitional" means: "Chief executives are chosen by designation within the political elite, without formal competition. Also coded for transitional arrangements intended to regularize future transitions after an initial seizure of power."

Competitiveness of recruitment of chief executive ranges from 1 = selection to 3 = election. 3 = election means: "Chief executives are typically chosen in or through popular elections matching two or more major parties or candidates." 2 = dual/transitional means: "Dual executives in which one is chosen by hereditary succession, the other by competitive election. Also used for transitional arrangements between selection and competitive election."

Openness of recruitment of chief executive ranges from 1 = 5 closed to 4 = open. 4 = open means: "Chief executives are chosen by elite designation, competitive election, or transitional arrangements between designation and election."

Monocratism: characteristics of chief executive ranges from 1 = pure individual executive to 5 = collective executive with full power sharing.

Centralization of state authority ranges from 1 = unitary state to 3 = federal state. 3 = federal state means: "Most/all regional units have substantial decision-making authority."

EU scores are mine. Differences are emphasized.

executive, open recruitment of the chief executive, and regional units with substantial decision-making authority.

In a sixth indicator, "Monocratism: characteristics of the chief executive," Switzerland and the EU get the highest mark (5 = collective executive with full power sharing) while the United States gets only a 3 = qualified individual executive, "first among equals".

In two other indicators, the EU receives a lower rating than the other two polities. In "Constraints on the chief executive" Switzerland and the US get the top rating 7 = executive parity or subordination, which means "Accountability groups have effective authority equal to or greater than the chief executive in most areas of activity." The EU gets only a 6 = intermediate category.

In the other indicator, "Competitiveness of recruitment of the chief executive," the United States clearly receives the top grade of 3 = election, defined as "Chief executives are typically chosen in or through popular elections matching two or more major parties or candidates." Code 2 = dual/transitional is defined as "Dual executives in which one is chosen by hereditary succession, the other by competitive election. Also used for transitional arrangements between selection and competitive election." As we have seen, Switzerland's chief executive falls short of being popularly elected, but it goes beyond a dual executive. I code it as 2.5. Now the EU: if we say that a single executive (the Commission) is appointed and then approved by Parliament, then the EU should receive the same code as Switzerland: 2.5. If, on the other hand, we believe that the EU has a dual executive—the Commission and the Council of Ministers—of which one (the council) is elected, and the other (the commission) is selected and then approved by Parliament, then the EU should receive only a 2. To be conservative, I rate the EU at 2.

Switzerland and the United States receive a Democracy Score of 10 and an Autocracy Score of 0, while the EU receives a Democracy Score of 9 and an Autocracy Score of 0. This puts the EU also behind Australia, Austria, Belgium, Canada, Colombia, Costa Rica, Cyprus, Denmark, Finland, Germany, Ireland, Israel, Italy, Jamaica, Luxembourg, the Netherlands, New Zealand, Norway, Sweden, the United Kingdom; but on a par with Portugal and Spain (Democracy Score 9), and ahead of Greece (8) and France (6). If the EU is charged with a democratic deficit, then liberal democracies such as France or Spain should as well.[13]

CONCLUSION

Table 3.8 summarizes my findings. According to Alvarez et al.'s scale, the three polities are identical in their democracy ratings, since executive

Table 3.8. Overview of Democracy Scales

Democracy Scale	Emphasis	Finding
Alvarez, Cheibub, Limongi and Przeworski	Dichotomous indicators: democracy or dictatorship. Minimal criteria: chief executive and effective legislature filled by elections.	EU is as democratic as Switzerland and U.S.
Bollen	Continuous scale (1–100). 2 groups of indicators (building on Dahl's 8 criteria): political liberties and democratic rule. 2 variables for media freedom.	EU scores 94 compared to Switzerland and U.S. (both 100): equal to Finland, Greece, Malta, and Portugal; and higher than Germany (89) and Spain (83).
Coppedge and Reinicke	Based on Dahl's 8 criteria, but contestation is unidimensional (political rights and political liberties correlated). Indicators rated from 1 to 4. Fold Dahl's 4th, 5th, and 8th criteria into one FAIRELT indicator.	EU is as democratic as Switzerland and the U.S., but FAIRELT indicator is ambivalent.
Freedom House	Minimal definition of democracy. 2 groups of indicators: political rights and liberties. Indicators rated from 1 to 4. Western bias.	In 19 of 21 indicators, all 3 polities receive top ranking. In 2 indicators (Voters Able to Endow Freely Elected Representatives with Real Power? And Freedom from Extreme Government Indifference and Corruption?) EU is less democratic but still receives top score overall.
Gasiorowski	Most expansive operationalization of democracy, but not implemented. Based on Dahl's criteria. Both dichotomous and continuous variables.	In 33 of 35 indicators, EU equals Switzerland and U.S. In 2 indicators (Technocratic Leadership and State Role in Economic Planning) EU is less democratic.
Gastil	No definition of democracy. Western bias.	In 23 of 25 indicators, EU equals Switzerland and U.S. In 2 indicators (Fair

Table 3.8. Overview of Democracy Scales (*continued*)

Democracy Scale	Emphasis	Finding
		Reflection of Voter Preference in Distribution of Power and Freedom from Gross Government Corruption), EU is less democratic.
Gurr, Jaggers, and Moore	No definition of democracy, but 3 criteria (political rights, constraints on power, civil liberties).	EU gets overall rating of 9, while U.S. and Switzerland get top rating of 10. In 5 of 8 indicators, all 3 polities get top rating. In 6th (Monocratism) EU and Switzerland are more democratic than U.S. In 7th (Constraints on Chief Executive) and 8th (Competitiveness of Recruitment of Chief Executive), EU is less democratic than other polities.

selection in the EU virtually equals the one in Switzerland. Coppedge and Reinicke's scale also shows the three polities as virtually identical in democracy. In Gurr's "Monocratism" indicator, the EU and Switzerland even show a "democratic surplus" compared to the United States. Other scales show the EU as slightly less democratic than the other two polities. Using Gurr's scale, the EU receives a score of 9 compared to 10. In Bollen's scale, the EU gets 94 points compared with 100 for the other two polities. In the Freedom House scale, the EU falls short in two of thirteen indicators; in Gastil's scale, in two of twenty-five; and in Gasiorowski's, in three of thirty-five.

However important these differences are, they do not detract from the central finding of this chapter: based on widely accepted indicators for measuring democracy, EU institutions do *not* suffer from a democratic deficit significantly greater than that of most liberal democracies.

Some readers might object to some of my ratings. Yes, the rankings are subjective, but so are many widely accepted scores in the scales. Others might object that while the scales clearly measure dimensions 2 (lack of transparency) and 3 (lack of consensus) from chapter 2, they at least partly ignore dimensions 1 (lack of legitimacy), 4 (lack of accountability), and 5 (lack of protection).

We saw already in chapter 2 that for dimension 1 this does not matter. The lack-of-legitimacy argument does not hold up to scrutiny, since multiple *demoi* need not prevent multicultural integration, parties need not contribute to legitimacy, and a constitution is not necessary for legitimization.

Dimension 5 is measured by Gastil's and Gasiorowski's scales with their indicators "Freedom from Gross Socioeconomic Inequality" and "Extent of State Sponsored Social Welfare Program," but chapter 2 showed that this dimension is not necessary for democracy either, since open economies appear to be positively correlated with big governments (Rodrick 1996).

On the other hand, none of the scales measure dimension 4 (lack of accountability) *per se*, although Gurr et al. imply it with the indicator "Constraints on the Chief Executive." The very notion of "accountability" is muddled, and only otherwise democratic governments are also accountable (Alvarez et al. 1996:18–19). But EU agencies may pose agency problems or suffer capture by special interests; and they may not be held accountable if the European legislature is weak. Wherever possible, my ratings account for this possible democratic deficit. We will see in chapters 5 and 6 whether EU agencies are less accountable than national nonelected agencies. Before we do, we need to step back from our comparison and theorize the twin problems of agency accountability and agency independence. This is the purpose of the next chapter.

NOTES

1. Treating the Commission as EU executive is also more conservative in the framework of our inquiry. If the council were the executive instead of the Commission, this would lessen the democratic deficit, since the council is made up of cabinet ministers of elected member-state governments.

2. The U.S. executive is *de iure* indirectly elected through an electoral college; but only twice, in 1876 and 2000, did the college in fact elect a president who had not won the popular vote.

3. This democracy-enhancing practice developed under the Delors presidency and became a constitutional requirement under the TEU. The Parliament approved the Santer College by 417 votes to 104 in 1995 and the Prodi Commission by 404 to 153 in 1999. Those who see this appointment procedure as lacking legitimacy should explain why the U.S. government was seen as legitimate before 1913, when presidents were not elected but appointed by an electoral college which in turn was appointed by senators.

4. Post-Nice, thirty-five new issues require QMV, but taxation and social security, aspects of immigration and border controls, health and education, culture, and audiovisual services and broadcasting still require unanimity.

5. *New York Times*, 22 March 1999.

6. Interview with Commission, 14 December 2000.

7. But note that Parliament votes on the budget as a whole, not on line items.

8. In earlier scales (1980, 1990), Bollen constructed a composite variable "Poldem" from six Political Liberties and Popular Sovereignty indicators. In these scales, the EU would receive an overall "Poldem" score of 91.7—significantly lower than Switzerland (99.7) and slightly lower than the United States (92.4).

9. They do not code a separate variable for Dahl's eighth guarantee because in a more recent reformulation of his criteria, Dahl stipulated that officials who have "control over government decisions about policy," rather than the policies themselves, should depend on votes (Dahl 1982:10–11).

10. Answering this and a number of other questions in the Civil Liberties checklist with "yes" is of course to make a gross oversimplification. In no polity are people free from foreign powers, given globalization, or from economic oligarchies, given mergers of multinational corporations. In no polity are all media free and independent. Are all people respected by the security forces of Switzerland or the United States? Is there gender equality in Switzerland or the United States? Is there equality of opportunity? Hardly.

11. Even if the EU were rated 2 in political rights, its combined rating of 1.5 (2 in political rights + 1 in political liberties / 2 = 1.5) would still put it in respectable company with France, Germany, Italy, Japan, Spain, and the United Kingdom.

12. The EU can hardly be faulted for its lack of meaningful welfare programs, since welfare is provided at the level of its constituent member states—not unlike in Switzerland.

13. Another scale, by Vanhanen (1990), calculates the Index of Democratization ID = xy / 100, where x is the share of all smaller parties subtracted from 100, y is election turnout. Vanhanen rates Switzerland at 22.9 and the United States at 16.7. Since a center-right party grouping won the June 1999 EP elections, winning 35 percent of the vote (219 of 626 Parliament seats), the share of the smaller parties is 65 percent. With a voter turnout of 52.8 percent, The EU's ID would equal (65) (52.8) / 100 = 34.32. This would put the EU ahead of Switzerland and the United States! But Vanhanen's index measures *democratization* (after all it is aptly entitled *The Process of Democratization*), which of course proceeds much more rapidly in the EU than in Switzerland or the United States. Since we are interested in the democratic deficit, not in democratization, we must dismiss the Vanhanen scale for our purposes. We must dismiss it also for another reason: the validity of Vanhanen's variable for voter participation is questionable, since countries with low voting levels are not necessarily less democratic than countries with high turnout (Bollen 1980:373).

4

✣

Bureaucratic Democracy

Up to now, we have defined democracy roughly as a system in which parties lose elections in a competitive struggle for votes, but of course neither elections nor votes are given in the case of bureaucrats, who are not elected but appointed. Regulators can wield great power without being subject to elections, without even being directly accountable to elected officials. Max Weber had already warned in the nineteenth century, in his seminal study of bureaucracy, that democratic principles are incompatible with rational adjudication (Weber 1946:217).[1] What are the mechanisms for making agencies representative of the popular will? Asked another way: does electoral discipline also constrain bureaucracy? Since EU citizens lack the power to punish the Commission and its bureaucracy directly, by throwing them out of office, does the bicameral legislature of the European Parliament and the Council of Ministers have the power to control them? These are the main questions of this chapter—a theoretical intermezzo, an attempt at building a theory, including clear criteria, of bureaucratic democracy in the regulatory state—before we look at specific cases in chapters 5 and 6. Here, I will trace the origins of the regulatory state; juxtapose assumptions that underpinned democratic deficit arguments in chapter 2 against new assumptions appropriate to the regulatory state; review the existing theoretical framework, including theories of representation, principal-agent theory, and theories of legislative control; and derive indicators of bureaucratic accountability and independence.

THE RISE OF THE REGULATORY STATE

We can distinguish three socio-economic functions of governments: redistribution, stabilization, and regulation. Regulation has been defined as sustained and focused control exercised by a public agency over socially valued activities (Selznick 1985:363). There are two types of regulation (Majone 1997): direct regulation relies on orders, prohibitions, legally binding standards, and other command-and-control techniques. But exclusive reliance on such formal rules can lead to under-regulation. Consider the Occupational Safety and Health Administration (OSHA) in the United States: OSHA tends to wait until the evidence becomes strong before taking any action, while neglecting to address the much larger number of chemicals with lesser evidence of carcinogeneity (Mendeloff 1988:102). Therefore, a second type of regulation, indirect regulation by information or persuasion, attempts to change behavior indirectly, by changing the incentive structure or by providing suitable information.

As we saw throughout this book, U.S. scholars have referred to the United States federal government as a "regulatory state" (Seidman and Gilmour 1986; Sunstein 1990; Rose-Ackerman 1992), indicating that it has long emphasized the regulatory more than the redistributive or stabilizing functions (Majone 1998:8–17). The modern administrative state, in which a big bureaucracy does much lawmaking, is very different from the state of the American framers. The Constitution did not anticipate that the president, through executive agencies, would have de facto lawmaking capability, violating the nondelegation doctrine and creating multiple principals—Congress and president—monitoring an agent. One solution for this problem was for Congress to delegate lawmaking power to agencies not controlled by the president (Eskridge and Ferejohn 1992; Wood and Waterman 1994:142).

What are agencies? The U.S. Administrative Procedure Act (APA) of 1946 defines an agency as a part of government generally independent in the exercise of its functions and with the lawful authority to take final and binding action affecting the rights and obligations of individuals, particularly through rule making and adjudication (Majone 1998).

Before Franklin Roosevelt's New Deal in the 1930s and, more broadly, the fiscal revolution from the Hoover (1929–33) to the Johnson (1963–69) administration, the American government played a very limited role in redistribution and macroeconomic stabilization. The United States lacks a tradition of absolutist state interventionism, as in France, or of a state bureaucracy to support domestic cartels while innovating in social policy, as in Germany. The small U.S. federal budget prevented economic and social policies even on a modest scale. As we have seen above, the EU should be seen as a regulatory state too: it has no general tax-and-spend powers analogous to those of a national government. Its budget is less than 1.3 percent of Union GDP (and 2.4 percent of member states' total public expenditure) and must always be balanced (Nugent 1994:340).[2] This allows the Community little leeway: it can undertake only limited, mostly regulatory, policies.

How did the European Union become a regulatory state? Why did it not adopt a tax-and-spend welfare state model, as after all its constituent members had? According to Majone, the driving factors for the European emphasis on regulation were several. First, European institutions imported and emulated the neoclassical free-market and deregulation ideology mainly from the United States. Second, in the 1970s and 1980s, stagflation exposed a crisis of traditional Keynesian welfare policies in Europe. Statutory regulation by independent agencies was increasingly perceived as less bureaucratic and more independent of European countries' strong parties. The problem solving, rather than bargaining, approach of agencies was seen as more protective of the diffuse interests of consumers than of the special interests of producers. Third, privatization made increased regulation necessary, since special interests were seen as an increasing threat both to market efficiency and to democratic legitimacy. Fourth, the European bureaucracy simply produced a rapidly growing volume of regulations. By 1970, the Community had issued an average of 625 directives and regulations per year. By 1991, that average had risen to 1,564 directives and regulations—more than the 1,417 French laws, ordinances, and decrees issued by the Paris bureaucracy in that same year (Majone 1996:49–57).

Why would EU member nations agree to outsource rule making to the Commission and to regulatory agencies? Functionalists would argue that the modern administrative state requires highly complex and technical expertise for many policy areas. Regulating and adjudicating are inappropriate for government departments. Regulatory agencies are separate from government and from partisanship; precisely because they are not elected, they are more committed to policy continuity. They are more flexible in policy formulation and execution, and they can handle controversial issues and enrich public debate. But still, functionalism cannot explain why some regulatory policies (namely transport, energy, research and development, education, and social policy) remain underdeveloped while others flourish (Majone 1996:63).

Another, less innocuous, explanation for the rise of delegation is blame-shirking. Fiorina asks: "What incentives lead legislators to delegate to unelected officials not only the administration but even the formulation of public policy?" (Fiorina 1981:176). His blame-shirking model assumes that benefits and costs of government programs are not perfectly perceived. Legislators spend considerable efforts improving perception of program benefits (Mayhew 1974) or lessening their own responsibility for failed programs in the eyes of their constituents. Fiorina argues that legislators delegate to avoid or disguise their responsibility for failure. (Unfortunately, shirking blame of course also lessens these legislators' ability to claim credit whenever success happens).

Theorists of the new economics of organization would say that agencies developed in order to lower transaction costs. Delegation to specialized bureaus is rational: it reduces decision-making costs that rise as legislation becomes more detailed and complex. Legislators have limited resources, so they must leverage them by delegating the details. If consumers are poorly organized in relation to a firm, lack the relevant information, and are unknown to one another, then "a bilateral governance structure between firm and consumers may fail to materialize." A regulatory agency equipped to receive complaints and screen products could serve to infuse confidence in markets (Williamson 1985:309).

But while delegation to agencies lowers some transaction costs, it raises others, both *ex ante*—costs of selecting the right agents, of providing incentives for their performance—and *ex post*—costs of monitoring their performance, of punishing them when they shirk, of their deviation from a ratified policy (Horn 1995). In short, delegation increases uncertainty.

We can assume an inverse correlation between uncertainty and representation. The more uncertainty, the less likely is representation; the more ignorant citizens are about issues, the more rulers can switch policies with impunity (Stokes 1999). Uncertainty is bound to be greater around policy issues that transcend the borders of a citizen's own country, for example carbon dioxide emission ceilings, multinational mergers, or the composition of imported foods.

Uncertainty permits politicians to incur rents: benefits from holding office other than total representation in the best interest of the public. Rents range from perks, to preventing the success of rivals, to simply shirking rather than working. Rent seeking tends to be correlated to uncertainty: the more hidden their actions are from the public eye, the more likely officials can get away with shirking.

If the citizenry is heterogeneous, as in the EU, spanning many national and ethnic constituencies, yet another result of uncertainty may be multidimensionality (Ferejohn 1999): representation breaks down as soon as there is no longer a one-dimensional issue-space. A government makes several thousand key decisions during one term. The problem of multidimensionality is that citizens have only one vote to respond to multiple policy stances of the government. If a government promises lower inflation rates, a restrictive immigration policy, and better schools, and that government keeps only one of these promises, what are citizens supposed to do? They must use one plebiscite to vote up or down an entire mix of policies—a very crude instrument indeed. And EU citizens don't even have that instrument as long as they cannot vote the Commission, the European executive, out of office.

Delegation makes sense only if its benefits outweigh these agency costs. One important agency loss is that while democratically elected principals can delegate policy-making powers to nonelective agents, they cannot transfer their own legitimacy to these agents. This legitimacy loss may be the most expensive agency cost (Majone 1998:7). John Locke, in his Second Treatise on Civil Government, saw this more than three centuries ago:

> The legislative cannot transfer the power of making laws to any other hands, for it being but a delegated power from the people, they who have it cannot pass it over to others. The people alone can appoint the form of the commonwealth, which is by constituting the legislative, and appointing in whose hands that shall be. And when the people have said, "We will submit, and be governed by laws made by such men, and in such forms," nobody else can say other men shall make laws for them; nor can they be bound by any laws but such as are enacted by those whom they have chosen and authorised to make laws for them. (Locke 1690:XI, 141)

Locke's phrase, "chosen and authorised to make laws for them" brings up a key issue: how do you control those to whom you have delegated authority?

DELEGATION AND CONTROL

Already Marx, and before him Montesquieu and the American Federalists in their own words, had argued that governments are merely executive committees of the bourgeoisie and big business. In 1971 Stigler showed that interest groups influence politics rationally, meaning, at a level where marginal benefit equals marginal cost. Not only a large corporation, but also small industry can acquire and operate regulation "primarily for its benefit" (Stigler 1971:3). But such positive models of regulation had two shortcomings. First, they ignored information asymmetries; as already Weber saw, bureaucrats can maintain their power because they make themselves the real experts and keep and control virtually all information (Warren 1982:51). Second, these positive models focused on internal groups—for example, corporations—as the "demand side" of regulation and ignored or treated as a black box the "supply side" of regulation—the bureaucrats themselves (Laffont and Tirole 1993:475).[3] A theory of bureaucratic democracy would need to focus on the agency relationship between bureaucrats and politicians. And not only that: a chain of delegation reaches from voters to the legislature, from the legislature to the executive, from the executive to the bureaucracy, and perhaps from the bureaucracy to a separate regulatory agency.

In the same year as Stigler, Niskanen provided a forerunner of formal models of bureaucratic delegation (Niskanen 1971). His basic model analyzed the budgetary relations between a legislature and an agency. The agency promises an amount of services in exchange for funding from the legislature. Two assumptions give the agency the upper hand: it knows the legislature's demand for its services; and it need not reveal a cost schedule but can present all-or-nothing offers to the legislature. The only constraint on the bureau is that it must deliver the services it has promised; its budget must cover the costs of its output. In sum, the agency can offer the legislature a price-output package that the legislature just barely prefers to zero output and budget. Economically speaking, the agency charges the maximum price the legislature is willing to pay, and produces up to the point where the legislature no longer values its services at all: where the marginal value of output is zero. This means the agency produces more than the socially optimal output where marginal cost equals marginal value.

Delegation, though not inherently incompatible with representation, presents the issue of information asymmetries. Elected officials face problems in controlling regulatory agencies that possess superior information about the effects of their policies (Wildavsky 1964; Schultze 1968).

Consider the principal-agent relationship in the abstract. Principal-agent models have two essential components: asymmetric information and conflict of interest. The agent knows something the principal does not know, which poses the danger that the agent will exploit this edge strategically. A critical requirement of principal-agent models is that the principal can precommit to what she promises the agent. Without this precommitment, the model would be a simple prisoner's dilemma, where both sides are better off if they cooperate than if they defect, but each party is tempted to double-cross the other (Bendor 1988).

Without information asymmetries between firms and regulators, there would be no rents for captured agencies to distribute, and without asymmetries between regulators and the public, it would be much easier to ensure that regulators fulfill their mandates—though even without such asymmetries there might still be organizing costs to the public to enforce that mandate (Neven, Nuttall, and Seabright 1993:170). But "when governments know what voters will be satisfied with and voters do not know what governments can do for them, room is opened for moral hazard" (Manin et al. 1999:9–10). Moral hazard and adverse selection[4] result because firms and regulators share private information that neither legislators nor consumers know and because regulators are not necessarily benevolent (Laffont and Tirole 1993:35–45).

Building on Niskanen's precursor, the U.S. congressional control literature began in earnest with an article by Weingast and Moran, who extended Stigler (1975) and Peltzman's (1984) approach to regulation by incorporating a legislature. They tested two opposing assumptions: that agencies operate independently of the legislature (bureaucratic discretion), or that Congress controls agency decisions (congressional control). Their case was the behavior of the Federal Trade Commission (FTC). Tracing the membership of subcommittees, Weingast and Moran found substantial evidence for systematic congressional influence on FTC decisions. They cautioned against the impression that the absence of active monitoring by Congress equals congressional ineffectiveness in controlling bureaus. Their analogy was the firm: under separation of ownership and control in companies, shareholders need not monitor the day-to-day performance of managers because market institutions allow shareholders to remain ignorant (Weingast and Moran 1983:792).[5] This finding is consistent with a result by Radner, who found that over time, the principal will infer the agent's actions more and more precisely. In an infinitely repeated game, the less the players discount the future, the more they can approach a fully efficient contract (Radner 1985).

A year later, Weingast drew an analogy between profit-maximization by firms and vote-maximization by Congress, since the principle of survival works in business competition as well as in electoral competition. Agencies depend on Congress as much as firms depend on consumers. There are many substitutes for direct, continuous congressional surveillance of agencies. The "decibel meter" or constituency-trigger mechanism can keep agencies on track. Congress can channel resources to those agencies that provide benefits. Alternatively, Congress can apply or threaten sanctions as "the big club behind the door." Finally, ambitious bureaucrats know that they must cater to congressional interests. These solutions need not be costly: they involve little direct congressional participation. Weingast stressed that *"the smooth operation of these institutional arrangements (i.e., agency policy equilibrium) involves little direct participation by Congress. The more effective this system, the less direct and visible the role of Congress in agency decisions"* (Weingast 1984, emphasis in original).

Later, Calvert, McCubbins, and Weingast largely concurred with this optimistic conclusion. They suggested that even if bureaus are the only active participants in policy making, their choices are traceable entirely to the preferences of elected officials because of ex ante appointment power, which gives them the last word on appointments of key officials, coupled with the threat of ex post sanctions if the agency does not perform or deviates from its contract. The more important a policy area to politicians, the less agency discretion they will permit, since politicians will seek to reduce the uncertainty that affords bureaucrats discretion (Calvert, McCubbins, and Weingast 1989).[6]

Similarly, McCubbins and Schwartz argued that same year that Congress is far from neglecting its oversight responsibility, though a few hundred elected officials face millions of bureaucrats that must be monitored. Rather, Congress rationally prefers a more effective form of oversight that the authors called fire-alarm oversight[7] to a less effective form they call police-patrol oversight. But McCubbins and Schwartz concluded pessimistically that fire-alarm oversight, the more effective option, tends to be particularistic, emphasizing the interests of individuals and interest groups rather than those of the public at large (McCubbins and Schwartz 1984).

Gilligan, Marshall, and Weingast traced the history of the Interstate Commerce Act of 1887 (ICA) and found also that multiple-interest-group analysis is frequently necessary to understand the inception of regulation (Gilligan, Marshall, and Weingast 1989). In addition, Banks and Weingast also found that organized interest groups, distinct from their electoral effects, influence policy making based on their ability to provide politicians with information about regulatory performance. Organized constituents with sufficient resources (for example multinational firms) often have access to expertise and information rivaling those of the agency (Banks and Weingast 1992).

Interest groups will be relevant in the next chapters when we look at specific cases involving legislative oversight of regulatory agencies. If special interests wield this much power, what instruments does the legislature have at its disposal to control their influence on regulators? Congress has several options to control agency rule making. It may require consultation between the agency and a study group; it can impose a particular sequence on agency policy making, thus creating an early-warning system; it may impose delay, or it can stack the deck in favor of certain constituencies. But under certain conditions, even with perfect monitoring, no legislative remedy is available for an agency's deviation from agreed-upon policy, which McCubbins, Noll, and Weingast call "policy drift." They review the organizational and procedural history of air pollution legislation in the United States and argue that effective political control of an agency requires ex ante constraints on the agency's decision-making flexibility *before* it makes policy choices. By contrast, they see ex post solutions as cumbersome and generally ineffective against policy deviation by agencies. They offer several prescriptions. The best ex ante remedy for policy drift is legislative specificity: writing precisely into law what the agency is to achieve and how it is to do so. Another solution is to constrain the agency through structure and process. A case in point, the role of the Environmental Protection Agency (EPA) was restricted to merely assuring compliance with the law (McCubbins, Noll, and Weingast 1989), rather than making laws or rules.

In contrast, Ferejohn and Shipan criticize models that give Congress the last move and hence overstate the level of congressional influence over agency decisions (Ferejohn and Shipan 1990). This is a valid objection: being the last mover is not necessarily advantageous in a strategic interaction. Both strategy and negotiation theory tell us that the opposite is true: the first mover, *not* the last, gains a strategic advantage, since the first mover can "anchor" the negotiation or frame the game with an initial proposal (Porter 1985:29; Bazerman and Neale 1992).

Also, we need to distinguish statutory policy making, in which the preexisting status quo prevails unless the legislature agrees on an alternative, from agency policy making, which permits an agency to make the first move and generate a policy which, unless stopped, will prevail (Ferejohn and Shipan 1990). These distinctions are nontrivial: they matter when we apply congressional control to the EU, given the European Commission's agenda-setting power. For example, in the EU, first-mover advantage would mean that the Commission, with its initiative monopoly, is able to create policy momentum that is hard to stop.

AGENCIES IN EUROPE

Several EU scholars have advocated a principal-agent view of the Commission (Majone 1996; Moravcsik 1995; Pollack 1997a). In the case of the EU, who is the agent and who is the principal? We can distinguish at least three principal-agent relationships. First, officials elected to political office in member-state governments and in the European Parliament or council act as agents of their constituents. The reelection process and the career opportunities afforded by the hierarchy of political offices make for a deal: citizens enforce compliance by elected officials with their policy preferences. In return, they vote for elected officials.

Second, regulatory agencies act as agents for politicians in the legislature (European Parliament and Council of Ministers) and the executive (European Commission). In this second principal-agent relationship, elected officials have a range of means of enforcing compliance with their policy preferences: legislation, executive orders, appointments and dismissals of agency leaders, the budgetary process, or direct intervention in decisions. For example, the European Parliament must approve the Commission president, the College of Commissioners, and the EU budget; and the Parliament demonstrated its powers of dismissal when it forced the wholesale resignation of the Commission in March 1999.

Third, delegation of responsibility may take place within the legislature itself. Legislatures normally delegate day-to-day policy oversight, annual budget review, and responsibility for initiating legislation to committees—or in parliamentary systems to ministers or subministerial members of parliament. The Council of Ministers, for example, delegates much legislation to its national staffers at COREPER (Comités de Représentants Permanents).

Schmidt offers a concise application of congressional control theories to the European Commission. In her analysis, there are at least three reasons for agency loss (Schmidt 1998:171). First, bureaucrats and politicians may have different time horizons for planning (Moe 1990:124; Pierson 1996). Politicians may hide long-term consequences of policies from voters, giving the Commission an opportunity to realize its own interests. Commissioners simply serve longer than do most politicians. Since European integration is not a one-shot game, the Commission may expand its powers incrementally. Second, the neutral agent may profit from information asymmetries (McCubbins et al. 1987:247): the Commission can exploit its privileged knowledge of the situation in all member states to advance its agenda (Héritier 1993:441). Third, the agent, in this case the Commission, can exploit differences in interests among multiple principals (Schmidt 1998:171–72).[8]

BUREAUCRATIC ACCOUNTABILITY

We can now derive a structure of bureaucratic democracy according to agency theory. Such a structure should contain several specific dimensions, since the term "democratic deficit" refers to such defects of public policy making as lack of transparency, insufficient public participation, insufficient reason giving, excessive technical and administrative discretion, and inadequate mechanisms of control and accountability (Horn 1995, Majone 1996):

Appointment

A key mechanism of checking bureaucratic discretion is appointment and removal power (Moe 1985). How is key agency personnel appointed, and what is the agency's governance structure (single-headed agency, multiheaded commission, self-regulatory organization, etc.)? Are key prospective agency officials subject to vetting by the directly elected legislature? Do principals have a "club behind the door" to throw agents out if those agents fail to perform (Laver and Shepsle 1997)?[9]

Participation

Does the system amplify signals from the electorate (Sutherland 1993)? For example, is the agency required to hold public hearings, and does it encourage and/or financially sponsor the participation of diffuse, weakly organized interests? What are the requirements for public participation in decision making? The task of public policy is not preventing interest group pressures from affecting regulation (a virtual impossibility), but rather to ensure that the pressures to which regulators respond are reasonably representative of society at large. An effective government must help enfranchise underrepresented interests such as shareholders, consumers, and potential employees, and must ally with these groups that are excluded from the alliance of managers and politicians in the modern state. It can and must strengthen its "output legitimation" by granting individual rights and access to information on policy implementation. "Policy networks" of actors with a stake in a policy must involve public scrutiny (Héritier 1999:24–27). Also, is the power to decide on a policy decentralized—devolved to some mechanism of local public choice (Seabright 1996)? Decentralization can reduce the likelihood of regulators being captured by particular interest groups (Neven et al. 1993:3, 11, 166).[10]

Transparency

How can the public observe government behavior under incomplete information (Minford 1997)? What are the decision-making procedures? Are they clear and accessible to the public? For example, does the agency hold votes on its decisions, and is it required to make these votes public? Transparency is necessary for the agency's credibility; its aim is not to banish the influence of political pressures, but to make those pressures visible (Neven et al. 1993:219).

Reason-Giving

The reason-giving requirement is a necessary condition for public accountability (Majone 1998:13–14). "Giving reasons is a device for enhancing democratic influences on administration by making government more transparent. The reason-giving administrator is likely to make more reasonable decisions than he or she otherwise might and is more subject to general public surveillance" (Shapiro 1992:183). Is the agency required to publish reasons for its decisions and are these reasons widely and easily accessible, for example on the Internet? Paradoxically, an agency with a commitment to objective analysis has an interest in increasing the potential for embarrassment by making its procedures as clear as possible in order to signal to firms its unwillingness to be manipulated (Neven et al. 1993:205).

Overrule

A crucial feature of checks and balances is the capacity to overrule (Bulmer 1994). What are the procedures for agency decisions being overruled by principals or by judicial review (Sutherland 1993), and which principals have overrule powers? Are political decisions to overrule the agency taken transparently and according to clearly defined and generally known rules?

Monitoring

A key agency problem is monitoring, since specialists are usually better informed than principals. The intensity of monitoring is the probability that the legislature, an interest group, or another affected party discovers that the agency has not carried out the legislative intent (Bendor 1988). What is the extent of ex post monitoring through ongoing legislative and/or executive oversight (Finer 1940/41), the budgetary process, citizens' complaints, or peer review (Shapiro 1997)? How directly can the legislature monitor the agency? For example, are there regular, institutionalized meetings and reports where the agency must account for its work to its principals?

BUREAUCRATIC INDEPENDENCE

But these criteria by themselves may not suffice for bureaucratic democracy, for two reasons. First, accountability per se is not tantamount to democratic accountability. Executive influence may deepen bureaucratic accountability, but to whom? To the executive, not to diffuse interests. A strong political leader might single-handedly exert influence on an agency's policies, as happened in France, Spain, or Germany (Majone 1996). Such influence would increase accountability but reduce bureaucratic democracy.

Second, already John Stuart Mill wrote that in a perfect agency relationship, "the rulers should be identified with the people, their interest and will should be the interest and will of the nation . . . let the rulers be effectively responsible to it, promptly removed by it, and it could afford to trust them with power of which it could itself dictate the use to be made" (Mill 1991:24). But is such perfect accountability desirable? Madison saw that a complete, one-to-one congruence between the popular will and policy decisions by rulers may not be in the best interests of the people, since public opinion can be uninformed and fickle. If representatives are 100 percent accountable, then the exact same passions and transient interests that affect the people will be transmitted to their delegates, the representatives (Sanchez-Cuenca 1997). The U.S. framers created both the Senate and judicial review as checks against too much accountability; and, Hamilton argued, "the courts were designed to be an intermediate body between the people and the legislature in order, among other things, to keep the latter within the limits assigned to their authority" (*Federalist Papers* LXIII and LXXVIII).

If it is true that too much accountability might be bad for democracy in the case of elected politicians, it is truer still for agency officials who own special expertise. For this reason we must add to the six criteria of bureaucratic accountability another: independence.

Independence

How independent is the agency from political processes? To what extent has the principal delegated decisions to the independent agent (Persson et al. 1993)? For example, does it depend on government funding or is it self-reliant? How independent is it in personnel matters (Eijffinger and de Hahn 1996:2)? How limited or expansive is the scope of regulation the agency enjoys, what instruments does it have at its disposal, and what is the duration of its regulatory contracts vis-à-vis the regulated industries (Laffont and Tirole 1993:4–5)?

The most prominent arguments for agency independence focus on central banks. *The Economist* once wrote: "The only good Central Bank is one that can say No to politicians." In the well-known Barro-Gordon model, the central bank wants to expand money supply if there are signals of an impending recession, but those signals may be difficult to describe in detail today. The central bank may want to keep its hand free rather than abide by a fixed rule that is sometimes inappropriate. A time-inconsistency problem arises: the policy maker has an incentive to deviate from the plan, while private actors expect it to be followed. Barro and Gordon find that the best solution for the time-inconsistency problem is a fixed monetary policy rule, meaning that the authorities commit themselves to abstain from discretion (Barro and Gordon 1983), but this brings up credibility problems. How can the public believe that the government will stick to its long-term contract and not reverse itself? To buttress their credibility, politicians delegate authority to a relatively apolitical institution with a longer time horizon, and accept restrictions on their future freedom of action (Eijffinger and de Hahn 1996:5–7). Similarly, Majone suggests that politicians in democracies have few incentives to develop policies whose success might not be recognized by voters before the next election; and since one legislature or majority cannot bind a subsequent majority or legislature, public policies lack credibility because they can always be overturned. Hence the move to independent agencies not subject to election cycles. A similar dynamic might be at work when national policy makers delegate policy making to European agencies, because they may lack credibility in the eyes of their peers in other EU member states (Majone 1998:3–4; 1997).[11]

We can distinguish between legal/formal and actual independence. Since actual independence is virtually impossible to quantify, research has emphasized legal independence: the appointment, dismissal, and terms in office of top officials; the presence of a statutory mandate to pursue a certain policy objective; the locus of final authority for policy; conflict resolution procedures between government and agency; and freedom from government influence (Eijffinger and de Hahn 1996:5–7).

Agencies also need to be independent of undue influence by special interests: in this sense, independence is the opposite of capture by private interest groups (McConnell 1966) whose lobbying power likely increases more than proportionately with the resources (including time) spent on lobbying, thereby disadvantaging other interest groups whose members have less at stake per capita (Krueger 1994). Regulators can be captured by the regulated industry, but also by government and even by the bureaucrats themselves (Noll 1989).

So isn't independence dangerous for democracy? To answer that, we will have a quick look at how agency independence originated in the United States and Europe. The American Constitution refers to the bureaucracy only in a handful of subordinate clauses, almost in afterthoughts (Krislov and Rosenbloom 1981:185). This relative lack of clear design and structural accountability probably allowed for "clientelism" (Wilson 1975) where special interests lobbied for preferred rules. In 1936, President Franklin D. Roosevelt sought to limit bureaucratic discretion by charging the U.S. Committee on Administrative Management (the "Brownlow Committee") with scrutinizing independent regulatory commissions (IRCs). The committee found that IRCs

> [a]re in reality miniature governments set up to deal with the railroad problem, the banking problem, or the radio problem. They constitute a headless "fourth branch" of the government, a haphazard deposit of irresponsible agencies and uncoordinated powers. They do violence to the basic theory of the American Constitution that there should be three branches of government and only three. (Brownlow Committee, cited in Litan and Nordhaus 1983:50)

Regulatory agencies have been accused of undermining democracy ever since that indictment. Their independence "represents a serious danger to the growth of political democracy in the United States. The dogma of independence encourages support of the naïve notion of escape from politics and the substitution of the voice of the expert for the voice of the people" (Bernstein 1955). In this view, regulators not subject to presidential or legislative oversight operate in a political vacuum, which can lead to their capture by the ostensibly regulated industries.

But ironically many contemporary features of the U.S. bureaucracy were instituted explicitly not to assure but to *limit* popular control. The 1883 Pendleton Act, designed to end some fifty years of rampant government corruption and inefficiency, created a merit system and career civil service based on expertise rather than political affiliation or ideology. The prototypical independent regulatory commission, the Interstate Commerce Commission (ICC), was designed at least in part to check the power of the political parties (Shapiro 1997). The 1921 Budgeting and Accounting Act placed the responsibility for formulating an executive budget on the president, whose interest was to be efficiency, not popular preferences or campaign agendas. The independence of the important regulatory bodies of the New Deal—such as the Federal Communications Commission, the Securities and Exchange Commission, and the Civil Aeronautics Board—were the price President Roosevelt had to pay for acceptance by Congress and Supreme Court of his far-reaching interventionist policies (Majone 1996:17). Even the 1946 Administrative Procedure Act (APA) laid down procedures for administrative policy making and adjudication in virtual isolation from electoral politics (Wood and Waterman 1994:6).

But U.S. independent regulatory commissions are independent only in the sense that they are autonomous from the executive and that commissioners cannot be removed for disagreeing with presidential policy (Shapiro 1997; Majone 1997). For example, in 1935, the U.S. Supreme Court ruled in *Humphrey v. United States* that the Federal Trade Commission was independent of the executive:

> The Federal Trade Commission is an administrative body created by Congress to carry into effect legislative policies embodied in the statute in accordance with the legislative standard therein prescribed, and to perform other specified duties as a legislative or as a judicial aid. Such a body cannot in any proper sense be characterized as an arm or an eye of the executive. Its duties are performed without executive leave and, in the contemplation of the statute, must be free from executive control. (U.S. Supreme Court, *Humphrey's Ex'r v. United States*, 295 U.S. 602 [1935])

In contrast to the United States, the problem in Europe is *not* one of too much independence but rather the opposite: too little. Political principals in Europe all too often interfere with decisions of regulators, whether because of a desire for expediency or because of a 200-year history of pervasive state interventionism ever since the days of absolutist states. Hence European agencies tend to enjoy *less* independence, both de facto and de jure, than do U.S. agencies.

To prevent this lack of independence from the beginning of the Community, the "Meroni Doctrine" prohibited the delegation of broad discretionary powers to bodies not envisaged by the Treaty on the European Coal and Steel Community—particularly agencies (Majone 1997b). For the Commission, Article 157 of the Treaty of Rome states that commissioners shall be "completely independent" in performing their duty. But in reality, commissioners are bound to pursue careers in their home countries after serving out their commission terms, and are not immune from influence from member states and from within the Commission itself (Majone 1998:10–12).

Martin Shapiro disagrees with this view. He argues that in the United States, keeping Congress happy is as important to most agencies as is pleasing the president, and more important to the independent agencies. No such check exists in Shapiro's view for the foreseeable future over EU independent agencies. In Europe, agencies are independent in that they are relatively free of control by other organs of the Community. The standard rationale for EU agencies is that they should be independent of the Commission because they are managerial, technical, or informational only. But Shapiro sees the managerial-technical-informational rationale for the separation of agencies from the Commission as "absurd." The very emphasis on technical expertise in the agencies poses coordination problems, he writes:

> A forest turns out to be a series of entirely different places to the timber manager, the recreation specialist, the fire control specialist, the fish and wildlife expert, the highway engineer, the water quality monitor, the range manager, the wilderness enthusiast and the land use planner. The attempt of the US Forest Service to generate multi-use forest plans has been an unending story of inability to resolve conflicts among experts. Far from resolving conflicts using objective science, the very expertise of agencies and their independence multiply the potential for conflict. . . . The point is that curing weak democratic legitimacy by a move to technocratic (and thus obviously élite) legitimacy has a certain 'out of the frying pan into the fire' aspect. (Shapiro 1997:281–284)

According to Shapiro, these severe problems of coordination, legitimacy, and control are not alleviated by the claim that EU agencies have purely informational roles because information is never purely technical but also political—a key element in policy making and policy controversy.[12] He writes that "technocracy is, these days, not perceived by the public as legitimate" and concludes that the proliferation and expansion of agencies is merely a strategy for enlarging the Union by evading the current popular hostility to the Commission (Shapiro 1997:287–290).

There is a middle way between these two views. It states that independence from direct political control does not mean independence from public accountability (Freedman 1978:72–73). In an effective accountability structure, accountability and independence must complement each other (Sutherland 1993). In Majone's words, "the key normative problem of the regulatory state is how agency independence and democratic accountability can be made complementary and mutually reinforcing rather than antithetical values" (Majone 1997a:28). Therefore the values of our seven criteria of bureaucratic democracy (appointment, participation, transparency, reason-giving, overrule, monitoring, and independence) must be assigned judiciously in order to achieve both accountability and independence. By doing so in chapters 5 and 6, we will see which of the theories in this chapter is supported by the facts. The above discussion will remain speculative unless we trace specific processes of legislation and examine to what extent they are democratic and to what extent undemocratic. Chapter 5 compares merger regulation, chapter 6 biotech regulation, in the three polities.

NOTES

1. This need not mean that bureaucracies are out of control. Wood and Waterman find in the U.S. case that the bureaucracy and its expertise can be a corrective that produces policy more consistent with the public good than elected politicians do, and stands as a check on the abuse of power by politicians (Wood and Waterman 1994:144).

2. But note that while much of the EU's activity is in regulation, that is by no means its sole focus. More than 80 percent of its budget is dedicated to redistributive policies ranging from agriculture to the European Social Fund, from economic and social cohesion to development cooperation (Majone 1996:61).

3. Some members of the so-called Virginia school (Tullock 1967; Buchanan 1980; Tollison 1982; Bhagwati 1982) make bureaucrats the causal variable and study how bureaucrats compete for rents such as bribes and kickbacks by creating and preserving a monopoly position.

4. Put simply, adverse selection in this context is the difficulty voters have distinguishing between "good" and "bad" regulators, which leads to the prevalence of low-quality regulators. Moral hazard stems from the fact that under asymmetric information, once the principal has accepted a contract with the agent, the agent will choose the level of effort that maximizes his utility, but the principal cannot verify whether the agent puts in low or high effort.

5. Weingast reaches a more balanced conclusion. Examining the history of the Securities and Exchange Commission (SEC), he finds that the SEC's program was

implemented when it provided political rewards to Congress, but concedes that his optimistic congressional-dominance hypothesis is an ideal type; reality may show a "shared-influence hypothesis" instead (Weingast 1984).

6. Banks and Weingast argued similarly that agencies hold differing values (for example the value of reelection) for politicians, who weigh those values against the auditing costs of monitoring agencies. If information asymmetries are potentially advantageous to agencies, then politicians will either look for ways to mitigate this advantage, or they will not create these agencies in the first place because they are not worth the costs of auditing them. This latter case is the source of the greatest inefficiencies (Banks and Weingast 1992).

7. Fire-alarm oversight has been called constituency-trigger mechanism by Weingast.

8. The rules in the 2000 Treaty of Nice slow down the Commission's activism. The leaders of the member states granted the Commission more scope in international trade by moving trade agreements from unanimity to QMV, but other important policy areas—such as taxation, social security, international transport, health, education, culture, certain aspects of immigration, border controls, audiovisual services and broadcasting—still require unanimity.

9. Note that the agent's accountability does not have to mean that the principal is happy with the agent's performance. It does mean that the principal, having the means to replace the agent with a feasible alternative, has no inclination to do so (Laver and Shepsle 1997).

10. However, decentralization need not enhance accountability. It may instead compound information asymmetries, and member states may leverage the threat of autonomous decision making to extract political concessions from the central authority (Neven et al. 1993:181).

11. Note that this explanation overlooks one simple actor: the citizen. Who says that citizens have as short a time-horizon as politicians? Their utility function is not necessarily geared to the election cycle.

12. Shapiro concedes, however, that "the mere existence of fixed agencies of defined structure and jurisdiction is an improvement in transparency over the comitology process" (Shapiro 1997).

5

Case 1—Regulating Mergers

European competition policy, codified in Article 3(g) of the Treaty on European Union in Articles 81–89 (formerly 85–94), is the European Community's "first truly supranational policy" (McGowan and Wilks 1995:142); this makes it a good case for our comparison. It is here that the commission enjoys the broadest authority and discretion—much broader than in other fields (Schmidt 1998) and checked by no other institution but the court. As the competition commissioner Mario Monti himself admitted: "The Union only has similarly broad supranational powers in trade policy and, more recently, since the creation of the European Central Bank, in monetary policy" (Monti 2000:2).

Competition policy can be divided into cartel (or restrictive practices), monopoly, and merger policy. This chapter compares merger regulation across the three polities—European Union, United States, and Switzerland. First we match merger policy in each polity with our criteria for bureaucratic democracy distilled in chapter 4; then we evaluate and compare the bureaucratic democracy of each polity. Table 5.1 shows the relevant actors by polity.

EUROPEAN UNION

Merger control was already part of the original 1951 Treaty of Paris establishing the European Coal and Steel Community (Article 66 ECSC)—not surprisingly, given concerns at the time with industrial concentrations in West Germany and the role of Germany's heavy industry in World War II.

Table 5.1. Key Actors in Merger Regulation by Polity

Case	European Union	United States	Switzerland
Regulation of mergers	Merging parties; Commission; DG Competition; Council of Ministers Court of Justice European (ECJ), Court of First Instance (CFI); consumer groups	Merging parties; Antitrust Division of Department of Justice (DOJ); Federal Trade Commission (FTC); Congress; Supreme Court; consumer groups	Merging parties; Competition Commission; Federal Council; Parliament; Federal Court; consumer groups

While the Paris Treaty established a *traité-loi* specifying the regulatory content, the 1957 Treaty of Rome, or European Economic Community (EEC) treaty, was a *traité-cadre*, a framework that needed further legislation to apply the principles (Bulmer 1994). Merger control was absent from the Rome Treaty, probably because of a new consensus in the 1950s that concentrations were not only unproblematic, but that economies of scale were actually good for industrial competitiveness and economic expansion.

Lacking clear rules, the Commission made do with the Rome Treaty's Article 82 (policy on dominant position, then called Article 86) to control mergers, and was backed in 1973 by the court's *Continental Can* judgment (Case 6/72, [1972] ECR 215) (Hölzler 1990:10). But Article 82 was restrictive: it permitted the Commission to investigate concentrations only given a clear abuse of dominant position, meaning *after* a merger had already been consummated. Realizing this, the Commission drafted a merger regulation in 1973, but it met stiff resistance from member states, especially the United Kingdom, France, and Germany. Over the next ten years, given declining merger activity, merger control was low on the agenda, and the council rejected three more Commission proposals in 1982, 1984, and 1986. But a merger boom in the 1980s and the Single European Act made a "level playing field" and a "one-stop shop" a priority. In the 1987 case *Philip Morris/Rothmans* (Case 156/84 [1987] ECR 4487), the court ruled that even Article 81 of the Rome Treaty (policy on cartels and restrictive practices, then called Article 85) was under certain circumstances appropriate for controlling mergers. In fact, the court's 1973 and 1987 precedents finally persuaded member states that a council regulation was needed for legal certainty and a coherent and effective merger regime. Less than two weeks after the 1987 court ruling, the council gave the Commission the green light to draft a merger regulation (Cini and McGowan 1998:27, 119), which came into force in 1990.

Articles 81 and 82 are remarkably similar to Articles 1 and 2 of the U.S. Sherman Antitrust Act below,[1] but not quite identical. Article 81 is weaker than the U.S. instrument, since it requires firms to be in a dominant position[2] before it can be invoked and excludes hostile takeovers. Similarly, Article 82 does not apply unless there is dominance; and it prohibits the *abuse* of a dominant position, not the dominant position *per se*. Also, unlike U.S. law, European law does not make a hard distinction between "competition" (the supposedly natural state of the market, unencumbered by regulation) and "regulation" (government intervention that displaces free competition) (Larouche, 2000:64, 318, 401). In the European tradition, competition and regulation are more compatible than in the United States. Table 5.2 shows the European procedure.

Table 5.2. The European Merger Procedure

1. Where worldwide turnover of all entities exceeds €2.5 billion and EU-wide turnover of at least two of the concerned undertakings exceeds €100 million (Council Regulation No. 1310/97), mergers have a "Community dimension" and are handled by Directorate B (formerly Merger Task Force) of the Commission's Directorate Competition. Merging parties must notify the Commission (and may also notify their member state government).[3] Below these thresholds, mergers fall under the jurisdiction of national authorities. The Council may revise these thresholds by qualified majority (based on Article 145, Rome Treaty).
2. The Commission distributes a copy of the notification to all member governments, and allocates the file to a *rapporteur*. The agreement is approved unless the Commission raises objections to the case within six months ("opposition procedure").
3. The Competition Directorate decides whether the case falls under the Regulation. If yes, it conducts a Phase I investigation for 1 month. If it has no concerns, its *cabinet* grants fast-track approval.
4. If the Directorate has concerns, the case goes into Phase II investigation for 4 months. During Phase II, the Commission may issue a Statement of Objections, hold oral or third party hearings, and consult the Advisory Committee on Concentrations (a member state committee).
5. An agreement qualifies for exemption under Article 81(3) if it meets four conditions: it must benefit the whole EU, and its advantages must outweigh its disadvantages; consumers must share fairly in the benefits; any restriction to competition must be indispensable for achieving the agreement's objectives; and there must be no substantial elimination of competition. Agreements can also be granted by "group" or "block" exemption (Regulation 1475/95).
6. The Directorate B makes a recommendation to the College of Commissioners.
7. The College votes in private (informal leaks, but no formal record of the vote). Neither Parliament nor Council hold binding votes.
8. The Commission rules: approval or prohibition, or approval with conditions or obligations.
9. The firms involved are entitled to an appeal to the European Court of Justice.

Source: Interview Commission, 22 September 2000; Merger Regulation

The timetable is more predictable in the EU than in the U.S., where cases tend to be in courts and more open-ended. All final decisions in competition cases are reached in a vote among all commissioners (Regulation 17, Article 9; Merger Regulation, Article 8). Except for two cases since 1990, the college always went along with the Competition Directorate's recommendation.[4] Most competition decisions are made with little or no debate: written proposed decisions are circulated to the *cabinet* of each commissioner and adopted unless objections are made within a limited period (Laudati 1996:236).

The Commission's assumption of powers was a sensitive matter, although some multinationals even favored *lowering* the thresholds for Commission intervention, triggering its intervention *more* easily. Why was the Commission able to push through its extraordinary regulatory competency? First, the Commission has been extremely lenient in permitting mergers (Neven et al. 1993). From 1990, when the Regulation entered into force, to December 2001, the Commission cleared 1,832 cases and prohibited only eighteen cases;[5] over 95 percent of cases were cleared in fast-track approval during Phase I and never made it into a detailed Phase II investigation. Second, more companies preferred the Commission's "one-stop shop" option to the cumbersome and costly alternative of having to apply in up to fifteen national jurisdictions.[6] The unified European rules proved more predictable than the politicized decisions often made by national authorities.

We can now apply the seven criteria of bureaucratic democracy from chapter 4 to merger regulation. I do this by loosely describing the features of the regulation in each of the seven dimensions. Of course these dimensions are not entirely distinct but overlapping (for example "monitoring" has implications for "transparency" and vice versa).

Appointment

Each commissioner has a secretariat-general and a cabinet that run the daily business of the directorate and function as liaisons between the commissioner and other directorates, other European actors, and national governments. Since 1995, Directorate B (formerly the Merger Task Force) within the Competition Directorate has been specifically charged with merger control, but the Commission collectively makes the final decision on competition cases. As we saw the commissioners are political appointees of the member-states governments (EC Treaty, Articles 157–158). After approving the president individually, commissioners are now vetted, and approved collectively, by Parliament. The 2000 Nice Treaty also submitted the Commission to designation by the Council of Ministers acting under qualified majority voting (QMV), but gave the Commission president the power to shuffle commissioners' portfolios and dismiss them if they do not perform satisfactorily.[7]

Participation

The actors at the heart of EC competition policy are the Commission and the European Courts; both chambers of the legislature, council and Parliament, have long been on the sidelines. But that changed in 1997 with the revised Merger Regulation, which gave the council the key power to legislate thresholds for Community intervention in mergers. Also, along with the Parliament's growing powers over time, its Committee on Economic and Monetary Affairs has grown in influence, too. It was Parliament that persuaded the Commission to publish an annual competition report beginning in 1972 (Cini and McGowan 1998:38–39).

Ever since the 1963 precedent of *Van Gend en Loos* (Laudati 1996:246–48), member-state competition authorities and courts have been empowered to apply Community competition law under the doctrine of direct effect.[8] In 1969, the court established the *de minimis* rule: "an agreement falls outside the prohibition in Article [81(1)] where it has only an insignificant effect on the market" (Case 5 [1969] ECR 295). The *de minimis* rule serves effectively as a decentralization vehicle, dividing responsibility between European and national cases. While Regulation 17 still centralized competition regulation in the Commission, by the early 1980s a policy of decentralization emerged. Realizing that it alone could never handle all competition cases or ensure effective enforcement, the Commission declared it would involve national courts more in enforcing competition policy (Cini and McGowan 1998:35).

The amended rules were prompted by the Commission's controversial prohibition (its first under the new Merger Control Regulation) of the DeHavilland merger, in which ATR, a joint venture of the Italian company Alenia and the French company Aerospatiale, sought to acquire the Canadian aircraft manufacturer DeHavilland.[9] Since the early 1990s, the Competition Directorate has followed a detailed consultation procedure involving national authorities before deciding on mergers. Article 19 of the Merger Regulation requires the Commission to stay "in close and constant liaison" with member-state authorities during an investigation and give them copies of all merger notifications and the most relevant documents. The regulation gives states a right to express their views "at every stage of the procedure up to the adoption of a decision," and to attend hearings in Phase II. After the hearings, the Commission must submit draft decisions for all Phase II cases to the member states' Advisory Committee on Concentrations, take "utmost" account of the opinion of the Committee, and inform it how it has taken its opinion into account (Laudati 1996:237–40). And in 2001, an overhaul of Regulation 17 empowered national authorities to apply Articles 81 and 82 themselves, eliminated the Commission's sole jurisdiction over Article 81(3) to grant exemptions (long a German criticism[10]), and freed the Commission to emphasize subsidiarity[11]—that the Community should enjoy only those competencies that are not satisfactorily exercised by member states (Commission 2001).[12]

In contrast to the member states, third parties (competitors, distributors, unions, consumer groups, and media) are aware of the issues, but have only limited access to Competition Directorate officials and background information (Laudati 1996:241). In the 1960s this was different: the Competition Directorate (then DG IV) was still marked by a consumer ethos (Goyder 1988:121), much like in the U.S. populist antitrust tradition that defended weak consumers against abuses by powerful firms or cartels. But this public-interest commitment diminished when consumer relations were transferred out of the Competition Directorate in 1967 (Cini and McGowan 1998:24, 108). Today, the speed of the procedure gives third parties very little time to make representations, let alone discuss remedies negotiated between the parties and the Commission (Neven et al. 1993:226). At an oral hearing at the end of the Phase II investigation, the parties can urge their interpretation of the evidence and expert witnesses can be called, but members of the public are not allowed to attend.

Transparency

Many aspects of the procedure are opaque to the public, not least because the law gives directorate officials ample discretion and flexibility to deal with each case on its own merits in prohibiting or exempting agreements. Before official notifications, officials and the companies tend to meet informally to anticipate possible issues, speed up the evaluation of non-controversial cases, and minimize any sunk costs of proceeding with a merger that will be prohibited. Since the overwhelming majority of cases are settled informally, this deepens legal uncertainty. Critics also charge that the public does not have sufficient access to information on the Commission's method for determining fines (House of Lords 1993:7; Korah 1997).[13]

The Advisory Committee may ask the Commission to publish its opinion (Merger Regulation, Article 19(7)), and though the Commission is not legally obliged to publish, it usually does, albeit often months later (Cini and McGowan 1998:123). The Commission must strike a delicate balance between transparency and business confidentiality, since disclosure of confidential competitive intelligence might severely damage the companies' viability. As a safeguard, the Commission and national competition authorities are prevented from using the information they gather for any purpose other than the case at hand.

The Merger Regulation provides some guarantees of transparency. The Commission must publish a notification when a proposed merger falls under the regulation. But the only information the Commission publishes before its final decision is a press release when it opens proceedings (Merger Regulation, Articles 4, 20). The process by which a judgment by Directorate B is transmuted into a political compromise in the Commission is opaque and risks distorting the character of the investigation (Neven et al. 1993:221). And the Court of First Instance (CFI), discussed below under overrule, reaches its majority-vote decisions in secret.

Reason-Giving

In Europe, reason-giving is ensconced already in the 1951 Treaty of Paris establishing the European Coal and Steel Community. Article 5 states that "the Community shall . . . publish the reasons for its actions." Article 15 provides that "Decisions, recommendations, and opinions of the High Authority shall state the reasons on which they are based."[14]

The Commission's decisions are not only legal documents, but also statements of its thinking and intentions—regulatory tools that shape rules and norms. It has stated its intention to explain whenever its decision departs from the opinion of the Advisory Committee (Commission 1993:24, 28). It has sought to make its publications more accessible. In 1996, it agreed to the Parliament's request to include in its annual report of competition policy a chapter on future policy initiatives (Commission 1997a:81), and has published Guidance Notices on important jurisdictional and substantive issues (Commission 2001:54).

But there is no case analysis independent of the Commission's rationale (Neven et al. 1993:224), so verification of its findings is next to impossible. Moreover, the Commission has been criticized for its overly juridical analysis. An economic analysis would, by contrast, "reveal that parallel conduct is innocent where the market is oligopolistic and the products homogeneous; alternatively it may suggest that there has been price fixing, where parallel prices have been charged over a long period in what would seem to be a competitive market" (Whish 1989:224).[15] Such an economic analysis is largely missing, which can give Commission decisions a somewhat arbitrary feeling.

Overrule

Two judicial actors have the power to overrule Commission decisions: the ECJ and the Court of First Instance (CFI), which began in 1989 as a European-level tribunal, mainly to reduce the ECJ backlog. The influence of the ECJ on competition policy used to be minimal until the mid-1960s, but ever since the landmark case *Etablissements Consten and Grundig v. Commission* (Cases 56 & 58/64 [1966] ECR 299) the ECJ has subjected Commission decisions to judicial review.[16]

The ECJ and the CFI have both been criticized for being too lenient with the commission. Indeed, the ECJ has been supportive of the commission's discretion in reaching settlements (Cini and McGowan 1998:55, 114) and has been reluctant to engage in the commission's limited economic analysis (Whish 1989:279). Worse, in 1995 the CFI upheld a Commission decision that left Nestlé and BSN with more than 65 percent market share (Cini and McGowan 1998:126). But especially since the mid-1990s, the ECJ has—at least partially—overridden Commission or CFI decisions.[17]

Monitoring

Parliament can monitor the Commission through its resolutions in response to the Commission's annual competition reports; through annual discussions with the competition commissioner of his report and activities; through the strategic use of written and oral questions that can approach 200 in number and are permitted whenever Parliament is in session; and through pressure on competition commissioners to report to Parliament regularly. But these parliamentary actions hardly constitute systematic control or scrutiny (Cini and McGowan 1998:39–40). As we have seen, Parliament is largely bypassed by Commission decisions. Member states, on the other hand, can monitor and constrain the Commission in the council, but only if they reach consensus on a treaty revision (Schmidt 1998).

Independence

Article 157 EEC provides that commissioners shall be "completely independent in the performance of their duties" and that they "shall neither seek nor take instructions from any government nor any other body." The Commission has fought hard for its autonomy from national interests in competition policy—perhaps rightfully: it has often been "prepared to proceed against alleged cartels where the domestic competition authorities might fear to tread" (Whish 1989:223).

But is the Commission independent? Some decisions suggest negotiations in which the firms had a strong hand, and the Commission has all too often been keener to clear deals than required by its criteria for analysis to which it is supposedly committed. One rapporteur was quoted as saying that "I sometimes get only ten minutes to present the outlines of a case analysis to the commissioner; and I know that after I've done so the firms will get half an hour to talk to him." Another said: "We often learn about the remedies after the handshaking has taken place" (Neven et al. 1993:160, 218, 223). For example, in 1991 the Commission, under pressure from France and Italy, struck a deal with both parties in the *Alcatel/Telettra* strategic alliance (OJ [1991] L122/48, [1991] 4 CMLR 778) *against* the recommendation by its own Competition Directorate. The controversial decision, probably based on the strategic value of creating a globally competitive European telecom player that would surpass AT&T as the world's largest telecom equipment supplier, resulted in the first conditional merger under the Merger Control Regulation (Cini and McGowan 1998:128).

On the other hand, as we have seen, the commission did narrowly prohibit the *De Havilland* merger. It also prohibited the joint venture *MSG Media Service GmbH* of two media companies and the German state telecom company (OJ [1994] L364/1). But both prohibitions happened because of the personal leadership of charismatic competition commissioners, not because of institutional independence, although the Commission recovered some of its credibility by prohibiting five additional mergers in 1995 and 1996 (Cini and McGowan 1998:129) as well as others, including MCI-Sprint in 2000 and General Electric-Honeywell in 2001.[18]

Corporate capture is one pitfall, government capture another. Although the need of independent agencies for policy credibility has become clear, agencies in some member states are less free from state intervention than are EU agencies. Even in Germany, which grants the *Bundeskartellamt* the most extensive powers of all national cartel offices in the EU, the government retains considerable powers of intervention with mergers. The minister of economics can overrule the cartel office at the request of the parties (but overturned only 6 of 108 cases from 1973 to 1994). For example, in the merger of Daimler-Benz with defense contractor MBB, the economics minister overruled the *Bundeskartellamt's* rejection and ignored the Monopoly Commission (Baake and Perschau 1996:144).

In this context, the Commission is a single enforcement body endowed with multiple functions: investigator, prosecutor, policy maker, decision maker, detective, judge, and jury. Its procedure has judicial or quasi-judicial features. If a single individual or institution acts as rapporteur, then develops a case file—and often prosecutorial zeal—then acts as objective decision maker, this conflation of roles makes it difficult to assess facts objectively or to protect the rights of the parties.[19]

UNITED STATES

In Europe, the overriding aim of competition policy has long been the integrity of the Common Market (Neale and Goyder 1980:189, 493). The basic concern in the United States, meanwhile, has been with illegal market power per se, regardless of whether such market power is mitigated by advantages to the economy as a whole. In contrast to European antitrust culture, the U.S. tradition began as an attempt to protect citizens from the overweening power of corporations (Neven et al. 1993:195) during massive capitalist concentration in the first half of the twentieth century. In 1909, the 200 largest nonbanking corporations owned about one-third of all corporate assets; in 1928 they owned 48 percent; by 1940, 55 percent. In the United States, antitrust is widely seen as a means of enforcing competition, which in turn enhances efficiency. The 1890 Sherman Antitrust Act embodied American values such as individualism, fairness, and free enterprise. Free and fair competition was seen as the economic equivalent of political freedom and democracy; unaccountable economic power of monopolists was counter to the ideological foundations of the U.S. state (Neale and Goyder 1980:16; Whish 1989:16). The 1914 Clayton Act embodies these values. Section 7 prohibits mergers or acquisitions "where in any line of commerce or in any activity affecting commerce in any section of the country, the effect of such acquisition may be substantially to lessen competition, or to tend to create a monopoly" (15 U.S.C. 18). Section 15 empowers the attorney general, and Section 13(b) of the Federal Trade Commission (FTC) Act, also of 1914, empowers the FTC to seek a court order enjoining consummation of a merger that would violate Section 7. Pri-

Table 5.3. The United States Merger Procedure

1. Merging commercial parties must notify the Department of Justice and the Federal Trade Commission[a] on merger plans if the proposed merger exceeds certain thresholds. The agencies split responsibility for merger cases between them.
2. The Attorney General and/or the Federal Trade Commission may take administrative action against violations of the Sherman Act, of the Clayton Act, or other violations of competition.
3. Private persons may also seek relief against anticompetitive practices.
4. Merging parties must provide information, then wait for a prescribed period (usually 30 days). The agencies may ask for further information and extend the waiting period by 20 more days. The agencies are empowered to subpoena information (e.g., through the Federal Bureau of Investigation and cross-examination of officers and employees).
5. The Antitrust Division of the Department of Justice or the Federal Trade Commission and the respective state attorney(s) general with jurisdiction over the merging parties jointly investigate the merger or antitrust violation. They collaborate closely and strategize jointly.
6. The Antitrust Division and/or the FTC provide certain otherwise confidential information with the consent of the merging parties to the state attorneys general.
7. The decisions of U.S. antitrust authorities are subject to judicial review.

[a]And in the case of a telecommunications merger, the Federal Communications Commission.
Source: U.S. Department of Justice, Antitrust, Division, 8 April 1997.

vate parties may also seek injunctive relief under 15 U.S.C. 26, and Section 5 of the FTC Act authorizes the FTC to take administrative action against unfair competition practices that violate the Sherman and Clayton Acts.

Much like the European Merger Regulation, the 1976 Antitrust Improvements Act (15 U.S.C. 18a), with a new clause 7a into the Clayton Act, requires merging persons to notify the agencies of a proposed merger or acquisition that would exceed certain thresholds.[20]

This court-based, adversarial process takes much longer in the United States than in Europe—usually five to ten years—and can cost both plaintiffs and defendants millions of dollars. Another difference is that 96 percent of U.S. civil antitrust suits are brought by private parties (Boner and Krueger 1991). Now, what does U.S. merger policy look like through the prism of the seven bureaucratic democracy dimensions?

Appointment

In the United States, unlike in Europe, not one but two bodies are responsible for antitrust policy. Cases are divided between the FTC, a regulatory agency, and the Department of Justice, a division of the executive branch, on a loosely sectoral basis. The attorney general, a cabinet member who heads the Department of Justice, the FTC commissioner, and their immediate deputies are not civil servants as in European agencies, but political officers, appointed by the president and vetted individually by Congress.

Participation

Few cases seem to result from complaints by members of the public (Neale and Goyder 1980:383); but the FTC can initiate a Special Report procedure and send out questionnaires for an industry-wide investigation (FTC Act, Section 6(b)). During the 1970s, consumers participated more actively in antitrust policy than in later years. Today the agencies are not required to involve the public, except in telecommunications, where the Federal Communications Commission must also approve mergers and hold public hearings. Also, if violations are deemed criminal, a grand jury is appointed to inquire whether the evidence warrants prosecution (Neale and Goyder 1980:376).

Transparency

The rules about whether and when regulators may meet with representatives of the industries concerned are much more restrictive in the United States than in Europe. Also, in the United States parties resort to adversarial procedures such as courts more than seeking negotiated solutions (Neven et al. 1993:169), which is good for transparency.

Reason-Giving

When the Clayton Act was passed in 1914, President Wilson knew that imperfect information might impair democracy. The president himself called for legislation "in such terms as will practically eliminate uncertainty" (Neale and Goyder 1980:182). The factors to be considered, according to Section 7, were whether the merger would be in an industry not yet concentrated; whether that industry had seen a recent trend toward domination by a few; whether suppliers had easy access to markets and buyers to suppliers; and whether new entry to the industry was possible without undue difficulty (Neale and Goyder 1980:187). Half a century later, in the 1963 case *United States v. Philadelphia National Bank*, the Supreme Court ruled that mergers "likely to lessen competition substantially" are illegal, and suggested that even as little as 20 or 25 percent combined market share was enough to convey illegality.

From its inception to the 1970s, the FTC had used a case-by-case approach to regulation. But with the increasing influence of the Chicago School in the 1970s and 1980s, and since the Reagan administration's sustained initiative to roll back the state in the 1980s, U.S. competition policy focused on market impact and efficiency (Cini and McGowan 1998:7). In the 1980s, the Reagan administration installed at the agency's helm a laissez-faire economist who believed that any regulation inhibited the operation of the free market. Requirements for evidence not only of market dominance but also of reduced consumer welfare were steep then; to justify even pursuing a case, attorneys had to present prima facie evidence (Wood and Waterman 1994:45).

On the other hand, unlike in Europe, a Bureau of Economics assists the FTC's Bureau of Competition in its economic analysis. The agency issues "Industry Guides" and advisory opinions, omitting only the names of the parties and any trade secrets, to clarify trade regulation rules (Neale and Goyder 1980:383, 390).

Overrule

American distrust of unchecked power is likely a more deep-rooted source of antitrust policy than economic or political ideologies (Neale and Goyder 1980:442). Unlike in Europe, judicial review is not occasional but common in the United States. The courts can and do overrule the agencies, and in *Federal Trade Commission v. Gratz* (1920) the Supreme Court held that "it is for the courts, not the Commission, ultimately to determine as a matter of law" what constitutes unfair competition. Nevertheless, until the late 1960s the agencies and the government lost hardly a Section 7 case, leading Justice Stewart to complain in *Von's Grocery*: "The sole consistency that I can find is that under section 7 the Government always wins." In the 1970s, Chief Justice Burger applied much more detailed economic analysis to each case and was less quick to apply presumptions of illegality based merely on market-share statistics (Neale and Goyder 1980:186).

Monitoring

The discretion of the FTC was a contentious matter until the Supreme Court in *Federal Trade Commission v. Sperry and Hutchinson & Company* (1972) reversed a Fifth Circuit Court of Appeals decision, ruling instead that the agency was entitled to "define and proscribe an unfair competitive practice even though the practice does not infringe either the letter or the spirit of the antitrust laws. . . ." This ruling gave the FTC vast discretion; to check that discretion, Congress monitors both agencies through oversight committees.

Independence

The FTC's wide discretionary authority under its vague statutory mandate (Katzman 1980) led some to see the agency as a prime example of agency capture (e.g., Stone 1977). But the evidence on who exactly influences the FTC is mixed: some found that the agency's case selection covaried with congressional ideology—a probusiness Congress meant probusiness case selection (Weingast and Moran 1983). Other studies found that FTC deceptive trade practice cases varied predictably with changing presidential administrations (Stewart and Cromartie 1982), or that the average level of FTC complaints was continually lower under the Reagan administration's appointee (Wood and Waterman 1994:46). Yet other studies found either no presidential effects (Yandle 1985) or even counterintuitive ones—Republican administrations correlating with *more* FTC complaints against businesses (Moe 1985). Thus the effect of legislative or executive influence is unclear.

But are the agencies susceptible to capture by special interests? No, it seems: interest groups lobbying congressional committees were unable to rein in the FTC and its activist policies (Wood and Waterman 1994:46), and based on anecdotal evidence, the Justice Department at least seems to withstand lobbying pressure.[21] Justice has pushed for heavy deterrent sentences in hard-core cases, including jail terms of up to eighteen months and fines of up to $1 million and 10 percent of a company's sales during an illegal agreement.

SWITZERLAND

Switzerland was relatively late in introducing a competition law. The first law of 1962 was revised in 1985 and again in 1995. The revised law (Bundesgesetz über Kartelle und andere Wettbewerbsbeschränkungen SR 251) is relevant here.[22] It applies whenever cartels have an impact on competition in Switzerland, even if these cartels originate outside the country (Kartellgesetz KG, Article 1.2).

Much like the European Commission, the Federal Council acts as the ultimate arbiter in competition matters, but the Swiss executive has delegated this function to the Competition Commission.[23] There are significant differences to U.S. or European Community rules. First, sanctions against Swiss cartels cannot be imposed retroactively after a merger, meaning that no fines equivalent to the economic damage can be imposed. Penalties can be imposed only if a cartel or monopoly has been certified as illegal and continues nonetheless. Thus, Swiss cartel law loses effectiveness not least in preventing cartels.[24] Second, unlike under U.S. law, responsible persons cannot be prosecuted. Third, while the European statute considers "significant impediments" to effective competition,

Table 5.4. The Swiss Merger Procedure under 1995 Cartel Law

1. For undertakings other than banks and insurance carriers, the Competition Commission (commission) must be notified of concentrations of enterprises before they are carried out when, in the last accounting period prior to the concentration: a) the enterprises concerned reported joint turnover of at least 2 billion Swiss francs or turnover in Switzerland of at least 500 million Swiss francs, and b) at least two of the enterprises concerned reported individual turnover in Switzerland of at least 100 million Swiss francs.
2. The Secretariat of the commission opens an evaluation whether effective competition is suppressed, notifies the public, and invites interested parties to come forward within 30 days.
3. The commission may hold public hearings and must complete its investigation within 4 months.
4. If the commission finds no suppression of effective competition, it examines economic efficiency criteria. If economic efficiency is positive, the commission closes the procedure. If economic efficiency is negative, the commission acts as if competition were suppressed. The commission renders a decision. It may require the parties to propose remedies for reestablishing effective competition.
5. Merging parties either accept the commission's decision or appeal to the Federal Court or to the Competition Appeals Commission.
6. If merging parties accept the commission's decision in 5., the Federal Council evaluates and can overturn the commission's decision based on public interest.
7. If the Federal Council overturns the commission's decision, the procedure is closed. If the Federal Council backs the commission, merging parties may appeal to the Federal Court.
8. If merging parties appeal in 5., the Federal Council can overturn as in 5, and close the procedure, or back the commission.
9. If merging parties appeal to the Federal Court in 4., that court can overrule the commission or back the commission.

Source: Bundesgesetz über Kartelle und andere Wettbewerbsbeschränkungen (Kartellgesetz, KG), 6 October 1995.

Swiss law insists on a higher threshold of effective competition being "suppressed" and is likely more permissive, since the freedom of contract is deeply rooted in the Swiss constitution.

We review Swiss merger regulation again along the bureaucratic democracy criteria.

Appointment

Switzerland after the 1848 constitution was guided by the motto "weak state—strong society," and the Federal Council played a coordinating-reacting, rather than a guiding-initiating role (Hug 1999). Since they expected the cantons to implement federal laws, the founders of the Swiss federal state did not think of a large federal administration. This division of labor is largely intact today (Linder 1999:138) much like in the EU. The number of departments of the federal administration has been fixed by the Swiss constitution since 1848, which has insulated the administration from political short-term interests, but also from organizational improvements. In most other states, central governments have much greater numbers of ministries, and reshufflings or restructurings are part of normal government business (Germann 1984).

The 1995 law authorizes the Competition Commission formally to issue binding decisions. The commission has a secretariat charged with the administration, coordination, and publication of cases. The Federal Council appoints the key agency officials, who are not subject to vetting or approval by the legislature.

Participation

As we saw, the Swiss constitution, not unlike the EU treaties, gives lawmaking power to the cantons unless a specific provision grants this power to the confederation. Even where the confederation is empowered to enact the law, it often restricts itself to the general principles and leaves implementation and detailed regulations to the cantons. Not surprisingly, Swiss cartel law reflects this decentralization culture: it grants the cantonal courts jurisdiction in "suits brought for restraint of competition" and related civil suits (Article 14.1). But in contrast to European antitrust law, and not unlike U.S. law, Swiss cartel law does not provide for public participation in the commission's deliberative process.

Transparency

The 1995 revision streamlined the commission's work, and its specific criteria for evaluating mergers now appear to be less prone to manipulation than under the 1962 and 1985 versions of the law. To be approved, mergers should add value to society by reducing distribution and production costs, improving quality, promoting research and diffusion of knowledge, and using resources more rationally.

The Federal Council's 1996 ordinance on merger control laid out the duties of the commission's secretariat to collect and publish rulings of the cantonal courts. The courts, without being asked to do so, must furnish a complete copy of their antitrust judgments, and the secretariat must collect these and publish them periodically.

The commission now has the right and duty to announce the initiation of an inquiry publicly. This enhances transparency, since the economics minister could previously block publication. Yet the commission still has no obligation to publish, and the public cannot always scrutinize, its analysis.

Reason-Giving

The Competition Commission must scrutinize a merger if it is concerned about market domination by the merged entity, or if the parties cannot show that the disadvantages of market dominance are outweighed by benefits for competition in another market (Article 4.2).[25] The commission can either prohibit the merger or admit it while stipulating conditions (Article 10.2). This provision is identical with EC competition law.

But both the criteria for the review of a concentration and those for their evaluation suggest that the treatment of mergers is significantly more lenient in Switzerland than in the EU or United States. "Competition" is a rather vague concept that leaves much discretion to the agency.

Overrule

The Federal Council can overrule the commission on the basis of a wider criterion, "the public interest" (Articles 8, 11); but the legislature implicitly anticipates this step only in exceptional circumstances. Since 1995, the minister of economics alone can no longer overrule the commission; only the whole seven-member Federal Council can, making it much more difficult for parties to persuade the collective executive than a single individual who traditionally catered to right-wing parties and corporate interests (Neven and Ungern-Sternberg 1997).

But federal court decisions are not binding on other courts in Switzerland. Although rulings by the Swiss Federal Tribunal—Switzerland's highest court—and by one of the cantonal appellate courts are generally followed, intentional deviation from such case law is not infrequent and at times even prompts the higher courts to revise their positions. Alternatively, the merging parties may appeal commission decisions to the Rekurskommission (Competition Appeals Commission, Article 44), whose rulings may in turn be appealed to the federal court.

Monitoring

One Swiss institution is unique among the three polities. *Preisüberwacher*— Price Supervisor—is a government watchdog agency in the Department of Public Economy whose mandate is to observe consumer prices, "to inhibit or eliminate abusive price increases or maintenance" and to orient the public about its activities (Preisüberwachungsgesetz [PüG] 942.20, 1985). The Rekurskommission has virtually always backed this watchdog agency's decisions.[26]

There is, however, no provision under Swiss law for the Swiss parliament or any other directly elected officials to monitor or check the commission's discretion—or its budget.

Independence

The Competition Commission is independent of the administrative authorities (Article 19.1) but is attached for administrative purposes to the ministry of the economy (Article 19.2). Although one could argue, from a majoritarian standpoint, that this attachment is good for accountability— the agency is accountable to an indirectly elected government—majority rule is not the only, or the best, way to guarantee democratic legitimacy. The nonmajoritarian model instead aims to limit and disperse power among different institutions. From the non-majoritarian standpoint it is doubtful that a conflation of regulatory functions in the executive is good for democracy (Majone 1996:285).

What is more, the Federal Council is not required to motivate its decision to overrule the commission, which makes the Swiss executive prone to capture by special interests. Worst of all, the Competition Appeals Commission is a *judicial* body that takes its decisions independently, but it too is part of the Federal Department of Economic Affairs—a red flag for the lack of independence of Swiss competition agencies.

There is no hard evidence that the commission's decisions were closely associated with the views of particular interest groups. But the commission's independence leaves much to be desired. For example, the Swiss food retail market is highly concentrated: MIGROS has a market share of approximately 40 percent and COOP one of approximately 30 percent. No other national retail market comes even close to this concentration. But the commission has never sought to prevent the dominance of these two firms. This comes as no surprise, as both COOP and MIGROS always have had their representative in the commission, not to speak of their superior resources for lobbyists to make their case (Neven and Ungern-Sternberg 1997).

FINDINGS: WHO IS WITHOUT GUILT . . .

Table 5.5 shows the ratings (weak = 1 point, medium = 2 points, strong = 3 points) for each polity in each dimension. This rating system is at best a rough approximation to reality. My ratings are subjective, and each indicator has equal weight. Both rating and weighting can surely be improved, but they give us at least a comparative impression of the democratic weaknesses and strengths—the democratic deficits and surpluses—in each polity's regulatory process.

U.S. merger control gets high marks in most, but not all, dimensions. Its *appointment, transparency, overrule, monitoring,* and *independence* indicators are all strong, because the heads of the antitrust agencies are each individually approved by Congress; the adversarial, court-based system pulls for disclosure; U.S. courts act as strong checkers of agency discretion through judicial review; congressional oversight committees monitor the agencies, whose budgets are subject to congressional approval; and the FTC (but not the Justice Department) is independent of the executive.

Table 5.5. Bureaucratic Democracy Ratings in Merger Regulation

Bureaucratic Democracy Indicators	Merger Policy—European Union	Merger Policy—United States	Merger Policy—Switzerland
Appointment	Medium = 2	Strong = 3	Weak = 1
Participation	Medium = 2	Weak = 1	Weak = 1
Transparency	Medium = 2	Strong = 3	Medium = 2
Reason-Giving	Medium = 2	Medium = 2	Medium = 2
Overrule	Medium = 2	Strong = 3	Weak = 1
Monitoring	Medium = 2	Strong = 3	Weak = 1
Independence	Weak =1	Strong = 3	Weak = 1
Cumulative Points = Average = Ranking	**13 points = 1.86 average = 2nd**	**18 points = 2.57 average = 1st**	**9 points = 1.29 average = 3rd**

But all is not well in the United States. In *reason-giving*, U.S. regulation gets only a medium rating, because criteria for agency decisions are likely influenced by the ideological bias of either Congress or the administration, although a Bureau of Economics assists in economic analysis. U.S. *participation* receives only a weak rating, since neither the Department of Justice nor the FTC are required to involve the public in their decision making. Nonetheless, on the whole, the United States is the most democratic of the three polities. The famous dictum "a Government of laws and not of men" seems deeply ensconced in U.S. merger policy.

Swiss merger policy, by contrast, is neither very accountable nor very independent. In *appointment, participation, overrule, monitoring,* and *independence*, it receives all weak ratings, because the executive appoints key Competition Commission officials, while the legislature plays no role in appointments; the commission need not seek public participation in its decisions; the legislature has no financial leverage over the agency; and the agency's independence is questionable—organized interests are overrepresented, and it reports to the economics ministry. Even the Appeals Commission is part of the executive!

Swiss *transparency* and *reason-giving* receive medium ratings: while its laws are now precisely defined, the Swiss government still largely adopts a reactive and laissez-faire policy of noninterference towards mergers. The agency is not obligated to publish its decisions, or even to give reasons; and the executive can override the agency without justification.

The "bureaucratic democracy" of European merger policy lies between U.S. and Swiss policy. The European Commission's *appointment, participation, transparency, reason-giving, overrule,* and *monitoring* are all medium, because Parliament can only vet the president and College of Commissioners wholesale, not individual commissioners; diffuse interest groups are not given as much voice as in the United States; the bureaucratic process is still opaque; the commission's criteria for decisions are overly juridical and unclear; only the European courts, whose agenda is close to the Commission's, can overturn Commission decisions; and the council of member states as well as Parliament can monitor, but not sanction the Commission.

Finally, the *independence* of European merger policy gets a weak rating, partly because of the Commission's weak financial independence, partly because the European executive has not delegated its merger control authority to an independent agency; executive and agency are one and the same in the EU.[27] But while the European Union is clearly less democratic than the United States in its merger regulation, it is clearly more democratic than Switzerland.

Let us now look at the second case—the hotly debated issue of biotech regulation. How democratic are European, U.S. and Swiss agencies in that policy area?

NOTES

1. Not surprisingly, since evidence suggests that in 1951, U.S. representatives insisted on the precise wording of the European Coal and Steel Community (ECSC) competition provisions (Berghahn 1986:118).

2. Dominance is likely where a company controls over 40 percent of a market, but according to the Commission 50 percent is usually adequate evidence of dominance (Commission 1994:114–21). But depending on the size of competitors and the firm's own structure and resources, market shares of 25–40 percent may already indicate dominance. For example, as guidance, the Commission used the U.S. Supreme Court's *Kodak* judgment in which Kodak was found to dominate a market with tying agreements (Cini and McGowan 1998:87, 93), much like Microsoft was found to tie its Internet browser to its software products.

3. Instead of with a notification, a competition case can also originate either with a complaint—by an individual or group with a "legitimate interest"—or with an *ex officio* (own initiative) action by the Commission.

4. Commission interview, 22 September 2000.

5. Commissioner Monti, Press release, 11 December 2001.

6. Commission interview, 5 January 2001.

7. The Commission does not prohibit "revolving door" appointments, where Commission officials may go on to the private sector. For example, the first head of the Merger Task Force left the Commission in 1993 to work for the Brussels office of a British law firm (Neven et al. 1993:228).

8. This authority is limited, though: member-state authorities may prohibit restrictive practices and abuses of dominant position (under Articles 81(1) and 82) only if the Commission has not already opened procedures on them. Also, one advantage of national courts is that they can award damages; but in practice plaintiffs are deterred from legal action by tremendous legal and information costs (Whish 1993:61).

9. Interestingly, had merger control stayed in member states' hands, the De-Havilland merger would have likely been approved (Neven et al. 1993:209), given national preferences for industrial policy at the time.

10. Other German contentions were that the Commission's merger policy enjoyed too much discretion and was too politicized.

11. Subsidiarity is codified by Article 9 (the "German clause") which permits a member state to investigate by itself a merger falling under the regulation if it fears a dominant position in a distinct market in that state.

12. But the Commission also enhanced its powers of search, inspection, and interrogation, and maintained its power to withdraw a case from national authority where there is "substantial disagreement within the network."

13. If undertakings intentionally or negligently fail to notify a concentration within the prescribed time period, the Commission may impose fines up to ECU50,000 or 10 percent of aggregate annual turnover (Fiebig 1998). In the 1990s, the Commission began imposing increasingly heavy fines on restrictive practices. The unprecedented fine of ECU75 million on TetraPak was appealed by the firm

because of a lacking precedent; but the Court of First Instance ruled that the Commission need not apportion the fine between alleged abuses, which made it difficult to say it was excessive (Korah 1997).

14. Incidentally, these reason-giving requirements were—and to some extent still are—not only different from, but also more advanced than national laws (Hartley 1988).

15. The commission defended its current analysis in a 1997 Green Paper: "economic policy can not be the only factor in the design of policy" since a full economic evaluation of each case would cost too much and lead to legal insecurity (Commission 1997b). In a 2001 Green Paper, it explored adopting the Substantial Lessening of Competition (SLC) test, an economic test used in other major jurisdictions such as the U.S., Canada, and Australia, but insisted that the SLC is substantively similar to its dominance test, and that most member states had already made their national rules consistent with its dominance criterion (Commission 2001).

16. Even the Commission's authority (under Regulation 17, Article 11) to request and then demand written information and carry out unannounced "dawn raids" is subject to judicial review, and the Commission must inform and consult national authorities beforehand (Cini and McGowan 1998:103).

17. Commission interview, 1 February 2002.

18. Even if the Commission is independent, the current bargaining process leads to firms making even more uncompetitive opening proposals: they know that by making concessions later, they can "buy" concessions from the Commission (Neven et al. 1993:225).

19. On the other hand, in competition policy, where concepts like competitiveness are much more fluid, contestable and discretionary, and where much information must be held confidential, such conflation of roles may be necessary: the only way for the commission to be sure of a fair analysis is to do it itself (Neven et al. 1993:182).

20. Unless exempted under the act, parties must notify the agencies pre-merger if persons of $10 million+ sales are being acquired by persons of $100 million+ sales—or vice versa if the acquiring person would hold 15 percent or $15 million of the acquired person (15 U.S.C. 18a(a) [1988]), but "The HSR rules are necessarily technical, contain other exemptions, and should be consulted, rather than relying on this summary" (DOJ and FTC Guidelines, April 1995).

21. In an interview, one Department of Justice official recalled only one attempt by politicians to pressure him directly into treating a case leniently. He had ignored the intervention without too much difficulty. But he added that politicians need not put pressure on Justice Department officials when they could do so directly via their political representative, the attorney general (Neven et al. 1993:227).

22. The Swiss merger law from 1936, in the process of revision, is not.

23. I refer to the Swiss Competition Commission as "commission" to distinguish it from the European Commission ("the Commission"). The Swiss will forgive me for this slight transgression, since all Swiss know that small is beautiful.

24. See http://www.wettbewerbskommission.ch/site/e/gesetze.html, 1999.

25. The Cartel Act defines "dominant position" as "one or more enterprises being able, as regards supply or demand, to behave in a substantially independent manner with regard to the other participants in the market." Article 10.4 also asks the commission explicitly to consider not only the market at the time of the merger, but to apply a "dynamic perspective" and watch market *trends* (Federal Council, 23 November 1994).

26. Price Supervisor Werner Marti, SonntagsZeitung, 7 November 1999.

27. A separate European Cartel Office, modeled after the German *Bundeskartellamt*, might introduce a much-needed separation of powers; but the European Cartel Office is not without opponents, who argue that competition policy is dependent on other Commission policies and must not be cut off from them.

6

Case 2—Regulating Biotech

This chapter compares biotechnology regulation, specifically the labeling of genetically modified (GM) foods, in our three polities. As in chapter 5, we review regulation in each polity, pit it against the seven bureaucratic democracy indicators, and then compare. Table 6.1 shows the relevant actors in each polity.

Genetically modified organisms (GMOs) are organisms whose genetic material (DNA) has been altered in a way that does not occur naturally by mating or natural recombination, but through a technology used to isolate genes from an organism, manipulate them in the laboratory and inject them into another organism.[1] Supporters argue that genetic engineering offers significant benefits to producers and consumers, from cost savings for farmers passed on to consumers, to increased yields benefiting poor nations, to environmental protection through reduced use of pesticides, herbicides, and other chemical sprays, to improved human health through new vitamins, nutrients, and pharmaceuticals (Pollack and Shaffer 2001:162).

There is so far no conclusive scientific evidence that the use of GMO technology is inherently unsafe, but skeptics point to studies that show possible dangers.[2] One former biotech engineer who became a vocal critic of GMOs asserted that they pose several health risks. First, mutations can damage genes naturally present in the DNA of an organism, alter the metabolism, produce toxins, and reduce the nutritional value of a food. Second, mutations can alter the expression of normal genes, leading to the production of allergens. Finally, mutations can interfere with other essential, but yet unknown, functions of an organism's DNA (Fagan 2000).

Table 6.1. Key Actors in Biotech (GMO) Regulation by Polity

Case	European Union	United States	Switzerland
Regulation of labeling foods that contain Genetically Modified Organisms (GMOs)	Biotech industry; Commission; DG Environment; DG Consumer Protection; ECJ; Council of Ministers; European Parliament; activists and consumer groups	Biotech industry; Food and Drug Administration (FDA); Department of Agriculture (USDA); Environmental Protection Agency (EPA); Congress; activists and consumer groups	Biotech industry; Federal Council; Parliament; Bundesamt für Gesundheit (BAG); activists and consumer groups

Whatever the scientific merits of these claims, the evidence that biotech foods and crops require stringent regulatory oversight is growing. In 1999, the British Medical Association called for an immediate moratorium on GM foods because of potential human health risks, including possible allergenic reactions and increased exposure to antibiotic resistance of genes that are spliced into every genetically engineered food (British Medical Association 1999). One study in the medical journal *Lancet* in October 1999 reported that a specific genetically engineered potato was causing rats to suffer substantial health effects, including weakened immune systems and changes in the development of their hearts, livers, kidneys, and brains (Ewen and Puztai 1999).[3]

In September 2000, a public outcry in the United States over the presence of genetically modified organisms (GMOs) in Taco Bell products led Kraft Foods to recall its genetically modified foods. The Taco Bell episode was only the last in a series of incidents. GMOs have become a salient and hotly contested issue for consumers and regulators worldwide. At an UN-sponsored meeting in Montreal in January 2000, 130 nations—including the European Union and Switzerland, but not the United States—adopted the Biosafety Protocol that requires exporters to label genetically engineered agricultural commodities.[4] In response to the rising "noise level" against GMO foods by activist groups and the media, brand-name companies around the world, including Gerber (Novartis), Heinz, Unilever, Nestlé, Seagram, the Japanese breweries Kirin and Sapporo, McDonald's, and Frito-Lay announced that their products would be GMO-free (University of Illinois 1999:72). Monsanto, Novartis, and Astra Zeneca announced that they would spin off their biotech agricultural divisions. Monsanto had already switched its stance on GMO labeling, advertising its support of labeling GM products in Europe (Williams 1998); its president went so far as to confess to a Greenpeace gathering that the company had "irritated and antagonized people" in failing to listen and engage in dialogue, and he pledged to change (Pollack and Shaffer 2001:169).

Meanwhile, the Biotechnology Industry Organization (BIO) continued promoting the beneficial effects of GMOs. "To date, more than 270 million people have benefited from drugs and vaccines created through biotechnology—that's more than a quarter of a billion. We fully expect that this is only the beginning of extending and improving our quality of life."[5] BIO argued that the increase in market presence of GMOs alone proved their value:

> about a quarter of the corn, and over half of our soybeans and cotton consist of varieties improved through biotechnology. The fact of this rapid market penetration speaks eloquently of the benefits provided to farmers in terms of reduced input costs, increased yields, and reduced chemical inputs.[6]

Why the case of labeling GM foods? The regulation of food safety is one of the most basic functions of governance in any polity, and potentially one of the most controversial (Pollack and Shaffer 2001:154). In 1999, the British survey institute Healey-Baker asked 6,700 Europeans in eight EU member states (plus in the EU candidates Czech Republic, Hungary, and Poland) whether they would eat GM foods. Sixty-one percent responded that they would prefer not to. Resistance was highest in Italy (79 percent) and lowest in the Netherlands (47 percent). More than 57 percent of respondents said they would like more organic foods on the shelves (Ammann 2000:18). GMO critics asserted that public aversion was even greater. The Campaign to Ban Genetically Engineered Foods cited surveys according to which 97 percent of European consumers wanted clear labeling of all genetically engineered foods and 80 percent did not want genetically engineered foods at all.

In the United States, it was estimated that by late 1999, some 60 percent of processed foods in U.S. food stores were derived from GM foods, which would make GMOs possibly "the most rapid adoption of new technology in the history of agriculture" (Hill and Battle 2000:5); but only about 33 percent of Americans knew that GM foods were already available in supermarkets, while 60 percent claimed that they would not buy foods labeled to contain GM ingredients (Pollack and Shaffer 2001:168).[7] And in Switzerland, a poll conducted by the weekly *Weltwoche* in 1999 showed that 71 percent of the Swiss population (and 82 percent of women) did not want to buy GM foods. Sixty-five percent of respondents said they would pay 10 percent more for traditional foods.[8] It is crucial to examine whether or not governmental regulation of this technology represents popular preferences, or whether it suffers from a democratic deficit. In all three polities, GMO foods are regulated by the executive or executive agencies. We review the EU, United States, and Switzerland in turn.

EUROPEAN UNION

The three key EU actors in our story are the European Commission, the Council of Ministers, and the European Parliament (as we will see later, the court has yet to rule on labeling GMO foods). The Commission has long walked the tightrope of protecting diffuse consumer interests without losing industry support. Already in the early 1970s, it organized and provided funds for a Consumers' Consultative Council of both national and European consumer organizations to consult on draft policies relevant to consumer concerns (Pollack 1997:580). In the next decade, the Single European Act recognized the danger of a regulatory race to the bottom: Article 100A(3) provides that Commission proposals "will take as a base a high level of protection." But the article covered only Commission proposals, not final legislation decisions, which rest with the council; hence the provision is not legally binding on member states (Eichener 1997:593). Another decade later, the 1997 Amsterdam Treaty included an amendment to that consumer protection provision. Now the Community pledged to "contribute to protecting the health, safety and economic interests of consumers, as well as to [promote] their right to information, education and to organize themselves in order to safeguard their interests" (EC Treaty, Art. 153 [ex art. 129a]).

On the other hand, the Commission has often been accused of being captured by industry interests. In April 1996 it formally approved the EU-wide import, storage, and processing of Monsanto's GM soybeans, Roundup Ready. Soybeans are used in 60 percent of all processed foods, such as bread, pasta, candies, ice cream, pies, biscuits, margarine, meat products, and vegetarian meat substitutes. Importers were not required to label GMO products as they entered Europe. The Commission also approved for sale a gene-altered maize strain developed by the Swiss pharmaceutical Ciba-Geigy (now Novartis) without requiring the specific labeling of these products. As of the fall of 1996, those products were available unlabeled in shops across Europe. Critics asserted that the Commission made these decisions without properly informing the public, and by ignoring public wishes.

Responding to those public wishes is the business of the legislature. The Council of Ministers, the upper chamber of the European legislature, has the last word on much European legislation, particularly GMO applications (see table 6.2).

Table 6.2. The European GMO Foods Labeling Procedure

1. The manufacturer or importer must submit a notification of a GMO product, with full risk assessment, to the member state competent authority (MSCA) where the product is first to be placed on the market.
2. The MSCA either accepts or rejects the application. If the MSCA rejects the application, it ceases.
3. If the MSCA accepts the application, it goes to the European Commission and all other competent MSCAs, which have the right to object.
4. Unless other MSCAs object, the original MSCA grants consent to place the product on the entire EU market.
5. If other MSCAs object, the Commission seeks the opinion of the Scientific Committee.
6. The Commission submits a draft decision to the Regulatory Committee of member states representatives (if the case is highly technical), or to the Council of Ministers (if the case is not highly technical), which vote under QMV.
7. Blocking an application in the Council requires unanimity.
8. If the Council does not decide within 3 months, the Commission decides.
9. Unless the Council rejects the GMO application unanimously, the Commission must authorize the GMO as long as it fulfills current EU legislation. Member states must comply.

Source: Regulation (EC) on Novel Foods and Novel Foods Ingredients 258/97, 27 January 1997

Article 5.3. of the 1979 council regulation states: "The name under which the product is sold shall include or be accompanied by particulars as to the physical condition of the foodstuff or the specific treatment which it has undergone (e.g., powdered, freeze-dried, deep-frozen, concentrated, smoked) in all cases where omission of such information could create confusion in the mind of the purchaser" (Council Regulation 79/112 EEC, 18 December 1978). In 1990, Council Directive 90/220/EEC stipulated that member states were to "take all necessary measures to ensure that products containing, or consisting of, GMOs will be placed on the market only if their labelling and packaging is that specified" between member state and producer (Art. 14, 23 April 1990). But environmental and consumer organizations criticized the directive for inadequate labeling rules. For example, the directive's Article 9 gives member states a choice rather than requiring them to involve diffuse interests in its decisions.

In May 1998, the council issued a regulation on compulsory labeling of genetically modified foods. It applied its earlier provision to biotechnology and recognized that "it is now urgent to lay down detailed uniform Community rules for the labeling" of GMO foods to ensure the proper functioning of the common market. Article 2.3 stipulated in great detail, down to the size and placement of the lettering, that where the food consists of more than one ingredient, the words "produced from genetically modified soya" or "produced from genetically modified maize," as appropriate, shall appear in the list of ingredients in parentheses immediately after the name of the ingredient (Council Regulation 1139/98, 26 May 1998).

In addition, a "de facto" moratorium on GMO products in member states was in effect since October 1998. In June 1999, environmental ministers in the council made it official: they moved to implement the legal equivalent of a three-year moratorium on any new approvals of GMO foods or crops.[9] Five member states—Austria, France, Germany, Greece, and Luxembourg—banned previously approved products under Article 16 of Directive 90/220, which permits member states to temporarily restrict the use or sale of specific GMO products on certain conditions.[10] The council decided this based upon its own regulation of a generation earlier, on approximating member states' laws on labeling and presentation of foods, and deemed Article 5.3 above applicable to GMO labeling.

What powers does the European Parliament, as the lower chamber of the EU legislature and the only supranational actor directly elected by and accountable to the European electorate, have in regulating GMOs? While the Parliament does not have approval power in individual GMO cases, it does share with the council the power to shape legislation that affects the GMO approval process. Both changes under the Maastricht Treaty—qualified majority voting (QMV) and codecision—permitted consumer protection directives under a new Article 129A (Pollack 1997:579). The Parliament also acted as a watchdog by issuing a plethora of nonbinding resolutions over the years, presumably in response to public pressure in the member states, and often to rein in unregulated GMOs. For example, in March 1996 the Parliament criticized the Commission for "glossing over" important elements, and asked it to urgently ensure the comprehensive labeling of GMO products, collect further information, launch a proper public debate, enforce existing GMO legislation, and create a stable legal climate on GMOs. But the Parliament itself voted against complete labeling of GM foods, and supported the view of the Commission and the council that food labels should display only major changes caused by GMOs in a product.

In April 1997, the Parliament voted with near unanimity (407 to 2 votes, with 19 abstaining) to suspend the admission of Bt-maize, but its resolution was nonbinding. In another nonbinding resolution in June that year, it called on the Commission to come up with clear labeling rules. Parliament members criticized the Commission's new rules, adopted the month before, for leaving too much room to interpretation by member states. The Parliament complained that "the current rules of the WTO oblige importing countries to prove that a product is harmful, rather than requiring the exporter to demonstrate that it is safe, thereby emphasising that commercial considerations take presidence [sic] in decision making." The Parliament charged the Commission with "lack of responsibility" for unilaterally deciding "to authorise the marketing of GMO maize in spite of all the negative positions of most Member States and the European Parliament." Worse, the Parliament charged that the Commission had acted "before the coming into effect of the European Parliament and Council Regulation on novel foods and novel food ingredients."[11]

In February 1999 the Parliament passed a resolution that, among some one hundred amendments to a proposal by the Commission, put the liability for human or environmental damage caused by the release of GMOs clearly on producers. And in December of that year, the Parliament banned genetically engineered foods from its own restaurants. Though largely symbolic, that new policy sent a clear message to the Commission. And the Parliament did not leave it at symbolism. That same month, it adopted a resolution calling on the Commission to come up with a new strategy and new proposals to deal with GM food labeling. It demanded that the Commission incorporate a time-limited review clause in a revision of Directive 90/220/EEC, so that the Commission's proposed 1 percent threshold of GMO content—below which producers need not report GMOs on product labels (Commission Regulation 49/2000, 10 January 2000)—could be reviewed in twelve months in light of new scientific evidence. The Parliament also asked that new legislation be accompanied by a list of products free of substances generated through DNA or genetic techniques, and that the Commission come up with proposals for GMO labeling in animal feed and clarification of the regulation relating to prepacked products.

To be sure, the Parliament has not been consistently anti-industry. Though it revised its earlier labeling directive in April 2000 to make the release of GMOs into the environment more difficult for producers, it failed to agree on liability rules and suggested that they be included in a special directive on environmental liability, which could take more than five years. Greenpeace responded promptly. "It is a scandal that the parliament failed to put the financial responsibility where it belongs, to the biotech industry," said the environment watchdog. "If these crops were as safe as companies claim them to be, they should have no problems in accepting full liability for them."[12]

In early 2000, like the Swiss executive below, and facing a potential collapse of consumer confidence in EU food safety, the Commission went through with its proposed 1 percent threshold value. On the same day, the Commission also required the labeling of GM additives and flavorings (Commission Regulation 50/2000, 10 January 2000). In a fifty-eight-page consultative White Paper, the Commission gave a critical analysis of the weaknesses of the existing system and proposed a radical overhaul, including the creation of a European Food Authority. While such an agency, in contrast to the U.S. Food and Drug Administration, would be a purely advisory body without regulatory powers, the Commission did uphold its precautionary principle, justifying EU regulation even in the absence of clear scientific evidence (Commission 2000b:9; Pollack and Shaffer 2001:159).

In July 2000, when growing resistance to GMOs in the member states threatened to erode its own legitimacy, the Commission proposed to the member states "a strategy to regain public trust in the approval procedure for Genetically Modified Organisms (GMOs)." The EU executive recommended the application of the revised directive on the release of GMOs in the environment to all new GMO approvals. Under the proposal, notifying companies would need to make, in their applications, voluntary commitments consistent with the new requirements. These commitments would become legally binding once authorization was granted. Environment Commissioner Margot Wallström conceded that "the EU needs to re-establish public confidence in our approval systems. Citizens must be allowed to choose for themselves whether they want products containing GMOs or not." Meanwhile, eighteen GMO products had been approved while fourteen other approvals were pending.[13]

In a background paper, the Commission presented the council with four options: (A) to maintain the status quo (since the 1996 Novel Foods Regulation, the seeds legislation, and the revised Directive 90/220 already provided for mandatory labeling of products containing above 1 percent live GMOs); (B) responding to the 1999 Parliament resolution, to maintain the status quo but introduce a "GMO-free" line (to provide consumers with a clear choice of products not derived from GMO technology); (C) to label all foods derived from GMOs (irrespective of whether final products contained traces of modified DNA or protein); and (D) to label all foods and ingredients produced with GMOs.[14]

In December 2000, the environment ministers in the council declared a preference for combining options (C) and (D) with a GMO-free line. Since the Parliament adopted twenty-nine amendments at its second reading, the final shape of the directive was decided in a conciliation committee of Parliament and council delegates, who agreed in February 2001 on tougher rules for mandatory labeling, monitoring, consultation of the EU public, and application of the precautionary principle (2001/18/EC). The new rules, to enter into force in October 2002, were greeted favorably by consumer organizations.

However, probably in an effort not to lose industry support, the Commission had announced in October 2001 that its fifteen-year biosafety research "has not shown any new risks to human health or the environment, beyond the usual uncertainties of conventional plant breeding."

The European executive also announced a roundtable on GMO safety research, including biosafety researchers, consumer organizations, national administrations, and industry.[15]

How democratic is the EU procedure? We match it with the seven bureaucratic democracy dimensions.

Appointment

As we have seen, the key actors in the European GMO procedure are the member-state competent authorities (MSCAs), the Commission, and the Council of Ministers or regulatory committee. Much of the authorization procedure is in the hands of ministers of member state governments in the council. Democratically elected governments appoint the MSCAs, council, and regulatory committee. By contrast, the Commission is vetted by the Parliament and approved wholesale (once its president is approved). Ideally the Parliament would vet the health or environment commissioners individually and have the powers to dismiss them individually. But it does have the power to dismiss the whole Commission.

Participation

The protection of diffuse interests from special, highly organized interests—the age-old problem of collective action—is a challenge in any system of governance; the EU is no exception. But Pollack argues that the EU is not a "businessman's Europe" privileging concentrated and mobile capital over other interests and precipitating a deregulatory race to the bottom. Rather, European institutions present opportunities as well as risks for diffuse interests—environmentalists, consumers, women—by offering multiple points of access which those diffuse interests can, and do, use effectively to ensure policy adoption and implementation. Pollack suggests four such access points for public policy advocates. First, they can take the "national route" and lobby their member-state governments for regulations and for representing these in the council. Second, they can take the "Brussels route" by lobbying the Commission to initiate a policy. The Commission's Environment Directorate, for example, has close ties to environmental activists such as Friends of the Earth Europe and Greenpeace (Mazey and Richardson 1993), and consumer groups have created a strong presence with the Directorate Health and Consumer Protection (Maier 1993; Young 1995). Third, activists can appeal to the Parliament, which has empathized with the demands of diffuse interests, especially in its Committee on the Environment, Consumer Protection, and Public Health. The Parliament regularly restores crucial funds for consumer groups that have been cut by the council. Fourth, they can appeal to the national courts and to the European Court of Justice (Pollack 1997). Together, these four access points constitute an "opportunity structure" (Mazey and Richardson 1993) that allows advocates to place issues on the Community agenda, have them adopted by the council and Parliament, and backed by the court.

Also, Eichener asserts that the Commission and the Parliament strategically support the evolution of European interest groups, including consumer, environmental, and worker interests. The Commission includes these nongovernmental groups in advisory committees, grants them privileged access, and gives them considerable financial support, for example to the European Bureau of Consumers' Unions (BEUC). The Commission's motives for doing so are not entirely altruistic, to be sure: in return it receives expertise, legitimacy for its proposals, and partnership of interest groups in promoting its preferred policies in member states (Eichener 1997:605).

Transparency

In May 1998, the European Commission published its Green Paper on "Efficiency and Accountability in European Standardization under the New Approach." The Green Paper concluded tersely: "the management of the standardisation process and transparency can be improved" (Commission 1998). Compared to the U.S. or the Swiss system, the EU food safety system has so far been a less centralized and more incomplete regulatory patchwork (Pollack and Shaffer 2001:158), which may raise information costs for principals, be they consumers or elected Parliament members. Also, policy networks, which Héritier views as a plus for legitimacy (Héritier 1999:24), do not help either in Shapiro's view, since they are not transparent or responsible to the public will. Shapiro would in fact fight these networks and redouble the conventional attempts to bring experts under the control of politicians, since "technocracy is, these days, not perceived by the public as legitimate" (Shapiro 1997:287).

Reason-Giving

To compensate for the EU's lack of transparency, the Commission takes pains to publish comprehensive explanations of its decisions, both in print and on the Internet. But the council does not publish a record of its own proceedings.

Overrule

Where does the European Court of Justice stand? The only indicative case of judicial review in GMO regulation so far was a court ruling in March 2000 that France had no right to block the sale of three GM crop strains once they had been approved by the Commission (Case C-6/99). The case dated back to 1998 when the French government, faced with growing public opposition to new GM crop varieties, had refused to ratify an EU decision clearing for sale new types of maize developed by the Swiss manufacturer Novartis. The court ruled that France could not unilaterally withdraw its own prior approval for Novartis maize, developed to resist corn borers. The Court's decision confirmed that once a member state approves a GMO, not that member state, but only EU institutions have the authority to approve or disapprove that GMO. Once the Commission has approved a GMO food, member states must comply with that decision. But the court also ruled that if new information indicates risks for human health and the environment, placing a GMO on the market can "be stopped pending a fresh Commission decision." This left the door open for France to ask the Commission to retake its decision based on new information. The Court even permitted that any member state with justifiable reasons to consider a GMO hazardous could restrict or prohibit use of the product on its territory, as long as it informed the Commission of that step.

Of course, one Court ruling is not enough to ascertain whether judicial review of the EU's GMO decisions is effective.

Monitoring

While the Parliament is effectively bypassed, the council has the last word on biotech regulation. Not only that: the council and the Commission are also subjected to much public scrutiny, be it from member states, from Parliament, or from watchdog groups and the media.

Independence

The Commission has not clearly delegated the approval process to an independent agency and suffers from a conflation of executive and bureaucratic functions. Just as in merger regulation, the Commission and the regulating agency are one and the same.

UNITED STATES

Already in May 1992, the U.S. Food and Drug Administration (FDA), which reports to the Department of Health and Human Services, issued a policy statement—not a formal regulation—on plants developed with GM organisms. The agency stated that "Under this policy, foods . . . derived from plant varieties developed using the new genetic modification

Table 6.3. The United States GMO Foods Labeling Procedure

1. The "decision tree" approach is based on voluntary self-testing by GMO manufacturers, which ask themselves in a questionnaire whether analytical or toxicological tests are required.
2. The companies themselves answer these questions and decide whether to consult with the FDA about the product. Companies need to certify to the FDA that they will comply with the guidelines.
3. Companies that choose to call the FDA's premarketing attention to their product supply testing summaries, not the full data.

Source: Federal Register, Vol. 57, Nr. 104, 29 May 1992

are regulated within the existing framework of the [Federal Food, Drug, and Cosmetic] act" (Federal Register, Vol. 57, Nr. 104, 29 May 1992). Table 6.3 summarizes the FDA procedure.

Touted by then-vice president Dan Quayle as a deregulatory initiative, this policy meant that the FDA need not scrutinize the provenance, but only the characteristics, of genetically engineered food. Since GMO foods were "substantially similar" to conventional crops, they were not required to be labeled or undergo special safety testing before entering the marketplace. While food additives are subjected to a rigorous round of testing and must meet the standard of "a reasonable certainty of no harm," the FDA determined that the GM foods currently on the market are not additives. Ever since 1992, the FDA designated all GM foods as "Generally Regarded As Safe" (GRAS), making the new foods exempt from mandatory premarket review.[16]

But just in case, the industry mobilized for a massive public relations effort to stem the type of negative public opinion on GMOs prevailing in Europe. In October 1999, BIO and the Grocery Manufacturers of America (GMA), a consortium of food, beverage, and consumer product companies that boasts combined "sales of more than $450 billion," joined forces to maintain that biotechnology was safe. "Scientific and regulatory authorities worldwide including the United States, Japan, United Kingdom, Canada and Europe have demonstrated confidence in the scientific principle of substantial equivalence as the basis to assess the safety of foods developed through biotechnology."[17] In September 2000, unfazed by the fact that the United States is far behind both the EU and Switzerland in regulating the labeling of GMO products, BIO insisted in a letter to the FDA: "Regulations in place have adequately addressed the scientific developments of the first generation of biotech products."[18]

In June 2000, the Society for In Vitro Biology, an organization of some 1,200 scientists, followed suit and endorsed the commercialization of GM crops at its annual meeting in San Diego. The society said: "The vast majority of crops used worldwide are the product of genetic modification and selection, both intentional and unintentional, which has taken place over the centuries." A resolution passed by the membership stated that "Scientific facts are often lost amidst the ensuing rhetoric and emotional debates."[19]

The month before, the FDA had taken its 1992 deregulation policy even farther. Asserting that "we believe our initiatives will provide the public with continued confidence in the safety of these foods," the agency announced that it would not require mandatory labeling, and instead proposed guidelines for voluntary labeling.[20]

As a result of the FDA's laissez-faire policy, regulators had approved some fifty GM plants for commercial production in the United States, and another 6,700 varieties had been authorized for field-testing as of October 2000. Even pro-biotech groups saw FDA oversight as so lax that they asked the agency at its Oakland public hearings in late 1999 to make the consultative process with the FDA mandatory for biotech companies. The industry groups, including the GMA and the National Food Processors Association, also urged that summary data be made available to the public.[21]

How does U.S. biotech regulation perform against our seven criteria?

Appointment

The hands-off U.S. regulatory regime is not by accident: the competencies of the agencies charged with regulating biotechnology are unclear. All three bureaus in charge of GM products—the FDA, regulating food safety; the Environmental Protection Agency (EPA), regulating the environment and pesticides; and the Department of Agriculture (USDA) regulating farms, poultry, and meat—utilize statutes designed for regulating products before the advent of GMOs. EPA officials said they would not permit any GM varieties not proven to be safe for human use.[22] But it is not clear whether EPA authority extends to include GMO labeling.

The USDA's most important regulatory role comes through its Animal and Plant Health Inspection Service evaluating the potential environmental impacts of field tests of GM crops. According to government estimates, the USDA had received notices of over 22,000 outdoor tests, authorized under 5,100 permits and streamlined arrangements called notifications, in which companies essentially tell the government what they are planting, but are not required to report the results.

So far, neither the EPA nor the USDA regulates genetic drift (GMO seeds carried by wind to GMO-free crops), and there are no existing regulations to deal with its associated problems. But the threat of unknown GM material flying through the air to another farmer's land is plausible, and organic farmers appear to be particularly vulnerable. One organic farmer in Texas supplied the Wisconsin chipmaker Terra Prima with organic corn; but on arrival in Europe in March 1999, the corn was returned after testing positive for GM material. The material had drifted from a neighboring farm and cost the company nearly $300,000. Another organic farmer told the FDA: "I literally can be put out of business in one breeze."[23]

What powers does the FDA have? The agency's authority has evolved in response to crises and reorganizations (Quirk 1980; Bryner 1987; Wood and Waterman 1994). Harvey W. Wiley, chief chemist of the Department of Agriculture's Bureau of Chemistry, joined the bureau in 1883 and soon experimented on live human subjects by feeding them small doses of poisons commonly found in foods and drugs. The resulting public awareness of health hazards led to the Food and Drug Act of 1906. In 1931 the bureau got its current name, and in 1938, in response to 107 deaths from a seemingly harmless cure-all elixir of sulfanilamide the year before, Congress passed the Food, Drug and Cosmetic Act, which expanded the FDA's powers by requiring manufacturers to prove the safety of a new drug before marketing it. In 1953 the agency was incorporated into what is now the Department of Health and Human Services (HSS). The FDA's regulatory authority was substantially broadened again in 1958 with the Delaney amendment to the Food, Drug and Cosmetic Act, requiring manufacturers to prove the safety of food additives; and in 1962 with the Kefauver amendments to the Food and Drug Act, requiring that producers prove the effectiveness as well as safety of products before they could be marketed.

The FDA broadly engages in two activities: analysis and enforcement. Some 1,000 inspectors examine more than 900,000 plants in the United States (Greer 1983) and have a full arsenal of administrative weapons against violations, from making informal visits or phone calls to writing formal letters, seeking injunctions, recommending voluntary recall, seizing hazardous products, filing lawsuits against negligent producers, or publicizing transgressions (Wood and Waterman 1994:54).

The secretary of Health and Human Service (HSS), a cabinet member, selects the FDA commissioner and delegates authority to him or her, but all the commissioner's decisions are subject to review and revision by the secretary. The president, not Congress, exercises clearance over the leadership of the FDA (Wood and Waterman 1994:52).

Participation

The FDA Modernization Act of 1997 (PL 105-115) mandated that "As determined to be appropriate by the Secretary," the agency carry out its mission "in consultation with experts in science, medicine, and public health, and in cooperation with consumers, users, manufacturers, importers, packers, distributors and retailers of regulated products." But the FDA has adopted a rather narrow interpretation of this clause. The consultation process is neither mandatory nor uniform. As table 6.3 showed, the agency's voluntary "decision-tree" approach allows each company to submit different types of tests, and only summaries of the data, not the entire studies. The tests are neither peer reviewed nor available for public scrutiny. The company seeking guidance from the agency is largely doing the testing itself.

The USDA has yet to deny a single notification from a biotech company. In April 1998 the agency, overwhelmed by 200,000 outraged responses to its Proposed Rule on Organic Standards, decided that the "organic" label should not include GM substances, irradiated foods, and crops grown using sewage sludge.[24] Activists claimed that if these rules had become federal law, the United States would have gained the dubious distinction of having the lowest organic standards in the world.[25]

What about participation by the public? While the debate over genetic engineering had been relatively tame in the United States, the public response to three public FDA hearings in late 1999 was overwhelming. One meeting in Chicago had to be moved to a much larger room, and many who had signed up to speak had to view the meeting in overflow rooms.[26] Regulators recognized enough concern to convene a special panel of the National Academy of Sciences to examine GMO issues. But in early 2000, that body also concurred with the biotech industry, saying it was "not aware of any evidence that foods on the market are unsafe to eat as a result of genetic modification."[27]

Transparency

The Administrative Procedure Act (APA) of 1946 was an attempt to subject the bureaucracy to clear rules. But FDA rules are not sufficiently transparent. The agency defended its antiprecautionary policy before a Senate Committee in October 1999: "FDA's 1992 policy statement and our guidance documents make clear that premarket clearance is required if there is scientific uncertainty about the safety of food derived from bioengineered plants." Yet, as we have seen, it is the biotech companies themselves that decide whether there is any such "scientific uncertainty,"[28] and the voluntary labeling policy places the costs of certifying, testing, and labeling foods on non-GMO producers—a burden they are likely to reject.[29]

Reason-Giving

Congress has delegated to administrative agencies its own legislative powers, but has often not defined clearly the content of what exactly these agencies should regulate. For example, the 1934 Federal Communications Act authorizes the Federal Communications Commission (FCC) to issue "such rules and regulations and prescribe such restrictions and conditions, not inconsistent with law" as "public convenience, interest, or necessity requires." But nowhere in the statute can be found a definition of public convenience, interest, or necessity that would guide the agency substantively or limit the scope of its rules. Hence its decisions sometimes have the appearance of being based on whim (McConnell 1966:285; Rosenbloom 1983:22). The FDA's mission is similarly unclear and does not require the agency to give reasons for its decisions.

Overrule

The U.S. government relies on the separation of powers to prevent the concentration of official authority in the hands of one group or a single political institution. Some (for example, executive-branch) agencies are subject to the president's tight control; some are closer to Congress; and some (for example, independent regulatory commissions) are virtually independent (Rosenbloom 1983:21, 26). But in GMO policy, neither the executive nor the judiciary ever overruled the FDA.

The U.S. State Department backed the FDA's hands-off approach in August 1999. Arguing from a strategic trade perspective, the undersecretary-designate of state for economic and business affairs reiterated Washington's stance against Japanese plans to require mandatory labeling of U.S. food products containing GMOs, asserting that such products do not pose any harm to humans. The official said the United States prefers voluntary labeling.[30]

In September 2000, the FDA scored a second victory when a federal court upheld the agency's 1992 policy on GM food and dismissed a lawsuit filed by biotech opponents seeking to require the FDA to enforce the labeling and testing for safety of GM foods. The lawsuit, filed by the Alliance for Bio-Integrity, Center for Food Safety, and some scientists and clergy members, had charged that the lack of labeling and mandatory safety testing violated food safety laws, and that the FDA had not allowed for proper public comment or filed an environmental impact statement on the new policy. But the federal judge ruled that the agency "was not arbitrary or capricious in its finding that genetically modified foods need not be labeled because they do not differ 'materially' from nonmodified foods." The judge added that the government did not have to follow procedures for public notice and comment or file an environmental impact statement, because the 1992 FDA announcement was a policy statement, not a formal regulation.[31] The court's ruling was cheered by the biotech industry organ, which called the summary dismissal "a huge victory for FDA and consumers."[32] But BIO failed to mention an important concession won by the plaintiffs: as part of the suit, the FDA was required to turn over to the plaintiffs 44,000 internal files, including memos of internal scientists critical of the agency's policy. Based on some of these internal files, it appears that there was little consensus within the ranks of the FDA on its own policy. For example, in one memorandum, a FDA microbiologist commented that a draft of the FDA policy "read very pro-industry, especially in the area of unintended effects." It is "industry's pet idea that there are no unintended effects that will raise the FDA's level of concern." But, the official wrote, "there is no data to back up their contention."[33]

Monitoring

Neither the executive nor the judiciary have meaningfully checked the FDA. What about the legislature? Congress, which is charged to oversee the U.S. regulatory agencies, has yet to pass a regulatory statute on GMO crops and foods, although individual members of Congress have shown some action. A letter circulated by Representative Bonior (D-MI) was signed by a bipartisan group of forty-six House members in November 1999. A bill, the Genetically Modified Foods Right to Know Act (HR 3377), sponsored by Representative Kucinich (D-OH) and nineteen other members, four of whom were Republicans, was launched in January 2000. As proposed by the bill, labels would read: "United States government notice: This product contains genetically engineered material, or was produced with a genetically engineered material."

Another bill, the Genetically Engineered Food Safety Act (S 2315) was introduced in the Senate by Democrats Moynihan, Reid, and Boxer in March 2000. The bill would require the secretary of Health and Human Services to establish, within a year, criteria for carrying out section 409 of the Federal Food, Drug, and Cosmetic Act (21 U.S.C. 349), which regulates additives. In effect, the bill, if passed, would mandate that the FDA treat GMOs also as additives, instead of as inherent food characteristics, which its 1992 policy does.

The biotech industry reacted promptly to the Moynihan draft legislation: "The principal impact of this proposed legislation would be to impose increased regulatory uncertainty and delay before important products, such as vitamin and nutrient enhanced rice, could reach the hundreds of millions of people in the developing world who so desperately need them," BIO wrote in a press release. "Food and Drug Administration regulations in place since 1992 provide rigorous protection for American consumers based on extensive evaluations of foods improved through biotechnology. This proposed legislation would not increase protection for consumers, but would promote bureaucracy, administrative delay, and confusion."[34]

But BIO needn't have worried. Although in October 2000 Senator Durbin (D-IL) introduced the Genetically Engineered Foods Act (S 3184), another GMO bill that would charge the secretary of Food and Agriculture to subject GMO food producers to a premarket consultation and approval process, Congress did not act on any of these bills. Far from putting pressure on agencies to regulate GMOs, Congress instead formed a Congressional Biotechnology Caucus in July 2000. This proindustry caucus was greeted enthusiastically by biotech firms, which pronounced themselves "delighted that members of Congress have joined together to educate their colleagues on the benefits and importance of biotechnology."[35]

Shapiro argues that the US Congress issues legally binding directives to federal agencies and enforces these directives through detailed agency oversight by its own highly specialized, intrusive, and numerous committees and subcommittees, each of which has jurisdiction over particular executive agencies; and through annual, intensive budgetary review of each executive entity by highly specialized subcommittees of the House and Senate appropriations committees (Shapiro 1997). But in GMO food regulation, ex post monitoring of the FDA by Congress is virtually nonexistent.

Independence

The degree of the FDA's independence is disputed. Some consider it an independent agency (Pollack and Shaffer 2001:156), while others see it as a semi-independent executive-branch agency (Wood and Waterman 1994:52). I concur with the latter view for two reasons. First, the agency is subject to clearance by the president. Second, in 1981 the Reagan administration put the FDA's drug approval process on its hit list of the top twenty government-wide regulatory problems, and the agency began a review of existing rules under a new commissioner ideologically aligned with Reagan's deregulation philosophy. That year, the FDA approved more new drugs than it had in any single year since the 1962 Kefauver amendments. Inspections declined by 60 percent, product seizures by 44 percent, and legal actions by 50 percent after the appointment of the new commissioner (Wood and Waterman 1994:55).

What is more, FDA policy has been virtually consistent with the views of the biotech industry.[36] The agency maintained that genetic engineering is more precise than traditional breeding because just the desired gene (or genes) can be transferred without extra unwanted genetic material and that this increased precision "increase[s] the potential for safe, better characterized, and more predictable foods" (57 FR 22986, 29 May 1992). BIO had campaigned aggressively for this view, through dozens of press releases, meetings, Biotech Legislator of the Year awards to members of Congress, and other public relations activities. In none of its many press releases did BIO ever come out openly against FDA decisions.

SWITZERLAND

Switzerland is more advanced in regulating GMO labeling than either the EU or the United States (see table 6.4). In fact, it may well be the only country in the world that explicitly mentions gene technology in its constitution (Die neue Bundesverfassung, 1998, Art. 119-120) due to a 1992 referendum. The Federal Council, the Swiss seven-member executive, translated this constitutional provision into law by adapting existing regulations. The federal law on foodstuffs of 1992 grants to the Federal Council the competence for regulating the use of gene technology in food production (table 6.4).

In 1993, the Federal Council proposed an amendment to the law on environmental protection and the law on epidemics to cover environmental and human health safety issues from the use of environmentally hazardous organisms. This legislation is compatible with both EU directives 90/219/EEC on the contained use of GM microorganisms and

Table 6.4. The Swiss GMO Foods Labeling Procedure

1. The applicant and the Federal Office for Public Health (Bundesamt für Gesundheit, BAG) enter into a preliminary dialogue.
2. The BAG checks whether GMOs are present. If no: no permission is necessary.
3. If yes: BAG internal experts examine the dossier. The BAG consults preliminarily with the Federal Office for Agriculture (Bundesamt für Landwirtschaft, BLW), Agency for Forests, Environment, and Landscape (Bundesamt für Umwelt, Wald und Landschaft, BUWAL), and Federal Veterinary Office (Bundesamt für Veterinärwesen, BVET) on specific information.
4. If necessary, the agency charges external experts and/or an expert commission, at the applicant's expense. The applicant submits additional materials at the agency's request. BAG experts test the toxicity of the GMO food on "mice, rats, cows, fish, chickens, and birds" for dangers to humans.
5. The BAG issues a report to BLW, BVET, BUWAL, as well as to the federal expert commission for biological security (Eidgenössische Fachkommission für biologische Sicherheit, EFBS). These agencies render their opinions.
6. The BAG decides and regulates (through ordinances, declaration, analysis, information).
7. The cantons execute the decision and/or regulation.

Source: Lebensmittelverordnung LMV, Article 15, 1 March 1995; ordinance on the permission procedure for GMO foods, GMO additives and GMO auxiliary processing materials, VBGVO, 19 November 1996

90/220/EEC on the deliberate release into the environment of GM organisms above. The Swiss executive's "ordinance on the authorization procedure for GMO foodstuffs, GMO additives, and GMO auxiliary processing materials" (VBGVO) regulates the extent of scientific materials that GMO product applicants must submit to the BAG for examination and the formal conditions for its permission.

A popular initiative the year before, in 1992, had sought to prohibit the release of GMOs into the environment. Although the Swiss electorate had rejected the initiative, it attests to the early and high level of awareness in Switzerland about GMOs, possibly as a result of a high concentration of leading pharmaceutical and biotech companies (Novartis, Roche, Lonza), as well as the presence of the world's largest food producer (Nestlé) in Switzerland. Also, increasing portions of the Swiss population had become sensitized, even suspicious, of Swiss industry and the existing regulatory landscape after a chemical spill by Sandoz (which later merged with Ciba-Geigy into Novartis) had killed life in the Rhine River at least for several years in the 1980s.

Swiss biotech critics used rather graphic arguments to mobilize and sustain this popular discontent. One activist wrote:

> Consumers face the question whether they really need tomatoes that don't get mushy for weeks in transport, on the shelf or in the kitchen, or potatoes that don't turn brown after peeling, or baguettes that are double or triple their length with the same amount of dough, thanks to built-in biotech-enzymes. (Amman 1999:7)

But no image could rouse Swiss popular disgust with biotechnology more than the one publicized by Greenpeace: a patent application at the European patent office in Munich for a mixture between a human and a pig. The creature had reportedly grown in the laboratory for one week.[37]

In July 1999, the Swiss executive amended its earlier food regulation, declaring in great detail that foods, additives, and substances that are, contain, or are derived from GM organisms, are to be marked with a label "produced from genetically modified X." The same rule applied to GM microorganisms. If a food contained less than 1 percent of its mass in GMOs or if the food had been severed from the GMO and cleaned, no label would be necessary (Lebensmittelverordnung LMV, Art. 22). As we saw above, the EU was to follow suit in adopting the 1 percent thresholds. The Federal Council explained the threshold rule in a media release: it was to ensure that normally and biologically produced foods need not be declared if they contained GMO traces because they might have accidentally been mixed with GMOs. The Swiss executive argued that alcoholic beverages require a similar 0.5 percent threshold below which beverages are not deemed "alcoholic": "The terminology is being adapted to the one in the EU" (Eidgenössisches Departement des Innern/Federal Department of Home Affairs, 14 June 1999).

As before, we now turn to the seven criteria of bureaucratic democracy. How does Swiss regulation do in each?

Appointment

The Federal Council appoints key agency personnel, and each member of the seven-head Swiss executive presides over one department. Studies of the Swiss bureaucracy's composition showed that language groups are more or less represented proportionally, but women and Social Democrats have been vastly underrepresented in the federal bureaucracy elite and in the independent commissions (in 1979, 4.5 percent Social Democrats and 1.9 percent women), while almost half of top federal officials have been Free Democrats (Germann 1984).

On the other hand, the Swiss executive appoints expert commissions on a voluntary basis. In the late 1970s there were 373 extraparliamentary commissions with 5,306 seats manned by 3,866 experts. Seventy percent of these commissions were standing, the others sporadic (Frutiger 1983). Some standing commissions, such as the Competition Commission, persist for decades and take on complex tasks; the Federal Council discharges others after they complete their tasks. It names commission members based on their expertise, but also along political criteria, such as equal regional and language, gender and party representation (Linder 1999:231). The Swiss Parliament has no role in appointing or approving agency personnel.

Participation

Recall the popular 1992 initiative we discussed above. While Swiss voters rejected the initiative as too far-reaching, the fact that Swiss citizens voted directly on a proposed GMO policy (and Switzerland appears to be the only country worldwide in which voters had this option) speaks volumes about Swiss, compared to EU or U.S., democracy in this policy area.

Nevertheless, the Federal Office for Public Health (BAG) saw itself faced with a hostile climate of public opinion. In September 1998, it responded by issuing an invitation to a public hearing on GMO declaration thresholds, and in January 1999 urged speedy adoption of a GMO regulation. The executive agency cited a nascent "consensus" on limits "supported by representatives of consumers, industry and authorities."[38]

Transparency

The BAG is integrated in a relatively transparent procedure of checks and balances, as table 6.4 showed. The greatest weakness in the procedure is that the BAG, as an executive agency, is not required to report to the Swiss legislature.

Reason-Giving

There is no formal requirement for the BAG to give reasons for its decisions, but in practice its superior, the Federal Council, does so frequently, not least in response to popular initiatives or referenda.

Overrule

The Swiss political system is a mixture between the basic models, the parliamentary system of Great Britain or Germany on the one hand and the presidential system of the United States on the other. Much like in parliamentary democracies, the Swiss Parliament elects the seven-member executive; but much like in presidential systems, once the executive is elected, it is free to govern and can afford conflicts with the parliamentary majority without fear of being toppled, as, say, an English prime minister or a German chancellor might be. The fact that the Federal Council is a collective body composed for many years of two Free Democrats, two Christian Democrats, two Social Democrats, and one Social People Party minister, acts as check on the power of each party. All seven ministers vote on all government business, which reduces the autonomy of individual ministers in their own portfolios, and has led to the outvoting of individual ministers even in matters within their own sphere of authority (Linder 1999:219, 224).

Another potential overrule vehicle is the Swiss referendum, since anybody who collects 50,000 signatures can challenge a law or regulation and bring it to a popular vote. But the procedures for judicial review and overruling agency decisions are not airtight. Despite an August 2000 ruling by a federal judge that the use of transgenic products needs a full environmental impact assessment before its introduction into the country, the Ministry of Agriculture had already authorized the liberation of transgenic corn.

Monitoring

Sister agencies such as the Federal Office for Agriculture (BLW), the Federal Veterinarian Office (BVET), and the Federal Office for the Environment (BUWAL) are authorized to monitor the actions of the BAG. But since these federal agencies all report to the executive, not to the legislature, ex post monitoring by directly elected representatives is not part of the procedure.

Independence

Expert commissions are not independent of the Swiss executive, but they do expand the representation of society and industry in Swiss politics. Industry associations in particular have dominated economic legislation since the beginnings of cartel protectionism in the late nineteenth century (Gruner 1964), sometimes with disastrous consequences. During the economic crisis of the 1930s, some corporate interest groups made increasingly extreme demands for protectionism on the state, but blocked each other with referenda. The bourgeois parties were split between protectionism and free market, and the Social Democrats were unable to command a majority for their Keynesian interventionism. Government was paralyzed until the Federal Council and Parliament ruled by emergency decree and suspended direct democracy. Only in 1947, the Federal Council granted to "accountable organizations" a "hearing" in legislation and "participation" in the execution of questions of political economy at the constitutional level (Art. 32 BV) (Linder 1983:276).

These arrangements could be called "consensus democracy" (Lijphart 1984; in German, "Konkordanzdemokratie") in which minorities can veto decisions that go against their interests, thereby transforming zero-sum games into positive-sum games, cultivating consensus and compromise, even building trust and learning (Linder 1999:309). But a less euphemistic interpretation is that Switzerland is a strongly corporatist system (Schmitter 1981; Katzenstein 1984) in which employers and corporate interests outweigh the influence of trade unions (Linder 1999:298). Recall that Swiss elections do not throw governments out of office; they only shift representations in Parliament. If the same power asymmetries persist over decades, consensus democracy is a thin veil for the dictatorship of a majority.

CONCLUSION

Now that we have reviewed the three GMO regulations separately, we can compare. Again, I use a simple rating system to rate each polity in each of the seven indicators as "strong," "medium," or "weak." Again, the ratings of bureaucratic democracy are subjective and imprecise, and can

Table 6.5. Bureaucratic Democracy Ratings in GMO Foods Labeling Regulation

Bureaucratic Democracy Indicators	GMO Regulation— European Union	GMO Regulation— United States	GMO Regulation— Switzerland
Appointment	Medium = 2	Medium = 2	Medium = 2
Participation	Strong = 3	Medium = 2	Strong = 3
Transparency	Medium = 2	Weak = 1	Medium = 2
Reason-Giving	Medium = 2	Weak = 1	Medium = 2
Overrule	Medium = 2	Medium = 2	Medium = 2
Monitoring	Strong = 3	Weak = 1	Medium = 2
Independence	Weak =1	Medium = 2	Medium = 2
Cumulative Points = Average Ranking	15 points = 2.14 = 1st	11 points = 1.57 = 3rd	15 points = 2.14 = 1st

surely be improved; but they give at least a good comparative sense of bureaucratic democracy in action. Table 6.5 summarizes my findings.

Applying the bureaucratic democracy indicators to the case of GMO food labeling, the bottom line is that EU regulatory processes appear to be virtually as democratic as those in Switzerland, while the United States suffers from a democratic deficit relative to the other two polities. The United States receives no strong rating in any indicator. Its *appointment, participation, overrule,* and *independence* indicators are all medium, because the president, not Congress, exercises clearance over the leadership of the FDA; the relevant agencies' responsibilities are not clearly delegated; the agencies involve the public only reluctantly and only in response to activist pressure; neither the executive nor Congress nor the judiciary ever overruled the FDA; and independence from capture by the regulated industry is far from assured.

Other indicators—*transparency, reason-giving,* and *monitoring*—are even rated weak: the FDA shows continued propensity for permitting industry self-regulation, where biotech companies themselves decide what and how much to report to the agency; the FDA's mission does not require it to give reasons for its decisions; and ex post monitoring by Congress has been virtually absent.

While there is room for improvement and further democratization, Swiss and EU institutions appear to be better equipped to represent and protect diffuse interests than are U.S. institutions. The EU's *participation* and *monitoring* ratings are strong, because it encourages and even subsidizes consumer involvement, and because the Council is strongly involved in GMO legislation and decisions.

The European *appointment, transparency, reason-giving,* and *overrule* dimensions in biotech policy all get a medium rating, since democratically elected governments appoint the decision makers in the council, but the Commission is not directly elected; policy makers are far removed from the electorate; the council's deliberation process is secret, and it gives no reasons for its decisions, while the Commission does; and decisions are taken not by a specialized regulatory agency but by political bodies: the Commission and the council.

The only weak rating for the EU is in *independence,* since the Commission and the agency are one and the same.

By contrast, Switzerland gets no weak rating anywhere. It gets medium ratings in six of the seven indicators, because the Swiss parliament has no role in appointing agency officials, but the executive does appoint expert commissions; because the health agency reports only to the executive and not to parliament; the agency is not required to publish reasons, but the executive does so frequently; the Swiss public can use referenda to overrule policies, but the executive can also overrule decisions of its own agency; because mutual monitoring by all relevant sister agencies allows them to check each other, but none of them are checked by the legislature; and finally, because the Swiss "consensus democracy" tends to encourage "old boys' networks" that maintain old power asymmetries.

One indicator, *participation,* is rated strong because Swiss citizens have the opportunity to vote not only for politicians but directly for policies.

A possible objection to these findings is that we cannot conclude from insufficient U.S. regulation of GMOs—or relatively advanced EU and Swiss regulation—that the United States is insufficiently democratic. After all, American GMO policies currently in place might be fully representative of U.S. voters' preferences. According to a survey, some 75 percent of Americans "believed that biotechnology would provide benefits for their family within the next five years" (Hill and Battle 2000: 8). But as we have seen above, 60 percent of Americans said they would not buy foods labeled to contain GMOs (Pollack and Shaffer 2001: 168), and 85 percent oppose labeling GM foods as "organic." A clear majority of U.S. respondents appear to favor labeling GM foods.

Why is GMO regulation in Europe—both in the EU and in Switzerland—more representative of consumer interests than regulation in the United States? We can only speculate. Are European activists and NGOs like Greenpeace and Friends of the Earth the independent factor? Some European environmentalists do come up with creative ways to protest biotech foods. For example, Greenpeace activists went to fields in Germany and France owned by Novartis, which grows GMO maize; they cut 4.5 tons of maize, packed it in bags marked "WARNING GENE-MANIPULATED," and delivered the bags to company headquarters in Basel—of course with reporters and cameras in attendance. But it is unclear whether activist NGOs are the driving factor, since Greenpeace-USA had organized a similar action to "quarantine" a biotech soy field in Iowa in 1996 and did not come close to mobilizing U.S. public opinion as much.

Are the European Parliament and Commission, and the Swiss Bundesversammlung and Bundesrat, more activist and public-minded than the U.S. Congress and executive? Congress can send signals of concern; this puts pressure on agencies to regulate. In this case Congress sent no such signal, while the European Parliament and the Commission were much more responsive to diffuse public opinion.

Is the U.S. regulatory process governed by whoever has more resources? Already in January 1996, some 1,300 biotech companies in the United States outnumbered some 500 biotech companies in the EU (Stewart and Johanson 1999:265). In May 2000, the U.S. industry association BIO commissioned a study by the consulting firm Ernst & Young, entitled "The Economic Contribution of the Biotechnology Industry to the U.S. Economy" to demonstrate the industry's supposed benefits. The financial resources at the disposal of the U.S. biotech industry seem enormous. U.S. public opinion seems malleable by whoever flexes the stronger marketing muscle. Does the European biotech industry have or deploy less marketing resources, or does the European industry have less influence on the regulatory process than does the American industry? Perhaps; but socially (or image-) conscious corporations like the food giants Gerber or Nestlé that refused GMOs, and Swiss wholesalers like the omnipresent Migros chain, which in 1996 began siding with biotech critics, may be a strong causal factor.

Is there a cultural difference in consumers' relationships with corporations? In a September 2000 speech to the FDA, BIO's president asserted:

> Right now the furor in the United Kingdom and continental Europe over biotech foods, or as they call them "GMO foods" is, in some part, attributable to the fact that while in the United States, citizens are skeptical about the government in general, we do trust the FDA to protect the public health. That is a long—and hard-earned—trust. Most European citizens, however government-centric or even socialist they may be, do not share such trust in any government agency devoted to protecting their public health, and they have been unnerved by their experience with tainted blood supplies and widely perceived government bungling over "mad cow" disease.[39]

The more liberal U.S. approach to regulating GMOs reflects more faith of U.S. regulators in the free market and in the safety of new technologies (hence the U.S. emphasis on science-based and self-regulation by producers), as well as more confidence of U.S. consumers in the independence of regulatory institutions like the FDA. By contrast, European political economy has a history of more intrusion by governments into the market, coupled with more mistrust by consumers of new technologies, industry, and their governments, especially given recent food safety scandals ranging from mad cow disease in the United Kingdom to dioxin-contaminated feed for livestock in Belgium, to the contamination of Coca-Cola products in northern Europe, to sewage in animal feed in France. A legacy of genetic testing in Germany, Austria, and elsewhere during the Nazi era does not exactly help to instill confidence either. Instead, Europeans tend to trust environmental and consumer organizations most deeply (Echols 1998; Hill and Battle 2000: 6; Pollack and Shaffer 2001).

In sum, the key independent variable allowing for, or pushing against, bureaucratic democracy in GMO regulation appears to be industry, compounded by the prevailing regulatory culture and lacking effective legislative oversight. We have to turn to macroeconomics for an explanation. When the EU Council of Ministers approved its three-year GM moratorium in 1998, one of the decision's most vocal adversaries was Charlene Barshefsky. The then U.S. trade representative complained that the GMO approval process in the EU had "completely" broken down and warned that the White House was considering economic retaliation by filing a formal complaint with the World Trade Organization. Stuart Eizenstat, the then-nominee for U.S. deputy treasury secretary, concurred:

> Almost 100% of our agricultural exports in the next five years will be genetically-modified or combined with bulk commodities that are genetically modified... The Europeans have an absolute fear, unfounded by any scientific basis, of accepting these products... The EU's fear of bioengineered foods... is the single greatest trade threat that we face.[40]

These complaints were understandable, given newspaper reports in Brazil and the United Kingdom claiming that major supermarket chains, food producers, and animal feed companies in Europe were turning to Brazil rather than the United States (where GMO and non-GMO soybeans continue to be comingled) for their soybean imports. Meanwhile prices paid to farmers for U.S. soybeans dropped to a twenty-seven-year low, with overall U.S. soybean exports declining by 38 percent. In addition the United States had lost $400 million in corn exports to Europe over two years because of the European public's rejection of GM corn, while Canada had lost over $500 million in canola (rapeseed) exports.[41] According to a Wall Street analyst, "if Europe doesn't accept GMOs, especially soybeans, it will hurt biotech seed markets in the United States."[42]

Multinational corporations are mobilizing to ensure that such horror scenarios do not become reality. Top executives of American and European multinationals meet annually with top U.S. and European regulators in the Transatlantic Business Dialogue (TABD) to advance their free-trade agenda and coordinate deregulatory strategies. TABD's 2000 midyear report stated simply: "The new obstacles to trade are now domestic regulations."[43] And the country whose deregulatory landscape is friendliest to the biotechnology industry is the United States—the very polity that suffers from the deepest democratic deficit among the three polities compared here.

NOTES

1. OECD, Biotechnology, Agriculture and Food, 1992:201.
2. Biotech critics say that although rDNA techniques may be more precise than traditional plant breeding in terms of the identity of genetic material transferred, they are less precise in terms of where the material is transferred. Conventional plant breeding shuffles around aberrant versions (alleles) of the same genes, which basically are fixed in the chromosomal locations as a result of evolution. With genetic engineering (or rDNA techniques), one inserts genes on essentially a random basis, using a gene "gun" or other techniques (e.g., Ti-plasmid, chemoporation, or electroporation) into a plant's preexisting chromosomes. Frequently the genetic material comes from living things with which the host organism(s) would never cross in nature. The variable insertion site can have a number of unpredictable, and potentially negative, consequences (Doerfler et al. 1997). The insertion site can affect expression of the inserted transgene itself as well as the expression of host genes (i.e., genes in the recipient organisms). The former is known as the "position effect". A classic example involved attempting to suppress the color of tobacco and petunia flowers via the transfer of a synthetically created gene designed to turn off (via antisense technology) a host pigment gene (van der Krol et al. 1988). The expected outcome was that all the transformed plants would have the same color, but the transformed plants varied in terms of the amount of color (or pigmentation) in their flowers as well as the pattern of color in the individual flowers. Not only that, but as the season changed (i.e., in different environments), some flowers also changed their color or color pattern. The factors contributing to the position effect are not fully understood (Consumers Union, Comment to FDA, FDA Docket 99N-4282, 13 January 2000).
3. The study's coauthor Arpad Puztai was fired by the director of his institute upon publishing his results. Several months later, twenty scientists published a memorandum to confirm Puztai's results and to rehabilitate him. The Royal Institute of Science ordered an examination of the results by six anonymous reviewers who concluded that the results do not form a reliable and convincing basis for proving negative effects. The controversy has not been resolved to date (Ammann 2000:9).
4. Consumers Union press release, 22 February 2000.
5. BIO press release, 20 July 2000.

6. BIO Senate testimony, 26 September 2000.

7. A U.S. poll commissioned by the Swiss biotech and pharmaceutical company Novartis in February 1997 showed that 54 percent of American consumers said they would like to see "organic" food production become the dominant form of agriculture in the United States. Another survey, commissioned by Environmental Media Services in Washington, DC, in 1998, found that one-third of Americans say they buy organic food regularly, while 40 percent buy organic at least a few times a year; 85 percent would support national organic standards, but oppose labeling as "organic" food that which has been genetically modified, grown with toxic sludge, irradiated or treated with antibiotics (*The Ecologist*, July-August 1998).

8. *Die Weltwoche*, 24 June 1999.

9. The Parliament endorsed the moratorium in a nonbinding resolution in March 2000, to remain in effect until more stringent EU safety rules would be put in place.

10. Commission press release, 13 July 2000.
11. EP resolution, June 1997.
12. Greenpeace press release, 12 April 2000.
13. Commission press release, 13 July 2000.
14. Commission background paper, 13 July 2000.
15. Commission press briefing, 9 October 2001.
16. *Multinational Monitor*, January-February 2000.
17. BIO/GMA joint press release, 7 October 1999.
18. BIO press release, 25 September 2000.
19. *PRNewswire*, 15 June 2000.
20. Consumers Union press release, 3 May 2000.
21. *Multinational Monitor*, January-February 2000.
22. *Houston Chronicle*, 22 October 2000.
23. *Multinational Monitor*, January-February 2000.
24. *Washington Post*, 1 May 1998.
25. *The Ecologist*, July-August 1998.
26. Organic Consumers Association, 17 November 1999.
27. *Houston Chronicle*, 22 October 2000.
28. *Multinational Monitor*, January-February 2000.
29. *Multinational Monitor*, November 2000.
30. BIO press release, 17 August 1999.
31. *New York Times*, 4 October 2000.
32. BIO press release, 4 October 2000.
33. *Multinational Monitor*, January-February 2000.
34. BIO press release, 30 March 2000.
35. BIO press release, 20 July 2000.

36. This congruence of agency and industry views is not entirely surprising, given the widespread "revolving door" practice where industry representatives become agency officials and agency officials return to industry. In one egregious example, the FDA's chief scientist who was instrumental in a pro-biotechnology ruling had reportedly worked for Monsanto before joining the FDA; he later left the agency to return to Monsanto (Robert Weissman, interview, 10 December 2000).

37. Greenpeace-Switzerland press release, 5 October 2000.
38. BAG, 28 January 1999.
39. BIO press release, 18 September 2000.
40. Senate testimony, 29 June 1999.
41. Campaign for Food Safety News No. 20, 14 July 1999.
42. *Multinational Monitor*, January-February 2000.
43. Robert Weissman, "TABD: Corporate Conspiracy," *Focus on the Corporation*, 19 November 2000.

7

✢

Democratic Surplus?

It is now clear that electoral democracies make their inhabitants better off than do dictatorships because they provide their voters with opportunity—the power to shape their own destinies (Zweifel and Navia 2000). But in the regulatory state, it is not that simple anymore. Here, classical theories of electoral democracy are no longer fully applicable without modification. Bureaucratic democracy must be measured with a different yardstick. Table 7.1 recapitulates my seven dimensions of bureaucratic democracy and the findings of chapters 5 and 6.

To reiterate: the ratings are subjective, and I have given each indicator equal weight. In the real world, some dimensions may weigh more heavily than others. Although both ratings and weightings are rudimentary and can certainly be improved, they give us a good impression of the relative democratic strengths and weaknesses—in other words, the democratic surpluses and democratic deficits—in each polity's regulatory processes. The overall finding is clear: in merger regulation, the United States bureaucracy is the most democratic; the Swiss bureaucracy is the least democratic; and the European Union lies between the two. In GMO regulation, the European Union and Switzerland are neck and neck, and both are more democratic than the United States bureaucracy.

The bureaucratic democracy indicators might do more than permit comparison. They also allow policy makers to pick, and perhaps emulate, best practices from each polity and each regulatory regime. The next section offers some recommendations building on these best practices. The remainder of the chapter offers new assumptions more suited to democracy in the regulatory state, anticipates possible objections to this study, and draws conclusions.

Table 7.1. Bureaucratic Democracy Ratings, Merger and GMO Regulation Combined

Bureaucratic Democracy: Indicators	EU Merger Policy	U.S. Merger Policy	Swiss Merger Policy	EU GMO Policy	U.S. GMO Policy	Swiss GMO Policy
Appointment	Medium	Strong	Weak	Medium	Medium	Medium
Participation	Medium	Weak	Weak	Strong	Medium	Strong
Transparency	Medium	Strong	Medium	Medium	Weak	Medium
Reason-Giving	Medium	Medium	Medium	Medium	Weak	Medium
Overrule	Medium	Strong	Weak	Medium	Medium	Medium
Monitoring	Medium	Strong	Weak	Strong	Weak	Medium
Independence	Weak	Strong	Weak	Weak	Medium	Medium
Cumulative Points = Average Ranking	13 = 1.86 2nd	18 = 2.57 1st	9 = 1.29 3rd	15 = 2.14 2nd	11 = 1.57 3rd	15 = 2.14 1st

weak = 1, medium = 2, strong = 3

NORMATIVE (AND TENTATIVE) RECOMMENDATIONS

The Westminster model of representative majoritarian democracy, with its elections that throw governments out of office, has become dominant in most polities worldwide and is seen as sufficient for assuring the legitimacy and stability of governments. Since direct political participation by most citizens in most polities is limited, this "thin democracy" (Barber 1984) appears to be conducive to a political culture that allows for the peaceful resolution of intrasocietal conflicts. But this study shows that the Westminster representative model need not be the only one. In Switzerland, and to a lesser extent in the EU, popular movements pushed through political rights beyond electoral rights for citizens. What is more, there is no trade-off between representative and direct democracy; the latter can complement the former and create a mixture of "sensible" (Cronin 1989) or "half-direct" (Linder 1999:335) democracy. Perhaps framers of regulatory regimes can learn something from the Swiss or EU best practices.

There is, of course, no reason to be complacent about democracy in the EU. Much remains to be done. Rather, my intention is to offer specific points where improvements can and must be made. Table 7.1 above implies best practices in one polity that another polity might adopt to strengthen its bureaucratic democracy and balance its own democratic deficit. (The ideal regulatory regime would combine all of the strong features of each polity.)

Appointment

The U.S. appointment procedure in merger policy is more accountable than analogous procedures in the EU or Switzerland, which would do well to adopt the public vetting and approval of individual agency officials by the directly elected legislature. Also, the fact that the Department of Justice and the Federal Trade Commission are both responsible for regulating mergers, indeed can be rivals competing for a case, acts as a useful check on agency discretion.

More radically, Wood and Waterman recommend, based on their study of bureaucratic democracy in the United States, a return to the two-tiered principal-agent hierarchy established originally by the U.S. constitution, with a clear division of labor between Congress (policy making) and president (administration). Policy orientation, rather than only qualification, should be the chief criterion for Senate approval of nominees (Wood and Waterman 1994:152).[1]

Participation

In GMO regulation, both Switzerland and the EU are strong in involving the public and diffuse interests in their decision-making processes. The United States (and the EU's and Switzerland's own merger policies) might benefit from adopting Swiss and European proactive consultation of diffuse interests (including consumers, environmentalists, and workers) in GMO policy. Another feature worth emulating is the EU's subsidies for weakly organized interest groups to participate in shaping policy. Most importantly, Switzerland allows its citizens to vote key policies up or down (through referenda) or even to initiate policy proposals (through popular initiatives, as happened with a proposed GMO policy).

Transparency

Given its adversarial court procedures, and given its stringent rules on whether and when regulators may meet with industry representatives, U.S. merger regulation is the most transparent of the three polities. Both the EU and Switzerland (and the United States in GMO regulation) should emulate the clarity and accessibility of U.S. merger regulation.

Reason-Giving

None of the polities in either regulatory regime receives a strong rating in reason-giving. All three polities and their six regulatory regimes would do well to adopt frequent and comprehensive press releases and public reports to educate the public and give understandable and widely accessible reasons and criteria for policy decisions.

Overrule

Both Switzerland and the EU would benefit from the strong overrule procedures and strong and frequent judicial review in U.S. merger policy, whose checks and balances are well established.

Monitoring

U.S. ex post monitoring of agencies through congressional oversight committees is strong in merger policy. EU monitoring is strong in GMO regulation, partly because of a deeply rooted public mistrust of European food regulation and industry. European and Swiss merger policy, as well as U.S. and Swiss GMO policy, should strengthen their ex post monitoring procedures, especially by their directly elected legislatures.

Independence

The independence of U.S. merger regulation is exemplary, since both the Justice Department's antitrust division and the Federal Trade Commission have reportedly withstood attempts of industry members to influence their decisions. Also, the Department of Justice has pushed for heavy deterrent sentences for antitrust violators.

There are other possible improvements. An urgent one would be the delegation of Commission competencies to specialized agencies. Regulation is not achieved simply by passing a law, but requires detailed knowledge of and intimate involvement with the regulated activity (Selznick 1985: 363–364). That is why specialized agencies are needed for fact-finding, rulemaking, and enforcement. The Commission would keep all the political responsibilities the treaties charge it with, but would delegate technical tasks to agencies. Agencies would no longer operate in an institutional vacuum, since national and Community representatives would sit on the management boards and scientific committees of each agency. As is current practice, the management board would be comprised of one representative from each country that belongs to the agency, plus representatives from the Commission and Parliament.

Other recommendations flow directly from the analysis of chapters 2 and 3. Above all, the EU must strengthen the European Parliament, make the Commission directly elective, and end the secrecy of council deliberations and votes (see Newman 1996:173). Information technology might make it physically possible to extend the direct democratic democracy of a Greek city-state to the citizens of a large nation-state or even a multinational federation (Dahl 1989:338–39; Held 1995:280).

Even more far-reaching changes have been suggested to improve democracy in the EU. One would be for any polity to require bureaucrats and judges to step down with each new election (Persson, Roland, and Tabellini 1996). This radical solution would clearly shorten the distance between principal and agent; whether it can be implemented, given currently existing political realities, is of course quite another matter.

Joseph Weiler suggested four quite creative proposals in his 1997 Jean Monnet Lecture at the London School of Economics. First, Weiler proposed a European legislative ballot along the lines of the type of direct democracy practiced in Switzerland. Direct referenda, for example around EP elections, would give individuals the chance to directly influence policy choices. The second proposal is to put all legislative deliberation on the Internet to socialize children to be more familiar with European governance. Third, a European constitutional council, modeled after its French namesake, would be chaired by the president of the court, and its members would be sitting members of the national constitutional courts or their equivalents in the member states. The fourth, and in my view most ambitious, proposal is direct taxation. Direct taxation by the EU of European citizens would instill accountability, provoke citizen interest, and become an electoral issue. Taxation would also establish a duty of citizens toward the polity. Elections of MEPs would become real choices among alternatives: "what are they going to do with my money?" (Weiler 1997).

In a more immediate vein, regulatory federalism in the United States may provide guidance for the cooperation between European and national regulators. Majone suggests that the democratic legitimacy of European regulatory bodies, nationally and at EU level, would improve greatly if these bodies adopted requirements similar to those stipulated by the U.S. Administrative Procedure Act (Majone 1998:10–12). The enactment of a European Administrative Procedure Act would create transparent and unified rules for rationalizing decision making, giving equal access to interest groups in the regulatory process, encouraging public dialogue with the Commission, and facilitating judicial review. For example, the Occupational Safety and Health Act (OSHA), passed in 1970 to assure safe and healthy conditions at work, did not provide for complete federalization. Instead, the objectives of OSHA were to be reached, in part, by "encouraging the States to assume the fullest responsibility for the administration and enforcement of state occupational safety and health laws" by means of federal grants and approved state plans (OSHA Act, section 2(b)(11)). Of course European conditions are radically different, since decentralized implementation is the rule rather than the exception; but an application of the OSHA example would be in line with the European subsidiarity principle (Majone 1996:278).

The American separation-of-powers system provides concentrated business interests with many veto points—in the executive branch, in committees of both houses of Congress, and in the courts—allowing them to block public-interest legislation (Pollack 1997:576). On the other hand, Pollack points out that the same American system provides important opportunities for diffuse interests, as we saw above. First, the separation of powers and the federal system, with its division between states and central government, provide a large number of access points within the executive branch, independent regulatory bureaucracies, congressional committees, and the courts. Second, once a public-interest policy has been adopted, the same multiplicity of veto points makes it hard to alter or roll back such legislation. For example, when the 104th Congress sought to weaken U.S. environmental legislation in 1994, the U.S. federal system provided checks against retrenchment, for example through the veto power of the Clinton administration (Vogel 1995:267–70).

NEW ASSUMPTIONS NEEDED

Whatever improvements can be made to maximize bureaucratic democracy, this much is clear: the regulatory state requires a new theoretical approach to democracy. Standards of legitimacy, developed to control an omnicompetent state with virtually unlimited powers to tax and spend, cannot be directly applied to a system of limited competencies and resources like the European Community (Majone 1998:19). In the regulatory state, the political contest shifts from the traditional arena of the budgetary process to the jurisdiction over reviewing and controlling the regulatory process (Majone 1997a:15). Table 7.2 bottom-lines the assumptions underlying most of the democratic deficit arguments we evaluated in chapter 2, and contrasts them with new assumptions suggested by Wood and Waterman (1994) and Majone (1997a).

Democracy is usually held to be government by majority rule. In an extreme formulation of this view, majorities ought to "control all of government—legislative, executive and, if they have a mind to, judicial—and thus to control everything politics can touch. Nothing clarifies the total sway of majorities more than their ability to alter and adjust the standards of legitimacy" (Spitz 1984). We have seen above that if the majoritarian model is the only yardstick for democracy, then European institutions indeed show a democratic deficit, since the Par-

Table 7.2. Assumptions: Traditional Democracy vs. Bureaucratic Democracy

Traditional Democracy Assumptions	Bureaucratic Democracy Assumptions
Positive, tax-and-spend state.	Regulatory state (Majone).
Majoritarian model of electoral democracy.	Madisonian model of democracy: checks and balances (Majone).
Bureaus enjoy undue discretion that must be reined in by majorities.	Bureaus and independent agencies are checks on the "tyranny of the majority" and protect minorities (Majone).
Responsiveness and accountability to voters.	Representation and accountability to end users for results (Majone).
Bureaucrats are self-interested agents.	Bureaucrats reflect past majorities (Wood and Waterman).
Procedural legitimacy.	Substantive legitimacy (Majone).

liament is the only directly elected supranational EU body, and it has yet to come into its full power to meaningfully check the European executive, bureaucracy, and judiciary. Not so fast, though. The majoritarian standard is not the only standard. In fact, it is the exception, not the rule: majoritarian democracy prevails mainly in the United Kingdom and in countries strongly influenced by the British tradition (Lijphart 1984, 1991; Lijphart, Rogowski, and Weaver 1993). Empirical evidence shows an overwhelming prevalence of nonmajoritarian principles in most political systems.

Another vital aspect of electoral democracy is accountability to voters. But in the regulatory state, accountability to voters may be complemented with, or replaced by, accountability for results, a type of accountability currently common in corporate settings, where managers must show results to their boards and shareholders. And in a media-inundated environment, at least some end users of services and some reporters are likely to make noise if they are dissatisfied with service quality.

Bureaus may exploit information asymmetries to their own advantage and therefore not be representative. But we need a better conception of the role of bureaucracy in democracies. Wood and Waterman point out that modern bureaucracy simply responds to and reflects public demands, laws, and majority coalitions of earlier periods. Bureaucracies were established by legislatures and by executives subject to the will of their electorates. They respond directly to courts, media, and issue salience. In the regulatory state, agencies might act as protectors against abuse of powers by rulers or special interests.

Majone distinguishes between procedural and substantive legitimacy. Procedural legitimacy requires four things. First, that agencies be created by democratically enacted statutes that define the agencies' legal authority and objectives. Second, that regulators be appointed by elected officials. Third, that regulatory decision making follows rules that include public participation. Finally, procedural legitimacy requires that agencies give reasons for decisions and be open to judicial review. But while procedural legitimacy—conferred by the consent of the governed—is a necessary aspect of democracy, it is not the only type of legitimacy. Legitimacy can also be substantive—an institution's capacity to engender and maintain the belief that it is the most appropriate one for the functions entrusted to it. Criteria of such substantive legitimacy are, first, policy consistency of regulators; second, their expertise and problem-solving skills; third, their ability to protect diffuse interests; fourth, their professionalism; and finally, a clear definition of their objectives and limits of their authority (Majone 1996:291–96; 1997:25–27).

The European Court of Justice, for example, may be making a move from procedural to substantive legitimacy. Shapiro has shown that the formula used by the court in *Germany v. Commission* (Case 24/62 [1963] ECR 63) "constitutes a transition from procedural to substantive reasons that is strikingly comparable to the American transition from procedural to substantive due process in the famous *Minnesota Rate* case" (Shapiro 1992:201). Article 190 of the Rome Treaty, "one of the world's central devices for judicial enforcement of bureaucratic transparency" (Shapiro 1992:220), might be used by the court to move beyond formal criteria toward substantive judicial review of regulatory decision making in the European Community.

CONCLUSION

As long as European citizens prefer the integration of European economies, but at the same time loathe the integration of European politics, a democratic deficit of some size is the inevitable outcome. This depoliticization of European policy making is the price Europeans pay for preserving national sovereignty in a European regulatory state. Since these are, at least for the moment, the preferences of the European electorate, the democratic deficit is, in the literal sense, democratically justified (Majone 1998:21). While this is a paradoxical outcome, it is not necessarily evidence for the absence of democracy. Neither is the fact that the EU is scrutinized and debated so heavily about its democratic credentials a sign of lacking democracy—on the contrary. The United States and Switzerland, and their political regimes, have been beyond doubt for so long that hardly anybody questions their democratic nature anymore. That absence of criticism and debate alone should raise suspicion. What if the very debate and controversy over the EU's democratic deficit, rather than being proof that the EU is democratically challenged, were instead evidence that the EU does *not* suffer from a democratic deficit greater than that of the most liberal democracies?

Nonetheless, I anticipate several criticisms of this study, as table 7.3 shows.

It is worth remembering that Switzerland and the United States are not exactly ideals of democracy. Actual political conditions in both countries raise

Table 7.3. Anticipated Criticisms

Anticipated Criticisms	Possible Responses
The comparison to the U.S. and Switzerland is strained, since the EU is *sui generis*.	Comparative analyses have been fruitful (Sbragia 1992, Peterson 1994 and 1995, Majone 1996, Goldstein 1997).
The study redefines EU actors as the same as nation-state institutions.	The EU can be seen as a regulatory state whose institutions were modeled after national institutions.
The absence of a single head of government makes the EU unique.	Wrong. Switzerland also lacks a single head of government; its *Bundespräsident* rotates.
The Commission is not an executive like in the United States or Switzerland.	The Commission is a weak executive, but an executive nonetheless. It executes legislation passed by the bicameral legislature (Council of Ministers of member states, and Parliament of representatives of the European electorate). It represents the EU in international treaties and organizations.
Why is the Commission, not the council, the executive? Executive responsibilities are split between council and Commission. The council is political, the Commission administrative. The Commission is not a political leader.	The council does have political functions. But taking the council as the EU executive would in fact lessen the democratic deficit, since member-state electorates can punish council members by throwing them out of office. Seeing the Commission as the executive makes it harder to disprove democratic deficit claims.

(*continued*)

Table 7.3. (*continued*)

Anticipated Criticisms	Possible Responses
EU parties are unlike American or Swiss parties.	Correct, but that does not mean the party systems cannot be compared.
The EU does not confer rights; only member states do. The EU is democratic because of the democracy of its member states.	Since the EU is based on democratic member states, that makes it only *more* democratic.
The democratic deficit lies neither in the EU's institutions nor in its decision-making processes, but in the lack of the EU's legitimacy.	The EU is legitimized by virtue of treaties ratified by democratic member states. Member states could leave the Union if their electorates preferred to stay out.
The case selection is such that the EU comes out looking democratic.	The case selection was based on the strongest democratic deficit arguments. I did not know in advance how the three polities would perform in the two cases.

doubts whether political competition is really fair and open. True, Switzerland's initiative and referendum system allows for direct popular policy input, and its decentralization of power to cantons and communities is a model for other democracies. True, the United States permits a degree of entrepreneurial freedom greater than that in most other states. But in the United States, incumbents are often favored over newcomers, Senate seats may be distributed unfairly, campaign finance rules are obsolete, and the courts are largely unchecked by other branches of government. The country's weak party system and relative lack of party discipline means that many members of Congress are not accountable to voters for the performance of successive governments. In Switzerland, the long-established coalition of the four leading parties breeds collusion, since they protect the seven-member Federal Council as a club from newcomers. Switzerland's grand coalition functions almost as smoothly as a one-party system. The media in both countries may be governed by money and taboos protected by the corporate sector or the bureaucracy that must not become public knowledge or enter the public debate. Both countries' institutions seem to suffer from a powerful bias toward the status quo.

In both the United States and Switzerland, the overwhelming majority of citizens have withdrawn into the privacy of their homes, leaving "democracy"—"the government of *the people*"—to others. I offer the possibility that *all three polities* suffer from a democratic deficit not because of their institutions or rules, but because "We the People" have let them. This state of affairs has been going on for quite a while. It predates the European Coal and Steel Community by 164 years. Consider this story, borrowed from Bruce Ackerman:

> in 1787, the framers of the American Constitution emerge from a summer of top secret meetings and announce that "We the People" want to eliminate America's first constitution, the Articles of Confederation. They propose to ratify their new announcements on behalf of "the People" in a way that is plainly illegal. The Articles of Confederation require agreement by all thirteen states for any constitutional change to be valid; yet the founders declare that their new constitution speaks for "We the People" if only nine states give their assent. Not only that, the convention on constitutional ratification refuses to permit existing state governments to pass judgment on its authority to speak for the people. Instead, only specially convened "constitutional conventions" will be allowed to determine the fate of the new Constitution. What in the world gives the framers the right to assert that they have a better claim to represent the people than the standing governments of the day? (Ackerman 1984).

It is, of course, this story that led the historian Charles Beard to argue that those who wrote the U.S. Constitution were an economic elite scheming to protect the interests of the wealthy, property-owning establishment (Beard 1913).

Is it really that simple? No, it is not. But let us not forget that the United States is founded on a revisionist history that somehow the revolution justified an undemocratic usurpation of power and legitimacy by a small group of people who took it upon themselves to speak as We the People. By contrast, the creation of the European Union is entirely based on legal treaties that were duly ratified by all member states. But I digress: this study did not aim to scrutinize the extent of democracy in the United States or Switzerland. Its main purpose has been a comparison between them and the European Union. And its finding is unequivocal: democracy in the European Union is close to being as great (or deficient, depending on one's viewpoint) as in most liberal democracies. If the EU suffers from a democratic deficit, it is hardly alone.

NOTE

1. On the other hand, Wood and Waterman themselves admit that multiple principals can have advantages for bureaucratic democracy: they make Congress and president more vigilant in monitoring the bureaucracy, and the media scrutinize government more carefully during controversial periods of divided government (Wood and Waterman 1994:148).

Bibliography

Ackerman, Bruce A. 1984. "The Storrs Lectures: Discovering the Constitution," *Yale Law Journal* 93 1013–1072.
Allen, David. 1983. "Managing the Common Market: The Community Competition Policy," in Helen Wallace, William Wallace, and Carole Webb (eds.), *Policy-Making in the European Community*. London and New York: John Wiley & Sons.
Alvarez, Mike, José Antonio Cheibub, Fernando Limongi, and Adam Przeworski. 1996. "Classifying Political Regimes." *Studies in Comparative International Development* 31:2 (Summer): 3–36.
Ammann, Daniel. 1999. "Gentechnik an Lebensmitteln," Manuscript.
Andersen, Svein. S., and Kjell A. Eliassen. 1993. *Making Policy in Europe: The Europeification of National Policy-Making*. London and Thousand Oaks: Sage.
Anderson, Benedict. 1983. *Imagined Communities*. London: Verso.
Baake, Pio, and Oliver Perschau. 1996. "The Law and Policy of Competition in Germany," in Giandomenico Majone (ed.), *Regulating Europe*, 131–56.
Baldwin, Robert. 1996. "Regulatory Legitimacy in the European Context: The British Health and Safety Executive," in Giandomenico Majone (ed.), *Regulating Europe*, 83–105.
Banks, Jeffrey S. 1971. *Cross-Polity Time-Series Data*. Cambridge: MIT Press.
———. 1989. "Agency Budgets, Cost Information, and Auditing," *American Journal of Political Science* 33:3 (August): 670–99.
Banks, Jeffrey S., and Barry R. Weingast. 1992. "The Political Control of Bureaucracies under Asymmetric Information," *American Journal of Political Science* 36:2 (May): 509–24.
Barber, Benjamin. 1984. *Strong Democracy: Participatory Politics for a New Age*. Berkeley: University of California Press.
Baron, David T. 1995. "The Economics and Politics of Regulation: Perspectives, Agenda, and Approaches," in Jeffrey S. Banks and Eric A. Hanushek (eds.), *Modern Political Economy*, 10–63. Cambridge: Cambridge University Press.

Barro, Robert J., and David B. Gordon. 1983. "Rules, Discretion and Reputation in a Model of Monetary Policy," *Journal of Monetary Economics* 12, 101–21.

Bazerman, Max H., and Margaret A. Neale. 1992. *Negotiating Rationally*. New York: Free Press.

Beard, Charles. [1913] 1986. *An Economic Interpretation of the Constitution of the United States*. New York: Free Press.

Becker, Gary S. 1983. "A Theory of Competition among Pressure Groups for Political Influence," *Quarterly Journal of Economics* 98, 371–400.

Bendor, Jonathan. 1988. "Formal Models of Bureaucracy," *British Journal of Political Science* 18, 353–95.

Berghahn, Volker R. 1986. *The Americanisation of West German Industry*. Leamington Spa: Berg.

Bernstein, Marver. 1955. *Regulating Business by Independent Commissions*. Princeton NJ: Princeton University Press.

Bogdanor, Vernon, and Geoffrey Woodcock. 1991. "The European Community and Sovereignty," *Parliamentary Affairs* 44:4. 481–92.

Bollen, Kenneth A. 1980. "Issues in the Comparative Measurement of Political Democracy," in *American Sociological Review* 45, 370–90.

———. 1986. "Political Rights and Political Liberties in Nations: An Evaluation of Human Rights Measures, 1950 to 1984," *Human Rights Quarterly* 8, 567–91.

Bollen, Kenneth A. 1993. "Liberal Democracy: Validity and Method Factors in Cross-National Measures," in *American Journal of Political Science* 37, 1207–30.

———. and Robert W. Jackman. 1989. "Democracy, Stability, and Dichotomies," in *American Sociological Review* 54, 438–57.

Boner, Roger A. and Reinald Krueger. 1991. "The Basics of Anti-Trust Policy: A Review of Ten Nations and the European Communities," Technical Paper No. 160. Washington DC: World Bank.

Brent, Richard. 1995. "The Binding of Leviathan—The Changing Role of the European Commission in Competition Cases," *International and Comparative Law Quarterly* 44(2): 255–79.

Bridge, John. 1981. "National Legal Tradition and Community Law: Legislative Drafting and Judicial Interpretation in England and the European Community," *Journal of Common Market Studies* 4, 351–76.

Brinkhorst, Laurens Jan. 1996. "The Future of European Agencies: A Budgetary Perspective from the European Parliament," in Alexander Kreher (ed.), *The New European Agencies*, EUI Working Paper RSC, No. 96/49, 75–81. Florence: European University Institute.

British Medical Association. 1999. "The Impact of Genetic Modification on Agriculture, Food and Health. An Interim Statement. Board of Science and Education, British Medical Association, May.

Bryner, Gary C. 1987. *Bureaucratic Discretion: Law and Policy in Federal Regulatory Agencies*. New York: Pergamon Press.

Bulmer, Simon. 1994. "Institutions and Policy Change in the European Communities: The Case of Merger Control," *Public Administration* 72:3, 423–44.

Bundesrat der Schweizerischen Eidgenossenschaft. 1994. "Botschaft zu einem Bundesgesetz über Kartelle und andere Wettbewerbsbeschränkungen." 23 November 1994.

Bundesversammlung der Schweizerischen Eidgenossenschaft. 1996. "Verordnung über das Bewilligungsverfahren von GVO-Lebensmitteln, GVO-Zusatzstoffen und GVO-Verarbeitungsshilfsstoffen (VBGVO)." 19 November 1996.

———. 1998. *Bundesverfassung der Schweizerischen Eidgenossenschaft*. Bern, Switzerland.

Burley, Anne-Marie, and Walter Mattli. 1993. "Europe before the Court: A Political Theory of Legal Integration," *International Organization* 47:1, 41–76.

Calhoun, John C. [1848] 1963. *Disquisition on Government*. Reprint. New York: P. Smith.

Calvert, Randall L., Matthew McCubbins, and Barry R. Weingast. 1989. "A Theory of Political Control and Agency Discretion," *American Journal of Political Science* 33:3 (August): 588–611.

Cary, William L. 1974. "Federalism and Corporate Law: Reflections on Delaware," *Yale Law Review* 83:4, 663–705.

Cases, Lluís. 1996. "Competition Law and Policy in Spain: Implementation in an Interventionist Tradition," in Giandomenico Majone (ed.), *Regulating Europe*, 180–201. Pub. info.

Christiansen, Thomas. 1997. "Tensions of European Governance: Politicized Bureaucracy and Multiple Accountability in the European Commission," *Journal of European Public Policy* 4:2 (March): 73–90.

Cini, Michelle and Lee McGowan. 1998. *Competition Policy in the European Union*. New York: St. Martin's Press.

Commission of the European Communities. 1990. Regulation no. 2367/90 of 25 July 1990 on the notifications, time limits and hearings provided for in Council Regulation (EEC) no. 4064/89, OJ L.219 of 14 August 1990.

———. 1993. Report from the Commission to the Council on the Implementation of the Merger Regulation, COM(93) 385 final: 4. Brussels, 28 July 1993.

———. 1994. Twenty-Third Report on Competition Policy 1993. Luxembourg: CEC.

———. 1997a. Twenty-Sixth Report on Competition Policy 1996. Luxembourg: CEC.

———. 1997b. Green Paper on Vertical Restraints in EC Competition Policy, COM (96) 721 final. Brussels: CEC.

———. 1998. Efficiency and Accountability of Standardisation under the New Approach, DG III, 13 May 1998.

———. 2000a. Regulation (EC) No. 49-50/2000 on the labelling of foodstuffs and food ingredients containing additives and flavourings that have been genetically modified or have been produced from genetically modified organisms, 10 January 2000.

———. 2000b. White Paper on Food Safety, COM (719) Final, 12 January 2000.

———. 2000c. Guidelines on the applicability of Article 81 to horizontal co-operation agreements, Notice, 29 November 2000.

———. 2001. Green Paper on the Review of Council Regulation (EEC) 4064/89, COM(2001) 745/6 final. Brussels: CEC.

Coppedge, Michael, and Wolfgang H. Reinicke. 1990. "Measuring Polyarchy," in *Studies in Comparative International Development* 25, 51–72.

Council of the European Communities. 1971. First Regulation implementing Articles 85 and 86, 1959–62 OJ Special Edition 87, as amended by Reg. no. 59, 1959–62 OJ

Special edition 249; Reg. no. 118/63/EEC, 1963–64 OJ Special edition 55; and Reg. no. 2822/71, 1971 OJ Special edition (III) 1035 ("Regulation 17"), 21 February 1962.
———. 1989. Regulation 4064/89 on the control of concentrations between undertakings, OJ L395 (30 December 1989) ("Merger Regulation"), 21 December 1989.
———. 1990. Directive 90/220/EEC on the deliberate release into the environment of genetically modified organisms, 23 April 1990.
———. 1998. Regulation (EC)1139/98, concerning the compulsory indication of the labelling of certain foodstuffs produced from genetically modified organisms of particulars other than those provided for in Directive 79/112/EEC, 26 May 1998.
Cronin, Thomas E. 1989. *Direct Democracy. The Politics of Initiative, Referendum, and Recall*. Cambridge/London: Harvard University Press.
Czada, Roland. 1996. "Vertretung und Verhandlung, Aspekte politischer Konfliktregelung in Mehrebensystemen," in Arthur Benz und Wolfgang Seibel (eds.), *Theorieentwicklungen in der Politikwissenschaft*. Baden-Baden: Nomos.
Dahl, Robert. [1951] 1956. *A Preface to Democratic Theory*. Chicago: University of Chicago Press.
———. 1971. *Polyarchy: Participation and Opposition*. New Haven: Yale University Press.
———. 1982. *Dilemmas of Pluralist Democracy*. New Haven: Yale University Press.
———. 1989. *Democracy and Its Critics*. New Haven: Yale University Press.
Dashwood, Alan. 1996. "The Limits of European Community Powers," *European Law Review* 21/1, 113–28.
Dehousse, Renaud. 1995. "Constitutional Reform in the European Community: Are There Alternatives to the Majority Avenue?" in Jack Hayward (ed.), *The Crisis of Representation in Europe*, 118–36. London: Frank Cass.
———. 1997. "Regulation by Networks in the European Community: The Role of European Agencies," *Journal of European Public Policy* 4:2 (June): 246–61.
Dehousse, Renaud, C. Joerges, G. Majone, F. Snyder, and E. Everson. 1992. "Europe after 1992: New Regulatory Strategies," EUI Working Paper, LAW 92/31.
Demarigny, Fabrice. 1996. "Independent Administrative Authorities in France and the Case of the French Council for Competition," in Giandomenico Majone (ed.), *Regulating Europe*, 157–79. Pub info.
Dixit, Avinash K., and Barry L. Nalebaum. 1991. *Thinking Strategically: The Competitive Edge in Today's Business, Politics, and Everyday Life*. New York: Norton.
Dixon, Robert. 1968. *Democratic Representation in Law and Politics*. New York: Oxford University Press.
Docksey, C., and K. Williams. 1994. "The Commission and the Execution of Community Policy," in G. Edwards and D. Spence (eds.)., *The European Commission*. London: Longman.
Doerfler, Walter, et al. 1997. "Integration of foreign DNA and Its Consequences in Mammalian Systems." Trends in Biotechnology 312, 401–406.
Downs, Anthony. 1957. *An Economic Theory of Democracy*. New York: Harper and Brothers.
Dunn, John. 1999. "Situating Democratic Political Accountability," in Bernard Manin, Adam Przeworski and Susan Stokes (eds.), *Democracy, Accountability, and Representation*. Oxford: Cambridge University Press.

Earnshaw, David, and David Judge. 1995. "Early Days: The European Parliament, Co-decision and the European Union Legislative Process Post-Maastricht," *Journal of European Public Policy* 2:4 (December): 624–49.

Echols, Marsha A. 1998. "Food Safety Regulation in the European Union and the United States: Different Cultures, Different Laws," *Columbia Journal of European Law* 4, 525–43.

Eichener, Volker. 1995. "Die Rückwirkungen der europäischen Integration auf nationale Politikmuster," in Markus Jachtenfuchs and Beate Kohler-Koch (eds.), *Europäische Integration*. Opladen: Leske und Buderich.

———. 1997. "Effective European Problem-Solving: Lessons from the Regulation of Occupational Safety and Environmental Protection," *Journal of European Public Policy* 4:4 (December): 591–608.

Eskridge, William N. Jr., and John Ferejohn. 1992. "The Article I, Section 7 Game," *Georgetown Law Review* 80, 523–64.

Ewen, Stanley W.B., and Arpad Puztai. 1999. "The Health Risks of Genetically Modified Foods," *The Lancet* 354:9179, 684–689.

Fagan, John B. 2000. "Assessing the Safety and Nutritional Quality of Genetically Engineered Foods," mimeo/web report: http://www.netlink.de/gen/jfassess.htm

Ferejohn, John. 1999. "Accountability and Authority: Towards a Theory of Political Accountability," in Bernard Manin, Adam Przeworski, and Susan Stokes, *Democracy, Accountability, and Representation*. Chapter 4. Oxford: Cambridge University Press.

———. and Keith Krehbiel. 1987. "The Budget Process and the Size of the Budget," *American Journal of Political Science* 31:2, 296–319.

———. and Charles Shipan. 1990. "Congressional Influence on Bureaucracy," *Journal of Law, Economics, and Organization* 6, Special Issue, 1–21.

Ferry, Jean-Marc, and Paul Thibaud. 1992. *Discussion Sur L'Europe*. Paris: Calmann-Lévy.

Fiebig, Andre. 1998. "Extraterritorial Application of the European Merger Control Regulation and Suggestions for Reform," *European Competition Law Review* 19:6 (July): 323–331.

Finer, Herman. 1940/1941. "Administrative Responsibility in Democratic Government," *Public Administration Review* 1, 335–50.

Fiorina, Morris P. 1985. "Group Concentration and the Delegation of Legislative Authority," in Roger Noll (ed.), *Regulatory Policy and the Social Sciences*, 175–99. Berkeley CA: University of California Press.

First Regulation implementing Articles 85 [now 81] and 86 [now 82], 1959–62 OJ Special Edition 87, as amended by Reg. no. 59, 1959–62 OJ Special edition 249; Reg. no. 118/63/EEC, 1963–64 OJ Special edition 55; and Reg. no. 2822/71, 1971 OJ Special edition (III) 1035 ("Regulation 17").

Franklin, Mark, Cees van der Eijk, and Michael Marsh. 1996. "Conclusions: The Electoral Connection and the Democratic Deficit," in Cees van der Eijk and Mark Franklin (eds.), *Choosing Europe? The European Electorate and National Politics in the Face of Union*. Ann Arbor: University of Michigan Press.

Freedman, James. 1978. *Crisis and Legitimacy*. Cambridge: Cambridge University Press.

Freedom House. 1992. *Freedom in the World. Political Rights and Civil Liberties*. New York: Freedom House.

Frutiger, Andreas. 1983. "Les commissions extra-parlementaires de la Confédération en 1978," *Cahiers de l'IDHEAP* 9, Lausanne.

Gandhi, Jennifer. 1997. "Political Parties and Accountability," mimeo, May.

Garrett, Geoffrey and George Tsebelis. 1996. "An Institutional Critique of Inter-Governmentalism," *International Organization* 50, 269–99.

Gasiorowski, Mark J. 1990. "The Political Regimes Project," *Studies in Comparative International Development* 25, 109–25.

Gastil, Raymond Duncan. 1990. "The Comparative Survey of Freedom: Experiences and Suggestions," *Studies in Comparative International Development* 25, 25–30.

Gatsios, Konstantine, and Paul Seabright. 1989. "Regulation in the European Community," *Oxford Review of Economic Policy* 5, 37–60.

Genschel, Philipp, and Thomas Plümper. 1997. "Regulatory Competition and International Co-operation," *Journal of European Public Policy* 4:4 (December): 626–42.

Gerber, David J. 1994. "The Transformation of European Competition Law," *Harvard International Law Journal* 35(1): 97–147.

Germann, Raimund E. 1984. "Regierung und Verwaltung," in Ulrich Klöti (ed.), *Handbuch Politisches System der Schweiz*, Band 2: Strukturen und Prozesse, 45–76. Bern: Paul Haupt.

Gilligan, Thomas W., William J. Marshall, and Barry R. Weingast. 1989. "Regulation and the Theory of Legislative Choice: The Interstate Commerce Act of 1887," *Journal of Law and Economics* 32 (April): 35–61.

Goldstein, Leslie Friedman. 1997. "State Resistance to Authority in Federal Unions: The Early United States (1790–1860) and the European Community (1958–94)," *Studies in American Political Development* 11, 149–89.

Goyder, D.G. (1988) *EEC Competition Law*. Oxford: Clarendon Press.

Greenwood, Justin, Jürgen Grote, and Karsten Ronit (eds.). 1992. *Organized Interests and the European Community*. London and Beverly Hills: Sage.

Greer, Douglas F. 1983. *Business, Government, and Regulation*. New York: Macmillan.

Gruner, Erich. 1964. "100 Jahre Wirtschaftspolitik, Etappen des Staatsinterventionismus in der Schweiz," *Schweizerische Zeitschrift für Vokswirtschaft und Statistik* 100, 34–72.

Gurr, Ted Robert. 1990. *POLITY II: Political Structures and Regime Change, 1800–1986*, ICPSR 9263. Ann Arbor, MI: Inter-University Consortium for Political and Social Research.

———. Keith Jaggers, and Will H. Moore. 1990. "The Transformation of the Western State: The Growth of Democracy, Autocracy, and State Power Since 1880," in *Studies in Comparative International Development* 25, 73–108.

Hartley, Trevor C. 1988. *The Foundations of European Community Law: An Introduction to the Constitutional and Administrative Law of the European Community* (2nd ed.). Oxford: Clarendon Press.

Hayes-Renshaw, Fiona and Helen Wallace. 1995. "Executive Power in the European Union: The Functions and limits of the Council of Ministers," *Journal of European Public Policy* 2:4 (December): 559–82.

Held, David. 1987. *Models of Democracy*. Cambridge: Polity Press.

———. 1995. *Democracy and the Global Order: From the Modern State to Cosmopolitan Governance*. Cambridge: Polity Press.

Héritier, Adrienne. 1993. "Policy-Netzwerkanalyse als Untersuchungsintrument im europäischen Kontext: Folgerungen aus einer empirischen Studie regulativer Politik," *Politische Vierteljahresschrift* 34 (Sonderheft 24):432–47.

———. 1997a. "Market-Making Policy in Europe: Its Impact on Member-State Policies: The Case of Road Haulage in Britain, the Netherlands, Germany and Italy," *Journal of European Public Policy* 4, 539–55.

———. 1997b. "Policy-Making by Subterfuge: Interest Accommodation, Innovation and Substitute Democratic Legitimation in Europe—Perspectives from Distinctive Policy Areas," *Journal of European Public Policy* 4:2 (June): 171–89.

———. 1999. *Policy-Making and Diversity in Europe: Escape from Deadlock*. Cambridge: Cambridge University Press.

———. Christoph Knill, and Susanne Mingers. 1996. *Ringing the Changes in Europe: Regulatory Competition and the Transformation of the State. Britain, France, Germany*. New York: Walter de Gruyter.

Hill, Lowell B., and Sophia C. Battle. 2000. "Search for Solutions in the EU-US GMO Debate," Proceedings of a Conference—GMO Regulations: Food Safety or Health Barrier?—Chicago, October 22–23. Department of Agricultural and Consumer Economics, Agricultural Experiment Station/Office of Research, College of Agricultural, Consumer and Environmental Sciences, University of Illinois at Urbana-Champaign, AE–4731.

Hix, Simon. 1994. "The Study of the European Community: The Challenge to Comparative Politics," *West European Politics* 17:1 (January): 1–30.

———. 1998. "Elections, Parties and Institutional Design: A Comparative Perspective on European Union Democracy," *West European Politics* 21:3 (July): 19–52.

Hölzler, H. 1990. "Merger Control," in Peter Montagnon (ed.), *European Competition Policy*. London: Chatham House/RIIA.

Horn, Murray. 1995. *The Political Economy of Public Administration*. Cambridge: Cambridge University Press.

House of Lords Select Committee Report on the European Community. 1993. *Enforcement of Community Competition Rules: Report with Evidence*. Session 1993/4, First Report. London: HMSO.

Hug, Peter. 1999. "Innenansichten der Aussenpolitik—Akteure und Interessen," in Brigitte Studer (ed.), *Etappen des schweizerischen Bundesstaates. Staats- und Nationsbildung der Schweiz 1848–1998*, 203–36. Zürich: Chronos.

Hull, Robert. 1993. "Lobbying Brussels: A View from Within," in Sonia Mazey and Jeremy Richardson (eds.), *Lobbying in the European Community*, 82–92. Oxford and New York: Oxford University Press.

Huntington, Samuel P. 1991. *The Third Wave: Democratization in the Late Twentieth Century*. Norman: University of Oklahoma Press.

Inkeles, Alex. 1990. "Introduction," *Studies in Comparative International Development* 25, 3–6.

Jacobs, F. 1995. "The European Parliament's Role in Nominating the Members of the Commission: First Steps towards Parliamentary Government of US-Senate

Type Confirmation Hearings?" Paper prepared for the Fourth Biennial International ECSA Conference, Charleston, SC.

Jacobs, Jeffrey A. 1996. "Comparing Regulatory Models—Self-Regulations vs. Government Regulation: The Contrast between the Regulation of Motion Pictures and Broadcasting May Have Implications for Internet Regulation," *Journal of Technology Law & Policy* 1:1 (Spring): 1–19.

Johnson, Stanley P., and Guy Corcelle. 1987. *L'autre Europe 'verte'—la politique communautaire de l'environnement*. Brussels: Labour.

Katzenstein, Peter J. 1984. *Corporatism and Change: Austria, Switzerland and the Politics of Industry*. Ithaca/London: Cornell University Press.

Katzman, Robert A. 1980. "The Federal Trade Commission," in James Q. Wilson (ed.), *The Politics of Regulation*. New York: Basic Books.

Keohane, Robert O., and Joseph S. Nye, Jr. 2001. "Democracy, Accountability, and Global Governance," mimeo.

Kielmansegg, Peter Graf. 1996. "Integration und Demokratie," in Markus Jachtenfuchs and Beate Kohler-Koch (eds.) *Europäische Integration*. Opladen: Leske und Buderich.

Korah, Valentin. 1997. "Tetra Pak II: Lack of Reasoning in Court's Judgment," *European Competition Law Review* 18:2 (March): 98–102.

Krasner, Stephen (ed.). 1983. *International Regimes*. Ithaca: Cornell University Press.

Krislov, Samuel. 1997. *How Nations Choose Standards and Standards Change Nations*. Pittsburgh: University of Pittsburgh Press.

———. and David H. Rosenbloom. 1981. *Representative Bureaucracy and the American Political System*. New York: Praeger.

Krueger, Anne O. 1974. "The Political Economy of the Rent-Seeking Society," *American Economic Review* 64 (June): 291–303.

Laffont, Jean, and Jean Tirole. 1993. *A Theory of Incentives in Procurement and Regulation*. Cambridge: MIT Press.

Larouche, Pierre. 2000. *Competition Law and Regulation in European Telecommunications*. Oxford and Portland OR: Hart Publishing.

Laudati, Laraine. 1996. "The European Commission as Regulator: The Uncertain Pursuit of the Competitive Market," in Giandomenico Majone (ed.), *Regulating Europe*. London: Routledge.

Laver, Michael, and Kenneth A. Shepsle. 1997. "Government Accountability in Parliamentary Democracy," mimeo.

Leibfried, Stephan. 1992. "Towards a European Welfare State?" in Walter R. Heinz (ed.), *Status Passages and the Life Course Vol. III: Institutions and Gatekeeping in the Life Course*. Weinheim: Deutscher Studien Verlag.

Leibfried, Stephan, and Paul Pierson. 1995. *European Social Policy: Between Fragmentation and Integration*. Washington DC: The Brookings Institution.

Lijphart, Arend. 1984. *Democracies: Patterns of Majorities and Consensus Government in Twenty-One Countries*. New Haven CT: Yale University Press.

———. 1991. "Majority Rule in Theory and Practice: The Tenacity of a Flawed Paradigm," *International Social Science Journal* 129, 483–93.

———, Ronald Rogowski, and R. Kent Weaver. 1993. "Separation of Powers and Cleavage Management," in R. Kent Weaver and Bert A. Rockman (eds.), *Do Institutions Matter?* Washington DC: The Brookings Institution.

Linder, Wolf. 1983. "Entwicklung, Strukturen und Funktionen des Wirtschafts- und Sozialstaats Schweiz," in Alois Riklin (ed.), *Handbuch Politisches System der Schweiz*, Band 1, 255–382. Bern: Paul Haupt.

———. 1999. *Schweizerische Demokratie: Institutionen, Prozesse, Strukturen*. Bern: Paul Haupt.

Linz, Juan. 1984. "Democracy: Presidential or Parliamentary. Does It Make a Difference?" Manuscript, Yale University.

Lipset, Seymour Martin. 1960. *Political Man*. Garden City, NY: Doubleday.

Litan, Robert E., and William D. Nordhaus. 1983. *Reforming Federal Regulation*. New Haven, CT: Yale University Press.

Locke, John. [1690] 1996. "An Essay Concerning the True, Original, Extent and End of Civil Government." http://www.ilt.columbia.edu/publications/locke_understanding.html.

Lodge, Juliet (ed.). 1993. *The European Community and the Challenge of the Future* (2nd ed.). New York: St. Martin's Press.

Madison, James. [1787] 1981. "The Federalist, No. 10," in R. E. Fairfield (ed.), from the 1787 original texts by Alexander Hamilton, James Madison, and John Jay, *The Federalist Papers* (2nd ed.). Baltimore: Johns Hopkins University Press.

Maier, Lothar. 1993. "Institutional Consumer Representation in the European Community," *Journal of Consumer Policy* 16(3–4), 355–74.

Majone, Giandomenico. 1996. *Regulating Europe*. London: Routledge.

———. 1997a. "From the Positive to the Regulatory State: Causes and Consequences of Changes in the Mode of Governance." Working Paper 93. Madrid: Instituto Juan March de Estudios Investigaciones.

———. 1997b. "The New European Agencies: Regulation by Information," *Journal of European Public Policy* 4:2 (June): 262–75.

———. 1998. "The Regulatory State and Its Legitimacy Problems," Institut für Höhere Studien (HIS), Vienna.

Manin, Bernard. 1994. "Checks, Balances, and Boundaries: The Separation of Powers in the Constitutional Debate of 1787," in Biancamaria Fontana (ed.), *The Invention of the Modern Republic*. Cambridge: Cambridge University Press.

———. 1997. *Principles of Representative Government*. Cambridge/New York: Cambridge University Press.

———. Adam Przeworski, and Susan Stokes. 1999. *Democracy, Accountability, and Representation*. Oxford: Cambridge University Press.

Mattli, Walter, and Anne-Marie Slaughter. 1995. "Law and Politics in the European Union," *International Organization* 94:1, 183–90.

Mayhew, David R. 1974. *Congress: The Electoral Connection*. New Haven: Yale University Press.

Mazey, Sonia, and Jeremy Richardson. 1993. "Environmental Groups and the EC: Challenges and Opportunities," in David Judge (ed.), *A Green Dimension for the European Community: Political Issues and Processes*, 109–128. London: Frank Cass.

McConnell, Grant. 1966. *Private Power and American Democracy*. New York: Knopf.

McCubbins, Matthew D., and Thomas Schwartz. 1984. "Congressional Oversight Overlooked: Police Patrols versus Fire Alarms," *American Journal of Political Science* 28, 165–79.

McCubbins, Matthew D., Roger G. Noll, and Barry R. Weingast. 1989. "Structure and Process, Politics and Policy: Administrative Arrangements and the Political Control of Agencies," *Virginia Law Review* 75:1 (March): 431–82.

Michels, Robert. 1962. *Political Parties*. New York: The Free Press.

Mills, C. Wright. 1956. *The Power Elite*. New York: Oxford University Press.

Minford, Patrick. 1997. "Time-Inconsistency, Democracy, and Optimal Contingent Rules," *Oxford Economic Papers* 47, 192–210.

Moe, Terry M. 1985. "The Politicized Presidency," in John Chubb and Paul E. Peterson (eds.), *New Directions in American Politics*, Washington DC: Brookings Institution.

———. 1990. "The Politics of Structural Choice: Toward a Theory of Public Bureaucracy," in Oliver E. Williamson (ed.), *Organization Theory. From Chester Barnard to the Present and Beyond*, 116–53. Oxford: Oxford University Press.

Monti, Mario. 2000. "European Competition Policy for the 21st Century," paper delivered at the 28th Annual Conference on International Antitrust Law and Policy, Fordham Corporate Law Institute, 19–20 October.

Moravcsik, Andrew. 1995. "Liberal Intergovernmentalism and Integration: A Rejoinder," *Journal of Common Market Studies* 33:4, 611–28.

Mosca, Gaetano. 1923. *Elementi di Scienza Politica* (2nd ed.). Turin: Fratelli Bocca Editori.

Neale, Alan D., and D. G. Goyder. 1980. *The Antitrust Laws of the United States of America* (3rd ed.). New York: Cambridge University Press.

Neunreither, Karl-Heinz. 1994. "The Democratic Deficit of the European Union: Towards Closer Cooperation between the European Parliament and the National Parliaments," *Government and Opposition* 29:3, 299–314.

Neven, Damien, Robin Nuttall, and Paul Seabright. 1993. *Mergers in Daylight: The Economics and Politics of European Merger Control*. London: Centre for Economic Policy Research.

Neven, Damien J., and Thomas von Ungern-Sternberg. 1997. "Swiss Competition Policy in the Last Decade," in Philippe Bacchetta and Walter Wasserfallen (eds.), *Economic Policy in Switzerland*, 35–61. London: MacMillan Press.

Neven, Damien J., and Pascal Raess. 1999. "Politique de la concurrence on Suisse (1996–1998): Evaluation et perspectives d'évolution," Rapport présenté à la Commission fédérale des questions conjoncturelles. Université de Lausanne. Manuscript.

Newman, Michael. 1996. *Democracy, Sovereignty and the European Union*. New York: St. Martin's Press.

Niskanen, William. 1971. *Bureaucracy and Representative Government*. Chicago: Aldine-Atherton.

Nixon, Raymond B. 1960. "Factors Related to Freedom in National Press Systems," *Journalism Quarterly* 37, 13–28.

Noll, Roger G. 1989. "Economic Perspectives on the Politics of Regulation," in R. Schmalensee and R. D. Willing, *Handbook of Industrial Organization* 11. Elsevier Science Publishers B.V., 1253–87.

Nugent, Neill. 1994. *The Government and Politics of the European Union* (3rd ed.). Durham NC: Duke University Press.

———. 1995. "The Leadership Capacity of the European Commission," *Journal of European Public Policy* 2:4 (December): 603–23.

Page, Alan C. 1982. "Member States' Public Undertakings and Article 90," *European Law Review* 7, 19–35.

Peltzman, Sam. 1976. "Toward a More General Theory of Regulation," *Journal of Law and Economics* 19, 211–40.

———. 1984. "Constituent Interest and Congressional Voting," *Journal of Law and Economics* (April): 181–210.

Persson, Torsten, and Guido Tabellini. 1994. "Designing Institutions for Monetary Stability," in Persson and Tabellini (eds.), *Monetary and Fiscal Policy*, vol. 1: Credibility, ch. 12. Cambridge, MA: MIT Press.

Persson, Torsten, Gérard Roland, and Guido Tabellini. 1996. "Separation of Powers and Accountability: Towards a Formal Approach to Comparative Politics," Discussion Paper No. 1475, Centre for Economic Policy Research, London, September.

Peters, B. Guy. 1992. "Bureaucratic Politics and the Institutions of the European Community," in Sbragia (ed.), *Euro-Politics*, 75–122. Washington DC: The Brookings Institution.

———. 1994. "Agenda-Setting in the European Community," *Journal of European Public Policy* 1, 9–26.

Peterson, John. 1994. "Subsidiarity: A definition to Suit Any Vision?" *Parliamentary Affairs* 47, 117–32.

———. 1995. "Decision-Making in the European Union: Towards a Framework for Analysis," *Journal of European Public Policy* 2:1 (March): 69–93.

Pierson, Paul. 1996. "The Path to European Integration: A Historical Institutionalist Perspective," *Comparative Political Studies* 29(2), 123–63.

Pinder, John. 1998. *The Building of the European Union* (3rd ed.). Oxford/New York: Oxford University Press.

———. (ed.). 1999. *Foundations of Democracy in the European Union: From the Genesis of Parliamentary Democracy to the European Parliament*. London/New York: Macmillan/St. Martin's Press.

Pitkin, Hanna F. 1967. *The Concept of Representation*. Berkeley: University of California Press.

Pollack, Mark A. 1997. "Delegation, Agency, and Agenda Setting in the European Community," *International Organization* 51:1, 99–134.

———. 1997. "Representing Diffuse Interests in EC Policy-Making." *Journal of European Public Policy*, 4:4 (December): 572–90.

———. 2000. "The End of Creeping Competence? EU Policy-Making since Maastricht," *Journal of Common Market Studies* 38:3 (September): 519–38.

———. and Gregory C. Shaffer. 2001. "The Challenge of Reconciling Regulatory Differences: Food Safety and GMOs in the Transatlantic Relationship," in Pollack and Shaffer (eds.), *Transatlantic Governance in the Global Economy*, 153–78. Lanham, MD: Rowman & Littlefield.

Porter, Michael. 1985. *Competitive Advantage*. New York: Free Press.

Przeworski, Adam. 1991. *Democracy and the Market*. Cambridge: Cambridge University Press.

Putnam, Robert D., and Nicholas Bayne. 1984. *Hanging Together: Cooperation and Conflict in the Seven-Power Summits*. Cambridge: Harvard University Press.

Quirk, Paul. 1980. "Food and Drug Administration," in James Q. Wilson (ed.), *The Politics of Regulation*. New York: Basic Books.

Rodrick, Dani. 1996. "Why Do More Open Economies Have Bigger Governments?" NBER Working Paper No. 5537.
Rose-Ackerman, Susan. 1992. *Rethinking the Progressive Agenda: The Reform of the American Regulatory State*. New York: Free Press.
Rosenblum, David H. 1983. *Public Administration and Law*. New York and Basel: Marcel Dekker.
Ross, George. 1995. "Assessing the Delors Era and Social Policy," in Stephan Leibfried and Paul Pierson (eds.), *European Social Policy: Between Fragmentation and Integration*. Washington DC: The Brookings Institution.
Sanchez de Cuenca, Ignacio. 1997. "The Democratic Dilemmas of the European Union," Manuscript.
Sbragia, Alberta M. (ed.). 1992. *Euro-Politics: Institutions and Policy-Making in the New European Community*. Washington DC: Brookings Institution.
———. 1993. "The European Community: A Balancing Act," *Publius* 23, 23–38.
Scharpf, Fritz W. 1988. "The Joint Decision Trap: Lessons from German Federalism and European Integration," *Public Administration* 66, 239–78.
———. 1996. "Negative and Positive Integration in the Political Economy of European Welfare States," in G. Marks, F. W. Scharpf, P. C. Schmitter, and W. Streeck (eds.), *Governance in the European Union*, 15–39. London: Sage.
———. 1997a. *Games Real Actors Play: Actor-Centered Institutionalism in Policy Research*. Boulder CO: Westview.
———. 1997b. "Economic Integration, Democracy and the Welfare State," *Journal of European Public Policy* 4:2 (March): 219–42.
———. 1997c. "Introduction: The Problem-Solving Capacity of Multi-Level Governance," *Journal of European Public Policy* 4:4 (December): 520–38.
———. 1999. *Governing Europe*. Oxford: Oxford University Press.
Schelling, Thomas C. 1978. *Micromotives and Macrobehavior*. New York: Norton.
Schmidt, Susanne. 1998. "Commission Activism: Subsuming Telecommunications and Electricity under European Competition Law," *Journal of European Public Policy* 5:1 (March): 169–84.
Schmitter, Philippe C. 1981. "Neokorporatismus: Überlegungen zur bisherigen Theorie und zur weiteren Praxis," in Ulrich von Alemann (ed.), *Neokorporatismus*. Frankfurt: Campus.
Schneider, Andrew C. 1994. *Domestic Choices, International Markets. Dismantling National Barriers and Liberalizing Securities Markets*. Ann Arbor: University of Michigan Press.
Schultze, Charles L. 1968. *The Politics and Economics of Public Spending*. Washington, DC: Brookings Institution.
Schumpeter, Joseph A. [1942] 1976. *Capitalism, Socialism, and Democracy*. London: George Allen & Unwin.
Seabright, Paul. 1996. "Accountability and Decentralization in Government: An Incomplete Contracts Model," *European Economic Review* 40, 61–89.
Seidman, Harold, and Robert Gilmour. 1986. *Politics, Position, and Power* (4th ed.). New York: Oxford University Press.
Selznick, Philip. 1985. "Focusing Organizational Research on Regulation," in Roger G. Noll (ed.), *Regulatory Policy and the Social Sciences*. Berkeley and Los Angeles: University of California Press.

Shapiro, Martin. 1992. "The Giving-Reasons Requirement." *The University of Chicago Legal Forum*, 180–220.

———. 1997. "The Problems of Independent Agencies in the United States and the European Union," *Journal of European Public Policy* 4:2 (June): 276–91.

Shepherd, William G. 2000. "Wrong Numbers: MCI Worldcom, Sprint, and Monopoly Power in the Long-Distance Market." Washington DC: Economic Policy Institute Briefing Paper. http://epinet.org

Shepsle, Kenneth A., and Barry R. Weingast. 1987. "The Institutional Foundations of Committee Power," *American Political Science Review* 81, 85–104.

Slomanson, William R. 1995. *Fundamental Perspectives on International Law*. Minneapolis/Saint Paul: West Publishing Company.

Spitz, Elaine. 1984. *Majority Rule*. Chatham NJ: Chatham House Publishers.

Stewart, Joseph, Jr., and Jane S. Cromartie. 1982. "Partisan Presidential Change and Regulatory Policy: The Case of the FTC Deceptive Practices Cases, 1938–1974." *Presidential Studies Quarterly* 12, 568–73.

Stewart, Terence P., and David S. Johanson. 1999. "Policy in Flux: The European Union's Laws on Agricultural Biotechnology and Their Effects on International Trade," *Drake Journal of Agricultural Law* 4, 243–95.

Stigler, George J. 1971. "The Theory of Economic Regulation," *Bell Journal of Economics and Management Science* 6(2): 3–21.

———. 1975. *The Citizen and the State: Essays on Regulation*. Chicago: University of Chicago Press.

Stokes, Susan. 1999. "What Do Policy Switches Tell Us about Democracy?" in Bernard Manin, Adam Przeworski, and Susan Stokes, *Democracy, Accountability, and Representation*, chapter 3. Oxford: Cambridge University Press.

Stone, Alan. 1977. *Economic Regulation and the Public Interest: The Federal Trade Commission in Theory and Practice*. Ithaca: Cornell University Press.

Streeck, Wolfgang. 1996. "Neo-voluntarism: A New European Social Policy Regime?" in G. Marks, F. W. Scharpf, P. C. Schmitter and W. Streeck (eds.), *Governance in the European Union*, 64–94. London: Sage.

———. 1997. "Industrial Citizenship Under Regime Competition: The Case of the European Works Councils," *Journal of European Public Policy* 4:4 (December): 643–64.

———. and Philippe C. Schmitter. 1991. "From National Corporatism to Transnational Pluralism: Organized Interests in the Single European Market," *Politics and Society* 19(2), 133–64.

Sunstein, Cass R. 1990. *After the Rights Revolution: Reconceiving the Regulatory State*. Cambridge, MA: Harvard University Press.

Sutherland, S. L. 1993. "Independent Review Agencies and Accountability: Should Democracy Be on Autopilot?" *Optimum* 24(2): 23–40.

Swiss Federal Council. 1994. "Botschaft zu einem Bundesgesetz über Kartelle und andere Wettbewerbsbeschränkungen" [message on a federal law about cartels and other competition constraints], 23 November 1994.

———. 1996. "Article 48.2, Verordnung zur Fusionskontrolle" [ordinance on merger control], 17 June 1996.

Thomas, Robert. 1997. "Reason-Giving in English and European Community Administrative Law," *European Public Law*, 3:2, 213–22.

Tinbergen, Jan. 1965. *International Economic Integration* (2nd ed.). Amsterdam: Elsevier.
Treaty on European Union. 1992. *Official Journal of the European Communities*, C224, 31 August 1992.
Tsebelis, George. 1994. "The Power of the European Parliament as a Conditional Agenda Setter," *American Political Science Review* 88, 128–42.
———. and Geoffrey Garrett. 1999. "Legislative Politics in the European Union." Manuscript. UCLA and Yale University.
University of Illinois. 1999. *The Economics and Politics of Genetically Modified Organisms: Implications for WTO 2000*, Bulletin 809, November.
U.S. Department of Justice and Federal Trade Commission. 1995. *Antitrust Enforcement Guidelines for International Operations*. April. www.usdoj.gov/atr
Van der Krol, A. R., P. E. Lenting, J. Veenstra, I. M. van der Meer, R. E. Koes, A. G. M. Gerats, J. N. M. Mol, and A. R. Stuitje. 1988. "An Anti-Sense Chalcone Synthase Gene in Transgenic Plants Inhibits Flower Pigmentation." *Nature* 333: 866–69.
Vanhanen, Tatu. 1992. *The Process of Democratization*. New York: Crane Russack.
Vaubel, Roland. 1995. *The Centralization of Western Europe*. London: Institute of Economic Affairs, IEA Hobart Paper 127.
Veljanovski, C. 1987. *Selling the State*. London: Weidenfeld & Nicolson.
Vogel, David. 1995. *Trading Up: Consumer and Environmental Regulation in a Global Economy*. Cambridge, MA: Harvard University Press.
Volcansek, Mary L. 1992. "The European Court of Justice: Supranational Policy-Making," *West European Politics* 15:3, 109–21.
Wallace, Helen. 1983. "Negotiation, Conflict and Compromise: The Elusive Pursuit of Common Policies," in Helen Wallace, William Wallace, and Carole Webb (eds.). 1983. *Policy-Making in the European Community*. Chichester: John Wiley & Sons.
Warren, Charles. 1991. "Legislative and Judicial Attacks on the Supreme Court of the United States—A History of the Twenty-Fifth Section of the Judiciary Act," *The American Law Review* 47, 184–185.
Weale, Albert. 1996. "Environmental Regulation and Administrative Reform in Britain," in Giandomenico Majone, *Regulating Europe*, 106–30. Pub. info.
Weber, Eugen Joseph. 1976. *Peasants into Frenchmen: The Modernization of Rural France, 1870–1914*. Stanford, CA: Stanford University Press.
Weber, Max. 1946. "Bureaucracy," in Hans H. Gerth and C. Wright Mills (eds.), *From Max Weber: Essays in Sociology*. Oxford: Oxford University Press.
Weiler, Joseph H. H. 1991a. "Problems of Legitimacy in Post-1992 Europe," *Aussenwirtschaft* 46, 411–37.
———. 1991b. "The Transformation of Europe," *Yale Law Journal* 100:3, 2403–37.
———. 1992. "After Maastricht: Community Legitimacy in Post–1992 Europe," in William James Adams (ed.), *Singular Europe: Economy and Polity of the European Community after 1992*, 11–41. Ann Arbor: University of Michigan Press.
———. 1997. "To Be a European Citizen—Eros and Civilization," *Journal of European Public Policy* 4:4 (December): 495–519.
———. Ulrich Haltern, and Franz Mayer. 1995. "European Democracy and Its Critique," *West European Politics* 18:3, 1–39.

Weingast, Barry R. 1984. "The Congressional-Bureaucratic System: A Principal Agent Perspective," *Public Choice* 44, 147–91.

Weingast, Barry R., and Mark J. Moran. 1983. "Bureaucratic Discretion or Congressional Control? Regulatory Policymaking by the Federal Trade Commission," *Journal of Political Economy* 91:5, 765–800.

Weissman, Robert. 2000. "TABD: Corporate Conspiracy," *Focus on the Corporation*, 19 November.

Whish, Richard. 1989; 1993. *Competition Law* (2nd ed.; 3rd ed.). London: Butterworth.

Wildavsky, Aaron. 1964. *The Politics of the Budgetary Process*. Boston: Little Brown.

Williams, Nigel. 1998. "Agricultural Biotech Faces Backlash in Europe," *Science* (7 August): 768.

Williams, Shirley. 1991. "Sovereignty and Accountability in the European Community," in Robert O. Keohane, and Stanley Hoffman (eds.), *The New European Community. Decision-Making and Institutional Change*. Boulder: Westview Press.

Williamson, Oliver E. 1985. *The Economic Institutions of Capitalism*. New York: Free Press.

Wilson, James Q. 1975. "The Rise of the Administrative State," *The Public Interest* 41 (Fall): 77–103.

Wincott, Daniel. 1995. "The Role of Law or The Rule of the Court of Justice? An 'Institutional' Account of Judicial Politics in the European Community," *Journal of European Public Policy* 2:4 (December): 583–602.

Wood, B. Dan, and Richard Waterman. 1994. *Bureaucratic Dynamics: The Role of Bureaucracy in a Democracy*, chapter 5. Boulder: Westview Press.

Yandle, Bruce. 1985. "FTC Activity and Presidential Effects," *Presidential Studies Quarterly* 15, 128–35.

Young, Alasdair R. 1995. "Participation and Policymaking in the European Community: Mediating Contending Interests." Paper presented at the Biannual Conference of the European Community Studies Association, Charleston, SC, 11–14 May.

Zweifel, Thomas D. 2002. "Who Is without Sin Cast the First Stone: The EU's Democratic Deficit in Comparison," *Journal of European Public Policy* 9:3 (June).

———. and Patricio Navia. 2000. "Democracy, Dictatorship, and Infant Mortality," *Journal of Democracy* 11:2 (April): 99–114.

Subject Index

Accountability: bureaucratic, 65, 74–76, *141*; and independence, 76–77, 81, 99; indirect, 26; lack of . . . in EU, 12, 14, 17–21, 23, 26, 28, *41*, 42–43, 63, 114; measure of democracy *59*, *60*; regulatory state, xiii, 74–76, *141*; through checks and balances, 16, 31–33, 38; through elections, 14, 18, *141*; Administrative Procedure Act, United States (1946), 66, 79, 119, 139
agency theory, 65–74; as basis for bureaucratic democracy theory, 74–81
Alliance for Bio-Integrity, 120
AMEA. *See* European Agency for the Evaluation of Medical Products
Amsterdam, Treaty of, 25, *42*, 47, 50, 108
ANEC. *See* European Association for Representation of Consumers in Standardization
appointment: biotechnology policy, 113, 117, 122, 125, *128*, 128–129, *136*; of courts, 16, 38; dimension of bureaucratic democracy, 76, 78, 81; merger policy, 86–86, 93, 97, *101*, 100–101, *136*. *See also* European Parliament, appointment and dismissal powers

Barro-Gordon model, 77
Biotechnology Industry Organization (BIO), 107, 116, 120–123, 130
blame-shirking, 67–68
Brazil, 131
Brownlow Commission, 78
Bundesrat. *See* Swiss Federal Council
Bundesamt für Gesundheit (BAG). *See* Swiss Federal Office for Public Health
bureaucratic democracy, 135; assumptions, *141*; comparisons between polities, 83, *100*, 101, 127–131, *128, 136*, 136–138; seven dimensions of, 74–81; theoretical basis for, 69–74. *See also* agency theory; ways to strengthen, 136–138

"California effect," 39
Campaign to Ban Genetically Engineered Foods, 107
Cantons. *See* Switzerland, as decentralized

capital mobility, 40, 113
checks and balances, 3–4, 7, 15–16, 30, 32, 57, 76, 138, *141*
Clayton Act (1914), *92*, 92–93
Comités de Représentants Permanents (COREPER), 74; *See also* European Council of Ministers, delegation of power
Comité Européen de Normalisation (CEN), 20, 31–32, *41*
comitology, 27, 32, *41*
Commission of the EU: accountability of, 33–35, *41*, 86–87; agenda setter, 73–74; biotechnology policy, *106*, 108, *109*, 110–115, 130; captured by industry, *41*, 108; Competition Directorate, *84*, *85*, 85–89, 91; competition policy, 35, *84*, *85*, 84–91, 101, 135–136; Environment Directorate, *106*, 113; environmental policy 35; executive functions, 46–47, *143*; Health And Consumer Protection Directorate, *106*, 113; politicized, 18; powers of, 27, 31, 33–35, 43; recommendations for improvement of, 138; selection of, 18, 42–43, 49–50, 86; structure of, 33–34; support of non-governmental organizations, 108, 114; trust in, 19;
companies. *See* corporation
Common Agricultural Policy (CAP), 18
Common Market, proper functioning of, 109
Congress, U.S., 10n2, 26, 29, 49, 51, 82n5, 140, 144; approval of nominations, 93, 100; biotechnology, laissez-faire response to, *106*, 118, 121–123, 128, 130; compared to European Parliament, 49, 54; control over agencies, 69–73, 95, 130; delegation of powers, 66–67, 119–120; merger regulation, *84*, 94; 137; power of purse, 50, 100; oversight of agencies, 72, 79, 80, 120, 128, 145n1. *See also* Senate of the United States

congressional control theories, 71–74. *See also* agency theory
Consumer's Consultative Council, 108
Copenhagen Summit (1993), 23
Corporation: analogy for government, 16, 71; mobility of, 21, 39. *See also* globalization; public wariness of, 124, 130, 138; socially conscious 130; target of environmentalists, 106–107, 130; overly powerful, 64n10, 91–92. *See also* Industry
Court of First Instance (CFI), *84*, 89–90, 102n13

"Delaware effect," 21, 39–43
de Havilland merger, 87, 91
de minimus rule, 87
democracy, measures of: Alvarez et al., 46–47, *46*, *61*; Bollen, 47–51, *48*, *61*; Coppedge & Reinicke, 51, *52*, *61*; Freedom House, 51–55, *53–54*, *61*; Gasiorowski, 55, *56–57*, *61*; Gastil, 55–57, *58*, *61–62*; Gurr, 57–60, *59*, *62*; Vanhanen, 64n13
democracy, definitions of, 6–8, 46, 47, 51–52, 55, *61–62*
democratic deficit, xii–xiii, 2, 8, 9, 136; arguments, 11–43; causes of, 142, 145; contrasted with bureaucratic democracy, 74; democratization, 64n3; of the EU, xi, 14, 138–140
demos/demoi: in Europe, 12–15, 16, 24–26, *41*; in Switzerland/U.S., 24–25, *41*
diffuse interests: access to agencies, 67, 76, 142; represented by European Parliament, 22, 113. *See also* European Union, diffuse interests in; *and* United States, diffuse interests in, *and* Switzerland, diffuse interests in
direct democracy, 139. *See also,* Switzerland, referenda
direct effect (of EU law), 4, 20, 20–21, 36, 87
direct/indirect elections, 46–47
Directorate B, *85*, 86, 89

Environmental Protection Agency (EPA), 72, 117
Eurobarometer, 12, 19, 26, 41
European Agency for the Evaluation of Medical Products (AMEA), 31
European agencies. *See* European bureaucracy
European Association for the Representation of Consumers in Standardization (ANEC), 31
European bureaucracy: accountability of, 18; network coordinators, 32; commitment-holders, 32, 73–74
European Center for Drug and Drug Addiction, 31
European Central Bank, xii,8, 12, 16, 19, 83; as accountable, 30–31; as check on executive, 31; as federalizing agent, 4; as undemocratic 19
European Coal and Steel Community, xii, 25, 145; *See also* Treaty of Paris
European Community (EEC, EC), *See* European Union
European Constitutional Council, proposal of, 139
European Convent, xi–xii. *See also,* democratizing the EU
European Council of Heads of State and Government, 29, 33, 34; as executive, 46
European Council of Ministers, xi, 12, 15, 18, 29, 33; biotechnology policy, *106,* 108–110, *109,* 112–113, 128; delegation within 74; dominant role of 14; executive aspects, 46; legislative aspects, 48; *143;* merger policy, 84, *84, 85,* 87, 101; transparency in 15, 26–28, 43. *See also* Comités de Représentants Permanents; *and* qualified majority voting; *and* modified codecision
European Court of Justice, 22, 101; accountability of, 12, 35–36, *42;* activism, 20–21, 36–37; biotechnology, jurisdiction over, *106,* 108, 114–115; caseload, 20, 89; cases, 31, 48, 84, 87; compared with U.S. Supreme Court, 36–39, *42; Costa v. ENEL,* 4, 36; decision-making structure of, 37; *Etablissements Consten and Grundig v. Commission,* 90; federalist, 4; 20–21, 36–37; *Germany v. Commission,* 142; *Internationale Handelsgesellschaft v. EVGF,* 36; judicial review in, 4, 20, 83, 89–90, 94, 103n16, 114–115, 142; legitimacy of, 20–21, 142; merger policy, *84, 85, 85,* 89–90; *Meroni v. High Authority,* 31; *Phillip Morris/Rothmans,* 84; *Simmental II,* 36; *Van Gend en Loos,* 4, 87. *See also* direct effect, doctrine of, *and* supremacy, doctrine of
European Environment Agency, 31
European Food Authority, 112
European identity. *See* demos in Europe
European monetary union (EMU), xii, 2
European Parliament, xi, 15, 18, 29, 48; appointment and dismissal powers, 30, 49–50, 63n3, 73, 86, 113; budgetary powers, 32, 50; criticism of EU Commission, 110; codecision-making with Council, 49–50, 112; effectiveness of, 17, 22–23, 29–30, *41,* 43–48; GMO policy, 110–113; merger policy, 87, 89, 90, 101; as only elected supranational institution in EU, 12, 29, 42, 110, 141; political aspects, 33, 50–51; recommendations for improving, 138; voter turnout in elections for, 17–18, 26, 29–30
European Union: bicameral legislature, 46, 48–51, 52, *58, 63,* 65, *143;* biotechnology policy, *106,* 106, 108–115, *109, 128,* 128–131; citizenship of, 14, 25; civil society in, 13, 26; diffuse interests in, 67, 109, 113, 128, 137; decentralization in 75, 87, 139. *See also* subsidiarity; enlargement of, xii–xiii, 9, 14, 16,

23, 28, 34, *41;* as federal state, xii, 1–5, 83; intergovernmental aspects of, 1, 3, 22, 27, 29; legitimacy of, 12–15, 21–22; merger policy, xiii, 6, 35, 83–91, *85, 100,* 101;plural society, 80; principal-agent problem, 73–74; as regulatory state, xii, 1, 18–19, 42, 66, 142, *143;* social policy in 12, 21–23, 39–41, *42,* 64n12, 81n2; taxation, 3, 66–67, 139; transparency in, 12, 15–16, 88–89, 114; tripartite decision-making in, 34. *See also* Commission of the European Union, European Parliament; *and* European Council of Ministers; *and* Pillars of EU

FDA. *See* Food and Drug Administration
Federal Commerce Commission (FCC), 79, 120
Federal Reserve Bank, 8, 31
Federal Trade Commission (FTC), 71, 79, *84, 92,* 92–95, 100, 137–138
federalism, 5, 10n3, 30–31. *See also* European Union, as federal state
Federalist Papers. See Madison, James; *and* Hamilton, Alexander
Food and Drug Administration (FDA), *106,* 115, *116,* 118–123, 128, 130–131
Food and Drug Act (1906), 118
Food, Drug and Cosmetics Act (1938), 118
Fourth Research and Technological Development (RTD) Framework Programme, 30, 48
Friends of the Earth, 113, 129
functionalism, 67

genetic drift, 117–118
genetically modified foods (GMOs): arguments for, 105. *See also* Biotech Industry Organization; companies that will not use, 106, 131; definition of, 105; public views in EU of , 107, 115, 131; public views in Switzerland of, 107, 124, 126; public views in the U.S. of, 106, 112, 116, 119, 133n7
gender equality, 44n12, 64n10, 125
Germany, 5, 49, 84; cartel politics in, 66, 91, 104n27; constitution of, 3, 26
Giscard D'Estaing, Valérie, xi
globalization, 1, 21, 40
Greenpeace, 107, 113, 124, 129–130
Grocery Manufacturers of America, 116–117

Haider, Jörg, xii
Hamilton, Alexander, 77
harmonization of national policies, 34. *See also* Single Europe Act
Healy-Baker Survey, 107

independence: and accountability, xiii, 63, 65, 76; biotechnology policy, 115, 122–123, 127–129, *128, 136;* central bank, 19, 31; from popular pressures in early U.S. history, 76–79; legal/formal versus actual, 78; merger policy, 90–91, 95, 99–101, *101, 136,* 138
industry: advocacy of GMOs in U.S., 111, 117, 119, 120–122, 130–132; influence on agencies, 69, 78, *106,* 117–119, 121, 128, 137–138; interaction with EU Commission, 86, 88, 108, 112, 112–113; part of Swiss consensual politics, 125–127
information asymmetries, 8, 10n6, 69–70, 74, 81n4, 82n6, 141
information agencies, concept of, 31
integration: cultural, 63; economic, 21, 39, 142; European political, xi, 9, 13, 17, 23, 25–26, 36, 74, 142; linguistic, 6; negative, 12, 22–23, 42, 43; positive, 22–23; regional, 1
interest group politics, 69, 72, 78, 113–114, 127, 137
international law, 4
international organization, xii–xiii, 1, 3
international regimes, 1
Interstate Commerce Act (1887), 72

Interstate Commerce Commission (ICC), 79

judicial review, 30, 76, 94, 138–139, 142; in Switzerland, 126, 138; in the U.S., 77, 92, 94, 100. *See also* European Court of Justice, judicial review in

Kartellgesetz, *96*
Kefauver amendments, 118, 122
Keynesian economics, 3, 22, 67, 127
Legitimacy, 32, 37: Commission's, 112, 114; Council of Ministers', 17; demos as requirement of 12–14, 24–26, 62–63; popular vote as requirement for, 29, 49, 99; procedural versus substantive, *141, 142*; transfer of, 14, 69, *144*

Luxembourg Compromise, 16, 28, 37

Maastricht Treaty, 18–19, 25, 27, 63n3, 83; establishing codecision and other legislative procedures, 34–35, 40, 47; limiting the European Court of Justice, 37; viewed by critics, xii, 2–3; Social Protocol, 34; Madison, James, xi, 25, 76–77
majoritarian model of democracy, 17, 28–29, 30, *41*, 44n14, 55, 136, 140–141. *See also* non-majoritarian model of democracy
Martin v. Hunter's Lessee, 38
Member State Competent Authorities (MSCA), *109*, 113
Merger Regulation Act, 86–88
Meroni Doctrine 80
modified codecision, 50
monitoring: agents, by principal, 66, 68, 71, 76; biotechnology policy, 35, 112, 115, 121–122, 126–127, *128*, 128–129; by Congress, 71–72, 95, 118, 121–122; of member-state budgets by Commission, 18; merger policy, 35, 90, 95, 99–101; mutual, 25
Monnet, Jean, 34

Monsanto, 106, 108, 133n36
Montreal Biosafety Protocol, 106
moral hazard, 70, 81n4
Moynihan, Senator Patrick, 121

nation, as imagined community, 24–25
nation-state, xiii, 2–3, 21
neo-liberalism, 21–22, 66–67
New Economics of Organization, 68
Nice Summit and Treaty, 15–16, 44n16, 49, 82n8, 86–87
non-majoritarian forms of government, 2, 30, 99
Novartis, 106, 108, 115, 124, 129, 133n7

Overrule: Amsterdam Treaty, negated by, 50; biotechnology policy, 114–115, 120, 126, *128*, 128–129, 136; Court of First Instance (CFI), 89–91; dimension of bureaucratic democracy, 76, 81, 138; Merger policy, 89–91, 94–95, *96*, 98–99, 100–101, *101, 136*; by referenda, 126, 129

Pareto optimality, 22, 28, 32, 44n14
Paris, Treaty of, 80, 83–84, 89
participation: biotechnology policy, 113, 118–119, 125, 127–129, *128, 136*; and democracy, 7, *53, 56, 57, 59*, 64n13; dimension of Bureaucratic democracy, 74–75, 81, 137, 142; indirect, 71; merger policy, 87–88, 93, 99, 100–101, *100, 136*; voter, 17, 26, 30, 64n13. *See also* diffuse interests
Pendleton Act (1883), 79
Pillars of EU policy: Common Foreign and Security Policy (Second Pillar), 6, 17, 29, 49; European Communities (First Pillar) 17, 29, 49; Justice and Home Affairs (Third Pillar), 6, 17, 29, 49
political rights, 64n11, 136; as measure of democracy, *48*, 51–59, *53, 54, 58, 61–62*
policy networks, 75

Preisüberwacher. *See* Switzerland, Price Supervisor
Preisüberwachungsgesetz, 99
principal-agent theory. *See* agency theory
privatization, 67
proportional representation, 3. *See also* majoritarian model of democracy

Qualified Majority Voting, 12, 16–17, 39, 34–35, *41*, 49–50, 82n8, 86, *109*, 110. *See also* EU Council of Ministers, decision-making in

Reagan Administration, 94–95, 122
redistribution as aspect of legitimacy, 21–23, 28–29, 39–40, 42
regulation, definition of, 66; direct versus indirect, 66
regulators, capture of, *41*, 63, 70, 75, 78–79, 95
regulatory competition. *See* "Delaware effect"
regulatory state, 36, 65, 80–81, 135, 140–144, *141*; rise of, 66–69. *See also* European Union, as regulatory state *and* United States, as regulatory state
rent seeking, 68
Rekurskommission. *See* Switzerland, Competition Appeals Commission
Rome, Treaty of, 33–34, 38, 41, 80, 84–85, 142; Article 177, 4, 38; as constitution of Europe, 20, 22
Roosevelt, Franklin Delano, 66, 78–79
RTD. *See* Fourth Research and Technological Framework Programme

Schmidt, Helmut, xi
Schweizerischer Bundesrat. *See* Swiss Federal Council
Schweizerische Bundesversammlung. *See* Swiss Federal Constitution
Securities and Exchange Commission (SEC), 79, 81n5
Senate of the United States, 15, 37, 46, 51, 137, 144

separation of powers, 15, 30, 32, 104n27, 120, 140
Sherman Anti-Trust Act, 85, *92*, 92–93
Single European Act (SEA), 30, 41, 50, 84, 108
sovereignty, xii–xiii, 3, 5, 38–39, 142
statutory law, 6
strategy and negotiation theory, 73
subsidiarity, 27–28, 32, 102n11
sui generis school, l, 3, 5, *143*
supranational, xii, 12, 20, 25, 29, 83; supranational institutions, 29, 31, 33–34; supranationalism, 25. *See also* European Parliament, as only elected supranational actor in EU
Supremacy Clause, 36, 79
supremacy, doctrine of 20–21, 36, 37
Supreme Court of the United States, 16, *42*, 79, 84, *Chisholm v. Georgia*, 36; *Cohen v. Virginia*, 38; early ineffectiveness of, 36–38; *FTC v. Gratz*, 94; *FTC v. Sperry and Hutchinson & Company*, 95; *Humphrey v. United States*, 79; judicial review, 4, 16, 36, 94, 95; *Tassel v. Georgia*, 36–37; *United States v. Philadelphia National Bank*, 94; *Von's Grocery*, 94;
Swiss Federal Constitution, 5, 24, 47, 97, 123
Swiss Federal Council: activism of, 130; appointment of agency personnel, 125; biotechnology policy, *106*, 123–125; capture of, 100; merger policy, *84*, *96*, 96–99; selection of, 47, 126; structure of, 24, 125, 144
Swiss Federal Office for Public Health (BAG), *106*, *123*, 125–126
Switzerland: biotechnology policy, *106*, 106, *123*, 123–127, *128*, 129–130, *136*; Cartel Law (1995), 95–97, *96*; Competition Appeals Commission, *96*, 99; Competition Commission, *84*, *96*, 96–99, 101, 125; competition policy 9, 83, *84*, 95–101, *96*, *100*, *136*, 137; consensual democracy 127, 129; courts, *84*, *96*, 97–98;

decentralized government, 5–6, 97, 144; diffuse interests in, 128, 137; executive. *See* Swiss Federal Council; Federal Tribunal, 98; multicultural democracy, 24–25; national bank of, 8; Nationalrat, 51; referenda in, xii, 26, 123, 125–127, 129, 137, 144; Ständerat, 15, 46, 51; stasis in, 127, 144; taxation policy of, 5, 25

Technocracy, 55, 56, 80, 114
transaction costs, 68
Transatlantic Business Dialogue (TABD), 132
transnational problems and solutions, xiii, 1
transparency: in biotech policy, 114, 119, 126, 128, 128–129, 136; democratic deficit arguments, part of, 12, 15–16, 26–28, 41, 74; measure of bureaucratic democracy, 75, 81, 100, 128, 136, 142; in merger policy, 88–89, 93, 97–98, 100, 100–101
Treaty of European Community (TEC), *See* Rome, Treaty of
Treaty of European Union. *See* Maastricht Treaty

unanimity principle. *See* Luxembourg Compromise

United States Department of Agriculture (USDA), 106, 116, 117, 119
United States Department of Justice (DOJ), 84, 92, 93, 103n21, 137, 138
United States: biotechnology legislation, 121–122; biotechnology policy, 106, 115–123, 116, 128, 128–132; competition policy, 84, 85, 91–95, 92, 100, 135–137; Constitution of, 36, 66, 78–79, 137, 145; diffuse interests in, 128, 137, 140; election of President, 47, 63n2; judicial system, 4, 38, 77, 86, 92–93, 96, 100, 120, 138, 140, 144. *See also* Supreme Court of the United State; lack of faith in government, 130–131; merger policy. *See* United States competition policy; populism in, 88; as regulatory state, 1, 66; Supreme Court, 79
United States of Europe, xii

welfare state, viability of 39, 67. *See also* Keynesian economics
Westminster model of parliamentary democracy. *See* Majoritarian model
Westphalia, Treaty of, xii
World Trade Organization (WTO), 110, 131

Author Index

Ackerman, 145
Alvarez et al., 45–47, *46*, 60–63, *61*
Amman, 124, 132n3
Andersen and Eliassen, 5
Anderson, 24

Baake and Perschau, 91
Bane. *See* Putnam and Bane
Banks, *48*
Banks and Weingast, 72, 82n6
Barber, 136
Barro and Gordon, 77
Battle. *See* Hill and Battle
Bazerman and Neale, 73
Beard, 145
Bendor, 70, 76
Berghahn, 102n1
Bernstein, 78–79
Bhagwati, 81n3
Biotechnology Industry Organization, 107, 121–2, 130
Bogdanor and Woodcock, 23
Bollen, 26, 47–51, *48*, *61*, 64n13
Boner and Krueger, 93
Brent, 18
Brinkhorst, 50
British Medical Association, 106

Bryner, 118
Buchanan, 81n3
Bulmer, 76, 84
Burley and Mattli, 3, 12, 20–21, 37–38, 42

Calhoun, 37
Calvert et al., 71
Cameron, *41*
Cary, 21
Christiansen, 18, 33, *41–42*, 46
Cini and McGowan, 84, 87–88, 91, 94, 102n2, 103n16
Commission of the EU, 88–89,102n2, 103n15, 111–112, 114,
Coppedge and Reinicke, 45, 51, *52*, *61*
Cromartie. *See* Stewart and Cromartie
Cronin, 136

Dahl, 2, 7, 51, 55, 64n9,138–139
Dashwood, 32
Dehousse et al., 15, 32, 34, 46
Docksey and Williams, 30
Downs, 6
Dunn, 8–9

Earnshaw and Judge, 34, 48, 50
Echols, 131

Eichner, 12, 35, 47, 114
Eijffinger and de Hahn, 77–78
Eliassen. *See* Andersen and Eliassen
Eskridge and Ferejohn, 7, 66
European Court of Justice (ECJ), 4
Everson. *See* Dehousse et al.
Ewen and Puztai, 106

Fagan, 105
Federal Register, Vol. 57, 115–116, *116*
Ferejohn, 68. *See also* Eskridge and Ferejohn
Ferejohn and Shipan, 73
Fieberg, 102n13
Finer, 76
Fiorina, 7, 67–68
Franklin et al. 12, 15, *41*
Freedman, 81
Freedom House, 51–55, *53–54*

Gandhi, 44n11
Garrett. *See* Tsebelis and Garrett
Gastil, 45, 51, 55–57, *58*, 61–62
Gasiorowski, 55, *56–57, 61*
Gatsios and Seabright, 32
Genschel and Plümper, 39
Germann, 6, 97
Gilmour. *See* Seidman and Gilmour
Gilligan et al., 72
Goldstein, 4, 5, 27, 36–39
Gordon. *See* Barro and Gordon
Goyder, 88. *See also* Neale and Goyder
Greenwood et al., 5
Grote. *See* Greenwood et al.
Gruner, 127
Gurr et al., 45, 57–60,*59, 62*

Hahn, de. *See* Eijffinger and de Hahn
Haltern. *See* Weiler et al.
Hamilton, 77
Hartley, 36, 103n14
Hayes-Renshaw and Wallace, 12, 15, 17, 26, *41*, 46, 49
Held, 12, 21, 138–139
Héritier, 21, 25, 35, *42*, 74–75, 114
Hill and Battle, 107, 129, 131
Hix, 3–5, 10n2, 10n3, 57

Hölzler, 84
Horn, 68, 74
House of Lords, 88
Hug, 97
Hull, 33, *41*
Huntington, 6–7

Inkeles, 6

Jaggers. *See* Gurr et al.
Joerges. *See* Dehousse et al.
Johanson. *See* Stewart and Johanson
Judge. *See* Earnshaw and Judge

Katzman, 95
Keeling. *See* Mancini and Keeling
Kielmannsegg, 11, 13–14, 17–18, 26, *41*
Korah, 88, 103n13
Krasner, 1
Krueger, 78. *See also* Boner and Krueger
Krislov, 42
Krislov and Rosenbloom, 78

Laffont and Tirole, 69–70
Larouche, 85
Laudati, 86–88
Laver and Shepsle, 74, 82n9
Leibfried, 22
Leibfried and Pierson, 22, *42*
Lijphart, 30, 127, 141
Lijphart et al., 141
Linder, 3, 97, 125–127, 136
Linz, 7
Lipset, 6
Litan and Nordhaus, 78
Locke, 69
Lodge, 2

Madison, James, xi, 25
Maier, 113
Majone, 1–3, 5–6, 9, 18–20, 27–31, 34–35, 40, *41,*66–67, 69, 73–81, 99, 140, *141*, 142. *See also* Dehousse et al.
Mancini, 3
Mancini and Keeling, 4

Manin 16
Manin et al., 7–8, 70
Marsh. *See* Franklin et al.
Marshall. *See* Gilligan et al.
Marx, 69
Mattli. *See* Burley and Mattli
Mayhew, 67–68
Mayer. *See* Weiler et al.
Mazey and Richardson, 113–114
McConnell, 78, 120
McCubbins. *See also* Calvert et al.
McCubbins and Schwartz, 72
McCubbins et al., 72, 74
McGowan. *See also* Cini and McGowan
McGowan and Wilkes, 83
Mendeloff, 66
Mill, 76
Moe, 74, 95
Montesquieu, 69
Monti, 83
Moore. *See* Gurr et al.
Moravcsik, 73

Navia. *See* Zweifel and Navia
Neale. *See* Bazerman and Neale
Neale and Goyder, 91–95
Neunreither, 23
Neven et al., 70, 75, 82n11, 88–93, 102n7, 103n19, 103n21
Neven and Ungern-Sternberg, 98
Newman, 138
Niskanen, 70
Noll, 78
Nordhaus. *See* Litan and Nordhaus
Nugent, 27, 33–34, 46–47, 67
Nutall. *See* Neven et al

Peltzman, 71
Perschau. *See* Baake and Perschau
Pierson, 74. *See also* Leibfried et al.
Pinder, 2, 4
Persson et al., 77, 139
Peters, 34
Peterson, 3, 4, 30
Plümper. *See* Genschel and Plümper
Pollack, 4, 22, 73, 108, 110, 113–114, 140

Pollack and Shaffer, 105, 107, 112, 114, 122, 129, 131
Porter, 73
Przeworski, 7. *See also* Manin et al.
Putnam and Bane, xi, 46
Puztai. *See* Ewen and Puztai

Quirk, 118

Radner, 71
Reinicke. *See* Coppedge and Reinicke
Richardson. *See* Mazey and Richardson
Rodrick, 40
Rogowski. *See* Lijphart et al.
Roland. *See* Persson et al.
Ronit. *See* Greenwood et al
Rose-Ackerman, 1, 66
Rosenbloom, 120. *See also* Krislov and Rosenbloom
Ross, 35, *41*

Sanchez de Cuenca, 9, 12, 20, 77
Sandholtz and Zysman, *41*
Sbragia, 5, 12, 14, *41*
Scharpf, 3, 5, 12, 14–15, 18, 20–24, 35, 39–40, *41–42*, 44n18, 50
Schmidt, 74, 83, 90
Schultze, 70
Schumpeter, 6, 10n6
Schwartz. *See* McCubbins and Schwartz
Seidman and Gilmour, 1, 12, 36, *42*, 66
Seabright, 75. *See also* Gatsios and Seabright; *and* Neven et al.
Selznick, 66, 138
Shaffer. *See* Pollack and Shaffer
Shapiro, 12, *41*, 50, 75–76, 79–81, 114, 122, 142
Shepsle. *See also* Laver and Shepsle
Shepsle and Weingast, 35
Slomanson, 1
Snyder. *See* Dehousse et al.
Spitz, 140
Stewart and Cromartie, 95
Stewart and Johanson, 130
Stigler, 69–71

Stokes, 68. *See also* Manin et al.
Stone, 95
Streeck, 12, 21, 39, 42
Sunstein, 1, 66
Sutherland, 74–76, 81

Tabellini. *See* Persson et al.
Taylor, Martin, xii
Tinbergen, 22
Tirole. *See* Laffont and Tirole
Tollison, 81n3
Tsebelis, 49
Tsebelis and Garrett, 49
Tullock, 81n3

Ungern-Sternberg. *See* Neven and Ungern-Sternberg
University of Illinois, 106.

Van der Eijk. *See* Franklin et al.
Vogel, 21, 39, 140
Volcansek, 20

Wallace, 3. *See also* Hayes-Renshaw and Wallace
Warren, 69
Waterman. *See* Wood and Waterman
Weaver. *See* Lijphart et al.

Weber, Eugene, 25
Weber, Max, 65
Weiler, 4, 11–14, 16, 20–21, 139
Weiler et al., 13–15
Weingast, 71. *See also* Banks and Weingast; *and* Calvert et al.; *and* Gilligan et al.; *and* Shepsle and Weingast; *and* Weingast and Moran
Weingast and Moran, 71, 95
Weissman, 134n43
Whish, 89–90, 92
Wildavsky, 70
Williams, K. *See* Docksey and Williams
Williams, N., 23, 107
Williamson, 1, 68
Wilson, 78
Wincott, 3, 36
Wood and Waterman, 18, 41, 66, 79, 94–95, 118, 122, 137, 140–141, *141*, 145n1
Woodcock. *See* Bogdanor and Woodcock

Yandle, 95
Young, 113

Zweifel and Navia, 135
Zysman. *See* Sandholtz and Zysma

About the Author

Thomas D. Zweifel, Ph.D., is the CEO of Swiss Consulting Group (www.swissconsultinggroup.com), an international consulting practice headquartered in New York City. He teaches leadership in international and public affairs at Columbia University, publishes frequently on leadership and democracy, and is the author of *Culture Clash: Managing the Global High-Performance Team, Communicate or Die* (both Swiss Consulting Group, 2002), and *International Organizations: Accountability, Democracy and Power* (Lynne Rienner Publishers, 2003).